The Buffalo Ridge Cherok

A Remnant of a Great Nation Divided

Horace R. Rice, Ed.D.

HERITAGE BOOKS
2007

HERITAGE BOOKS

AN IMPRINT OF HERITAGE BOOKS, INC.

Books, CDs, and more—Worldwide

For our listing of thousands of titles see our website
at
www.HeritageBooks.com

Published 2007 by
HERITAGE BOOKS, INC.
Publishing Division
65 East Main Street
Westminster, Maryland 21157-5026

International Standard Book Number: 978-0-7884-0296-8

THE BUFFALO RIDGE CHEROKEE
[Ya (na) s se (Buffalo) Tsa la gi (Cherokee)]:
A Remnant of a Great Nation Divided

PREFACE

I first became conscious of an Indian connection in the Stapleton, Virginia, area and vicinity when, in 1976, the Fairmount Baptist Church's Centennial Committee asked me to research Fairmount's church history. I commenced the historical research in April, 1976, in preparation for Fairmount Baptist Church's Centennial Program, which was to be held on the same date that the United States of America would celebrate its bicentennial, Sunday, July 4, 1976. The senior church members believed that the church started around 1865, following the Civil War, since they had heard stories from their ancestors about slavery. While they knew some of their ancestors were free colored people, they believed that others had been slaves--and therefore assumed that the church did not start until after 1865. The officers were aware that the church was actually 109 years old in 1976 but this national celebration was a good time for the church to hold its official centennial celebrations, as well.

As I gathered historical information from interviews with senior members of Fairmount Baptist Church, I began to get the picture that this area, Stapleton, was not an ordinary community. Its members were bi- and tri-racial, with Indian characteristics taking predominance. While older members mentioned matter-of-factly during the interviews that they had Indian ancestry, the younger members looked on and often asked for additional information to quench their curiosity or to add new stories to their old oral traditions.

After completing the Fairmount Centennial Bulletin in July, 1976, I had planned to write a historical account of the area at a later date. This project, however, was delayed for approximately nine years and, in fact, almost forgotten. It was not until the November, 1985, flood in the Stapleton area that I seriously began to consider studying this location. The flood unearthed an area used by Woodland Indians around 900 A.D. Archaeologists indicated that the village near the banks of the James River in Stapleton may date from 900-1250 A.D. This incident, and the resulting historical information that supported my earlier belief that this area was not an ordinary location, forced me to take on the project immediately.

It seemed that God provided an opportunity out of a disaster to show Amherst County a part of history that would otherwise not have been recorded. Stapleton along the James River, like a refrigerator retarding food spoilage in a hot climate, has preserved Native American history for our "consumption" today. In a fast and technological society where people tend to look forward more than backward, the Stapleton vicinity appeared to be forgotten as an area of Indian culture. It appeared that

3

Divine intervention provided the setting for us to notice that Indians were here, more than the names remain.

Since 1985, I have been researching the genealogical records and history of citizens who lived in the Stonewall (Appomattox County)/Stapleton Area. During the years of my research, I have become acutely aware that many of Stapleton's senior citizens have valuable historical information that must be recorded before time or death steals their secrets.

This book is a revision of my book, The Buffalo Ridge Cherokee: The Colors and Culture of a Virginian Indian Community. As I continued my research after publishing my first book which covered the period from 1820 through 1990, I discovered that the Buffalo Ridge/Stonewall Mill people were in the area long before the 1820s. Actually, we find the Buffalo Ridge ancestors in the area as early as 1770, and it is believed that they were there prior to the mid or early 1700s.

This book is not an attempt to provide a general history of Stapleton and vicinity. It is a very small view of a generally bi-racial (Native American and Caucasian) and tri-racial (Native American, Caucasian, and African American) people who lived in Stapleton, and vicinity. Only a few of these families have been interviewed because of the enormous size and complexity of this very large tribal group. It is hoped that this book **will not** provide the closure that some readers are seeking but will help create further interest and excitement on the part of the descendants of Stapleton's Native American ancestors to the point that serious readers or researchers will attempt to fill the unending gaps that I have left. My research has provided information that reveals that these people were predominantly Cherokee Indians. Historical closure is not possible in any study of the past. I feel that this book is no exception because **they**, the Cherokee Indians, are a special people in history, with an enormous amount of history to be researched. This book's focus is on a small group of Native Americans, a small part of the once great whole and now **a remnant among many remnants whose ancestors were once part of the united and great Cherokee Nation.**

I am grateful to my wife, Gloria, for her continued encouragement and faith in my efforts. My children, Joylyn and Holli, must be commended for their patience in my absence as I sought to find some answers to their heritage. I appreciate the assistance of Chief Samuel Penn and the gracious and kind support of members of the Buffalo Ridge Band of Cherokee. This research could not have been completed without their helpful assistance. Special thanks is also extended to Chief Bernard Humbles Penn, United Cherokee Indian Tribe of West Virginia, for his valuable information and encouragement. I also appreciate the editorial assistance of Rebecca Averett and helpful suggestions of Wayne Rhodes, Certified Genealogist.

4

CHAPTER I
Sa quu i (One)

CHEROKEES IN
STAPLETON, VIRGINIA

A Remnant of a Broken Nation

"Amherst is the Genius of the Old Dominion.
A living, real, everlasting representative of the
State, to be seen and known of all men. Look at
her, the great, Giantess, sitting upon the highest
portion of central Virginia, with her back against
the Blue Ridge, and her feet dabbling in the noble
James. Mount Pleasant her head, lifted 4,090 feet
in the air, the Tobacco Row her fruitful breast:
"The Ridge," her knees holding under them a wealth
of minerals; the upper James her strong right
arm,..."(Blankenship, R.B., 1907, 15).

A new county was created from Albemarle County in 1761 and named
Amherst, after the hero of Ticonderoga, Sir Jeffrey Amherst, the most
successful and famous general of all of the English Colonial Governors.
Nelson County was taken from Amherst in 1808, leaving the county in
its present form.

"With its salubrious atmosphere, its beautiful scenery, its
beautiful scenery, its varied landscape, its pure water, its
temperate climate, its productive valley, its abundant forest, its
mineral hills, its towering mountains, its rapid streams, its
central location, there is no part of this grand old
Commonwealth that has received more of nature's endowments
and less of man's exploitation than the county of
Amherst..."(Blankenship, R.B., 2).

When did man first inhabit this attractive and fruitful county?
Archaeologists feel that Indians have been in Virginia for over ten
thousand years.

Indians were attracted to the beauty and wealth of this area from all
sections of the Commonwealth and country. Many forest fires were
caused by Indians burning the fields to prevent the development of
forest land and to encourage the growth of grass to attract elk and
other game. The Iroquois and other Indians did not want the grasslands
to become forest lands (Percy, 1961, 2). The Glades of Amherst and

Scenic View of Stapleton, Virginia

Stapleton, Virginia

THE BLUE RIDGE MOUNTAIN RANGE

Nelson Counties became the hunting grounds of the Indians. It is said that "all of (the glades) running along the north side of Buffalo Ridge and Findlay Mountain, that parallels the James River, was first known as the hunting grounds of the Indians" (Percy, 1950, 12). The Indians were known to create hunting grounds by the continuous burning of the land until the forest disappeared and became grassland. They shaped the land to draw buffalo and elk to this section. Percy noted that Cherokees came to the mountains of Amherst (Percy, 1952, 33) and that the northern boundary of the Cherokee Nation extended to the Peaks of Otter area where their markers were located. Percy noted the fact that the band of Cherokees who settled in the Amherst Blue Ridge after the Revolution should not be confused with the Monacan Indians who had settlements in the area (Percy, 1961, 2). The Monacans had several villages in the vicinity, including one near Richmond, one in the Goochland Courthouse area, and one site in Charlottesville. Manahassanugh, a village at Wingina (Nelson County), was located near Amherst County (McLeRoy, 1977, 12). McLeRoy suggested that the Monacans camped near Horseford Island in the town of Madison Heights in the early 1700s (McLeRoy, 12).

Local legend has referred to Amherst County Native Americans as descendants of Cherokee who avoided the "Oklahoma March" and returned home through the Blue Ridge Mountains (McLeRoy, 1977, 13). The McLeRoys indicated that these people may have some Cherokee ancestry but believe that they were "more likely" descendants of local tribes.

It seems, however, that most of the traffic and trouble in the Amherst area came about as a result of war parties traveling to and from the Cherokee Nation. One of the primary Indian routes led from Buchanan County over the Blue Ridge Mountains and down to Goose Creek in Bedford County (Percy, 1952, 45). The Cherokee Nation dominated the section covering the area of the Blue Ridge Parkway from the Peaks of Otter to the Great Smoky Mountains (Percy, 1952, 47).

There is, however, research that supports the fact that Cherokee were residents of Amherst County prior to, during, and after the American Revolution (Whitehead, 1896). Residents along the Blue Ridge Mountains and foothills, from South Carolina to Virginia, have strong Cherokee oral traditions, Native American physical features, and old Cherokee family surnames. It is believed that they traveled back and forth between Georgia, South Carolina, North Carolina, and Virginia, and that Cherokee bands lived in various areas of the mountains, including the Blue Ridge range and foothills, long before the Cherokee Removal and "Death March" to Oklahoma. While some of the residents in Amherst County are possibly descendants of Monacan ancestors, Amherst County had pockets of Cherokee families or bands before the Revolution. It is possible that some of the remnants of or last

Monacans in the area intermarried with some of the Cherokee residents.

A large Saponi tribe settled in the Peaks of Otter area of Bedford County. Remains of their settlements were discovered when the lodge and lake were constructed a few years ago. It is believed that this area was the westernmost village of the Saponi, who were generally concentrated closer to Richmond (McLeRoy, 1977, 12)

William J. O'Neill's Washington Post article in 1969 supported the view that Amherst Indians were descendants of the Cherokee who slipped through the nets as the Cherokees were being forced to move to Oklahoma in 1838. Although the Bear Mountain and Tobacco Row Mountain residents believed through oral tradition that they were Cherokee, they have generally accepted the fact that they are Monacan Indians today, as a result of the book, Indian Island in Amherst County (Houck, 1985). Phyllis Hicks, Spokesperson for the Monacan Tribe indicated that she thought they "were Cherokee until" Dr. Houck wrote the book, Indian Island in Amherst County (TV Interview, Good Morning Virginia, 1/28/91). The oral tradition is very strong in Amherst and vicinity regarding the Cherokee connection. Perry Tortelot, a state archaeologist who investigated the flood excavation in 1985 in Stapleton, noted that the fragments that were found in Stapleton could not be documented as Monacan items ("Good Morning Virginia," 1991). Dr. Claudia Chang, an archaeologist at Sweet Briar College and wife of Perry Tortelot, indicated that, since the fragments related to the Woodland Indian Period, a particular tribe could not be documented as the settlers on the river bank (Chang, 1990).

Stapleton, situated on the James River, has some Indian history of its own to share with readers. This little community, bordered on the eastern side of the James River by the Stonewall Mill area and on its western side by the Buffalo Ridge Mountain, has been referred to by many residents as "Indian Land"(Hesson, 1990). Before we visit the Stapleton Community, it would be wise to understand the full impact of the Cherokees on the United States and Virginia to gain a more realistic view of the Stapleton and vicinity connection and the special place of this area in history.

7

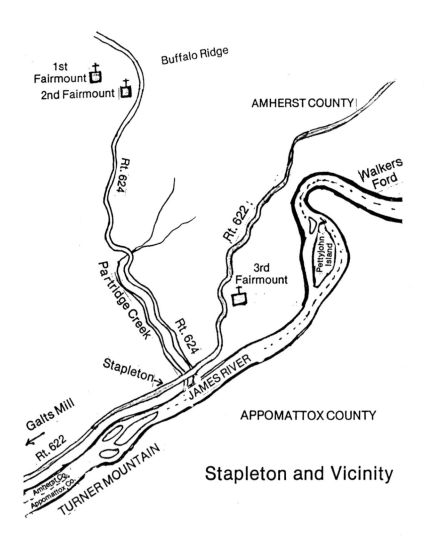

Stapleton and Vicinity

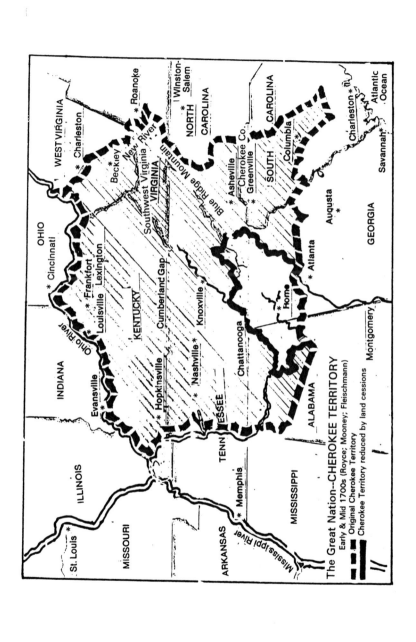

The Great Nation--CHEROKEE TERRITORY
Early & Mid 1700s (Royce; Mooney; Fleischmann)
▪ ▪ ▪ Original Cherokee Territory
▬▬ Cherokee Territory reduced by land cessions

CHAPTER II
Ta li (Two)

THE CHEROKEE IN THE
EASTERN UNITED STATES

A Great Nation

It is believed that the first Americans came from Asia as hunters in pursuit of big game. They traveled approximately 55 miles across a bridge of land joining Siberia to Alaska about 11,000 years ago. They came from northeastern Asia, probably following the route across the Beringian landmass. They moved southward during the years following their arrival in America. They quickly populated an area of North American from Maine to Florida (Gallant, 1989, 23 & 29).

The American Indians in America today and the northern Asians seem to be related in appearance, as their "coppery skin, dark eyes, wide cheekbones, and straight hair" indicate (Gallant, 28). It is believed that the early human beings came to America from another area, perhaps northern Asia.

The origin of the Cherokee has been placed in the Canadian north, the Great Lakes area, and as far as Middle and South America; however, it cannot be accurately stated where the Cherokee started as a Tribe. The Cherokees, who speak Iroquois, are believed to have accompanied the Iroquoian Indians on their travels. They probably left the Iroquoian group, after moving into the Ohio Valley area, about 3,500 years ago and traveled into Virginia and later into the southern Appalachian mountain region (Jacobson, 1970, 46). They were the strongest tribe of the Iroquoian group. Cherokee inhabited southwest Virginia, western North Carolina, northern Georgia, sections of South Carolina, and northeast Alabama, and claimed land as far as the Ohio River.

At one time in their exciting history, the Cherokee were a powerful and great nation. They possessed 135,000 square miles of area that covered eight states: North Carolina, Georgia, South Carolina, Alabama, Tennessee, Kentucky, West Virginia, and Virginia (Blankenship, B., Cherokee Roots, 1978, 5). This tribe, one of the largest in the Southeastern section of the United States, was the first to adapt to the arrival and civilization of the Europeans. In 1540, when Hernando De Soto explored the area of the Cherokee, he discovered that they had an advanced society in their capital city, Echota (Itsati), near the modern city of Madisonville, Tennessee (Yenne, 1986, 35). They lived in the section of the southern Allegheny and Great Smoky Mountains and nearby areas of Virginia, North and South Carolina, Georgia, Alabama, and Tennessee (Encyclopedia Americana, 1972, 399). They occupied the

8

high mountain region of the Southeast.

The Cherokee Nation was great in size (Terrell, 1971, 131). In 1650, the Cherokee population numbered near 22,500 within a 40,000 square mile area in the Appalachian Mountains (Goetz, 1989, 172). When De Soto, the Spanish explorer, first visited their location in 1540, he saw their advanced culture based on agriculture (O'Brien, 1932, 75). The Cherokees had already become very good farmers and were successful in passing their talents on to their children. DeSoto determined that they did not worship idols but believed in one God. The Cherokee were not ungodly but believed in a "Superior Being," their creator and master of their lives. They were content with their problems in life because it was God's will. They believed that misfortune in life was under God's Supreme control and that man had very little control. The Cherokee had faith in a judgment after death (Parris, 5 & 6). Their faith in God grew stronger over the centuries. The Cherokee were still maintaining their faith in God and Christ in 1828. The Cherokee Phoenix wrote, "The knowledge of Jesus Christ is a wonderful mystery...To know Jesus Christ for ourselves, is to make him a CONSOLATION, ---DELIGHT, ---STRENGTH, ---RIGHTEOUSNESS, COMPANION,--and END" (Vol., No. 4, New Echota, March 13, 1828, 4).

In the seventeenth century, their capital, New Echota, was moved to the present-day Calhoun, Georgia. In 1729, it is believed that approximately 20,000 Cherokee lived among 64 villages and towns (Yenne, 1986, 35). They remained friendly with the frontiersmen until two of their chiefs were charged with killing a settler. This accusation precipitated two years of war between the Cherokee and the British (O'Brien, 1932, 75).

During the French and Indian Wars, occurring from 1759 to 1763, the Cherokees fought with the English against the French. A large force of Cherokee troops assisted the British forces in the Virginia wilderness (Mooney, Myths of the Cherokee, 1982, 40). Their warriors engaged in battles on the side of the English. They even found themselves fighting on the side of their traditional rivals, the Iroquois, against the French. After an incident in what is now West Virginia, the English frontiersmen attacked some Cherokee and killed twelve warriors. This English attack was precipitated by a claim that Virginia settlers made upon horses which the Cherokee had captured on their way home from the battle in which they aided the English in the capture of Fort Duquesne. After this confrontation with the English settlers, several bands of Cherokees, with their leader Chief Oconostota, raided white settlements on a number of occasions. They captured Fort Loudon in the Appalachians.

The British defeated them after two years by destroying their villages and crops. They fought for a long time from their mountain retreats

(Waldman, 1988, 43-45).

It is interesting to note that the Cherokee continued to support the English in their attempt to defeat the American troops during the American Revolution of 1775-83. "Despite British attempts to restrain them, in July 1776, a force of 700 Cherokee under Chief Dragging-canoe attacked two U.S.-held forts in North Carolina: Eaton's Station and Ft. Watauga. Both assaults failed, and the tribe retreated in disgrace" (The New Encyclopedia Britannica, 1989, 173). The Cherokee lost almost half of their territory by the end of the Revolution (Blankenship, B., Cherokee Roots, 5). The North Carolina militiamen destroyed Cherokee villages in retaliation and also demanded land concessions (Waldman, 45).

As previously stated, the Cherokee language belongs to the Iroquoian linguistic group. It is believed that, during some prehistoric time period, they lived in the Great Lakes region. This belief is based on numerous generations of Delaware Indian historians who passed on the oral tradition of their ancestors to their descendants whenever they had the opportunity in the nothern woodlands (Terrell, 1971, 131). The tradition states that the powerful Delawares, whose ancient homeland was in New Jersey, eastern Pennsylvania, and New York, fought the Cherokees over a period of the reign of three chieftains before the Delawares could finally claim victory.

The Iroquois warriors joined with the Delaware to force the Cherokee south of the Ohio River. This oral tradition is documented by the physical evidence found in Ohio, Illinois, Virginia, and Tennessee. Archaeologists have found pipes and other artifacts that are identical or closely related to those possessed by the Allegheny Cherokee. These remains, it is suggested, were left by the Cherokees as they were forced to retreat southward after their major defeat by the Delaware and Iroquois. They were called "cave people" by the Wyandot (Hurons) who lived in the Great Lakes and in the St. Lawrence Valley. The Wyandot, who were members of the Iroquoian linguistic group, had two names for the Cherokee, **Uwatayo-rono**, and **Entari ronnon**, which refer to "cave people" and "mountain people," respectively (Terrell, 132). These names were probably applied to the Cherokee after their retreat to the Allegheny mountain country. The neighboring Creeks probably gave them their name **Cherokee-"tciloki** in its original form," which means "people of the different speech." In Iroquoian, they named themselves **Ani-yun-wiya**, or "real people" (Waldman, 43). The Eastern dialect, the Lower Cherokee dialect, pronounced the tribal name Tsaragi but the "English settlers of Carolina corrupted" the word to "Cherokee" (Mooney, 16). The Spaniards explorers wrote Cherokee as "Chalaque" (Mooney, 16).

During the 1800s, the Cherokees were successful in assimilating into

10

the culture of the white man (Moulton, 1978, 31). They set up a governmental system based on that of the United States. They modeled the settlers' methods of weaving, farming, and house building (Goetz, 173).

Chief Charles Hicks, in 1808, organized the Cherokee legal code in written form. During the same period, Sequoia (Sequoya), a half-blooded Cherokee, also known as George Gist, developed the first written language to originate in North America. This language had an 85 character alphabet and, by 1822, many Cherokees were communicating by reading and writing (Yenne, 36; Goetz, 173; Waldman, 45). The Cherokee Nation greeted the Cherokee alphabet with joy and Sequoyah told his people that he could "teach the Cherokee to talk on paper like the white man" (Parris, 1950, 53,56).

Although the Cherokee were successful in adopting some of the cultural styles of the settlers, they maintained their love of and skill in the martial arts. They sought or accepted almost any reason to enter into combat with their enemies. They were skilled in hand-to-hand fighting and seemed to have maintained their combat readiness because of their frequency or quickness in engaging in hostilities. White (1979, 118) noted that they often entered into battles because they enjoyed fighting. They enjoyed the act of fighting--it was not so much a chore or duty, it was a exciting.

The Cherokee owned as many as 1,275 slaves in 1825. After the Civil War, however, all Indian nations that owned slaves were required to provide their freedom. The Cherokee often adopted their freed slaves into their tribes.

The settlers who moved in and near the Cherokee territory were generally Scottish, Irish, and English. Fleischmann noted that the settlers entered the area from Maryland, Pennsylvania, and Virginia (Fleischmann, 1971, 10 & 11). Cherokee families of mixed blood with the white settlers included, for example, names such as Walker, Rogers, Ward, Davis, McDaniel, McCoy, and Bolinger (Fleischmann, 1971, 10 & 11). Mooney noted that one of the reasons for the Cherokee progression in civilization and development into a great nation was due to intermarriage with white traders. He suggested that the prosperous Cherokee making Cherokee history were generally mixed bloods (Mooney, 83; Clarke, 7).

The Cherokee desire to have its own nation was sabotaged as far back as 1789, when the United States Government declared that its new constitution had authority over the tribe. Ratifications by Virginia (June 26, 1788), South Carolina (May 23, 1788), and Georgia (January 2, 1788) permitted boundaries to be set through the Cherokee territory, "as if it did not exist" (Fleischmann, 1971, 5 & 6).

11

Tecumseh, the great Shawnee chief, conferred with the leaders of the Cherokee at Soco Gap in North Carolina. He pleaded with the Cherokee to unite with the "federated tribes in the Northwest Territory in an alliance against white aggression" (Parris, 35 & 36). Tecumseh knew that the great nation was headed for a great fall. The English-- the King's men and horses--would not be able to put the nation back together again. They actually assisted in the fall by sending settlers into Cherokee territory. The Cherokee Nation, by the end of the Revolution, would be reduced from 125,000 square miles to approximately 43,000 square miles (Parris, 34).

During the period of their land loss, to complicate matters more, gold was discovered on Cherokee land in Georgia (Blumenthal, 72). Frequently, armed men invaded territory. The Cherokee were robbed of their horses, cattle, and houses. The Cherokees were unable to retaliate effectively at this point because the State of Georgia annexed their land and claimed jurisdiction over the area. Georgia declared Cherokee laws "null and void" (Thornton, 115).

The Cherokee were harassed by the State of Georgia and Andrew Jackson of the United States Government and forced to give up their gold-rich and attractive farmland and move west of the Mississippi (Thornton, 116). In 1835, the Treaty of New Echota was signed by a minority group of the Cherokee. This treaty ceded to the United States Government all of their land on the eastern side of the Mississippi for the sum of $5,000,000. The Cherokee majority went to the United States Supreme Court to fight for its rights to keep its land. The Court supported the majority Cherokee and ruled that Georgia did not have any authority and claim over their land. The State of George refused to honor the Supreme Court decision and Andrew Jackson failed to enforce it (Goetz, 173). President Jackson was reported to have responded to Chief Justice Marshall's decision in Worcester vs. Georgia (1832) by challenging John Marshall, after he had made his decision, to "enforce it" (Thornton, 116). The Federal government made 40 treaties with the Cherokee and holds the record of breaking every one (Blankenship, B., Cherokee Roots, 5).

In 1838, a body of 7,000 soldiers arrived to enforce the fraudulent treaty and to remove the Cherokee to Indian Territory (now Oklahoma)" (Encyclopedia Americana, 1972, 400). The Cherokee, numbering approximately 17,000, were rounded up like cattle and forced to move westward to Oklahoma (Thornton, 117). This single Federal order changed the proud, indigenous tribe--those that were forced to leave their homes--into an indigent, destitute people.

Peter Nabokov tells of a young Cherokee child's ordeal during this removal period. It seems that when the military escort or enforcers arrived at her house, she remembered her father--who had wanted to fight the soldiers--yielding to her mother's request that he should save his life by surrendering (Nabokov, 1978, 189). This eviction and march to Oklahoma, which was known as the "Trail of Tears," occurred during the fall and winter of 1838-39. The march was poorly organized and managed. Inadequate supplies of food and clothing led to terrible suffering in the frigid climate that the Indians encountered on the westward journey. Approximately 4,000 died during the 116-day, 800-mile trip (Goetz, 1989; Yenne, 36).

Approximately 1,000 brave Cherokee refused to leave their beloved country and managed to escape the deportation to the west. They lived as fugitives in the mountains (Encyclopedia Americana, 400). Eluding the troops by hiding in the hills, even with calls by Chief Ross to return to the main body, they remained as a defiant band that refused to cooperate with the forced removal to Oklahoma (Moulton, 1978, 97). The descendants of these brave and committed Cherokee still reside "amid the mist-wreathed ridges today" (National Geographic Society,1974, 136).

The more than 1,000 Cherokee, who objected to the removal and were to remain, had been guaranteed citizenship under the Treaty of New Echota. They became subjected to the laws of North Carolina and, in breach of the guarantee, were not granted citizenship as provided by the treaty. North Carolina Legislature passed a law, however, permitting them to remain "permanently within the State." The Cherokee filed many lawsuits until they received a title to the land as a corporation in 1925. Approximately 56,572.80 acres of land over a five-county area near Cherokee, North Carolina, are held in trust by the United States Government. The control and management of the property has been entrusted to the Council of the Eastern Band of Cherokee (Blankenship, B. Cherokee Roots, 1978, 6).

Today, the Qualla Band of Cherokee have the unique status of being a sovereign body within the United States, as opposed to living on a reservation, due to the fact that the land does not belong to the State of North Carolina nor to the United States (Blankenship, B., 1978, 6).

The Cherokee Nation--like the planarian flatworm or Turbellaria, that reproduces itself by splitting into two parts and regenerating--has grown in size and in influence in spite of, actually as a result of, its numerous divisions. The Cherokee people will not die as a tribe, even when parts of its Nation have been severed from the main body. Each severed part has a self-reproducing power, like the Turbellaria which reproduces each half into a new whole.

CHAPTER III
Tso i (Three)

CHEROKEE IN VIRGINIA

Part of the Cherokee Nation

When European settlers first entered North America in the 17th century, they encountered the Cherokee, who occupied the Appalachian Mountains, specifically the territory of southwest Virginia, western North and South Carolina, eastern Tennessee, northern Georgia, and northeastern Alabama (Terrell, 131; Waldman, 43; Utley and Washburn, 92 & 93; Keel, 1; Thornton, 115; Mooney, 14; Egloff and Woodward, 51). Although very little archaeological research has been conducted in southwest Virginia, a Pisgah site at the mouth of Cave Creek in the New River area has been dated at A.D. 1390 (Swanton; Johnson). The Pisgah people were the prehistoric ancestors of the Cherokee. Cherokee archaeological studies have revealed the Lee-Pisgah ceramics around A.D. 1000 (Holland; Keel, 2,47,223). In 1876, Professor Lucien Carr discovered the Lee County, Virginia mound in which he found historical data that forced him to conclude that the mound was built by the Cherokee (75).

It is believed that the Cherokee exterminated the Xuala tribe in southwest Virginia, now Washington, Smyth, Russell, and Tazewell Counties and "held the country" until they were forced out by the English (Hale, 110). The Cherokee claimed superior rights to the land in Tazewell County and southwest Virginia (Bundy, 3). Mooney noted that the Cherokee claimed to have once lived near the Peaks of Otter in Bedford County (Mooney, 30; Roanoke Valley Historical Society Map of Botetourt County). The Cherokee controlled the Blue Ridge area from the Peaks of Otter to the Smoky Mountains (Percy, 1952, 47).

Haywood, in "Natural and Aboriginal History of Tennessee" (Report to the Bureau of Ethnology, 1823, 223), concluded that the Cherokee were settled in central Virginia before being driven back toward southwest Virginia. His assertions are as follows:

"Before the year 1690, the Cherokee, who were once settled on the Appomattox River, in the neighborhood of Monticello, left their former abodes and came to the west. The Powhatans were said by their descendants to have been once a part of this nation. The probability is that migration took place about, or soon after, the year 1632, when the Virginians suddenly and unexpectedly fell on Indians, killing all they could find, cutting up and destroying their crops, and causing great numbers to perish by famine. They came to New River and made a temporary settlement, and also on the head of the Holston."

14

There were some ongoing friendly tribal contacts between members of both groups. When the European settlers first arrived, Cherokee lived in central and southwestern Virginia and were at peace with Powhatan (M. Wilson, 1994). Virginia settlers and the Cherokee had early contact long before contact was made in South Carolina, Maryland, and North Carolina. Virginia has a long and rich archival history with the Cherokee (see Virginia Colonial Council minutes). Powell (138) noted that "whatever the degree of probability attending these legends, it would seem that the settlers of Virginia had an acquaintance with the Cherokee prior to that of the South Carolina immigrants, who for a number of years after their first occupation confined their explorations to a narrow strip of country in the vicinity of the sea coast, while the Virginians had been gradually extending their settlements far up toward the headwaters of the James River and had early perceived the profits to be derived from the Indian trade."

According to tradition, the Allegeni, the ancestors of the modern Cherokee, were defeated by the Delaware-Iroquois alliance and moved into Virginia. They settled in the New Holston Valley after residing for a period of time at the Peaks of Otter in Bedford County (Johnson, 34; Hamm, 1; BCEA, 5; Woodward, 19; Terrell, 131-132). In the late 1560s, a few traders from Virginia and the Carolinas ventured into the territory but frequent contacts by the English traders and settlers did not occur until the 18th century. Addington noted that "Virginians have always considered the Cherokee the original and rightful owners of the land of Southwestern Virginia" (1956, 6). The Cherokee, after losing possession of southwestern Virginia and other lands that had been a part of their Nation and land prior to the Removal, noted:

"When a nation finds a country uninhabited, and without a master, it may lawfully take possession of it, and after it has sufficiently made known its will in this respect, it cannot be deprived of it by another"(Cherokee Phoenix, 4, 1828).

Underwood, in The Story of the Cherokee People, noted that the earliest contact with British settlements occurred in Richmond, Virginia. The Cherokee replaced the Powhatans in their village site after the British had spent considerable time on its effort to dislodge the Powhatan Tribe. As soon as the British dislodged the Powhatans, the Cherokee moved in to take the site. The British, with the assistance of more than one hundred Pamunky warriors "to help them destroy the new intruders," the Cherokee, confronted the enemy. "The combined forces" attacked the Cherokee, lost the battle, and were "forced to sue for peace" (20). While there is some confusion among historians regarding the accuracy of this legend, there is very strong support for accuracy of the legend that Cherokee roamed and lived throughout Virginia, and that they were friendly with Powhatans. The descendants of Pocahontas in central and southwestern Virginia have a very strong Cherokee heritage. There are counties and cities that carry the princess' name, "Pocahontas," throughout the regions where the Cherokee traveled as they moved in a southwestern direction from Virginia. A large number of her descendants are members of Pocahontas societies and their ancestors were on Cherokee removal rolls (M. Wilson; V. Santini).

The Cherokee believed that southwestern Virginia and other areas of the southeast were still a part of their Nation theoretically, even though they ceded the land. Adair, an early trader and historian, indicated that the Cherokee gave more trouble to the settlers in Virginia than all of the other tribes combined (Summers, 30-31; Clement, 78 & 79; Martin, 2). The Cherokee often engaged in territorial conflicts with settlers, even if they came near the border of their Cherokee Nation. Morlin and Salling, for example, settlers from Williamsburg, ventured into the Salem area around 1732, a section that was close to but not a part of the southwestern Virginia section of the Cherokee Nation. They were attacked by a body of Cherokee (Brock, 2).

Before the explorers arrived in the Pulaski area, the Cherokee and Shawnee had well-traveled routes to the New River (Pulaski--Our County, Our Town, 1). The Cherokee engaged in numerous confrontations with settlers, soldiers, and other tribes as they trespassed on Cherokee territory (Smith, C.H., 38; Wilson, 45-46; Summers, 30; Addington, L., 91; Kegley, 264; Mapp, 337). As the settlers increased their movement into Cherokee territory and faced more hostility from Cherokee, leaders in Virginia, feeling the constant harassment and danger, decided to send expeditionary forces with aid from other states, against the Cherokee from four sides (Underwood, 22; Swanton, 112).

After numerous defeats in battle, the Cherokee ceded their ownership of or claim to southwestern Virginia as part of their Nation. They gave up an area in 1768 to the British that included the counties or sections of the counties of Washington, Grayson, Carroll, Floyd, Patrick, Wythe, and Smyth. In 1770, they ceded the counties of or parts of Giles, Montgomery, Bland, Smyth, Wythe, Tazewell, Buchanan, Russell, and Scott. Dickinson County was ceded in 1772 and Wise, Scott, and Lee Counties were given up in 1775 (Royce; Purdue; Waldman; Bauer, 35). In 1778, Virginia ignored the Cherokee Nation's claim to any of southwest Virginia and drew a line through its boundary as if the Nation had not existed (Fleischmann).

When the white man came to the Blue Ridge, where the Skyline Drive now runs, the Shawnees lived in three villages near the Winchester area. The Shawnees also had another village near Woodstock. Julia Davis, in The Shenandoah (1945, 18), noted that the Cherokee had a tradition of being residents of the Martinsburg area--where the

Tuscaroras had once lived--until they were driven farther south by the northern tribes. Nellie White Bundy, in Sketches of Tazewell County, Virginia (1976, 2), noted that the characteristics of the discovered Indian "pottery indicate connections with the early Cherokee..."

As already noted, the Cherokee sided with the British during the Revolution. Under pressure from the regular encroachment on their territory by settlers and, at the same time, provided with weapons by the British agents, the Cherokee engaged in a general war against intruders into their area in Virginia, Georgia, and the Carolinas. Militiamen from Virginia, Georgia, and the Carolinas engaged in expeditions to punish the Cherokee for their rebellion (Dictionary of American History, 14).

Virginia had three Iroquoian tribes in its midst: the Cherokee, the Nottoway (Mangoac), and the Meherrin. While the Cherokee had control of the Virginian territory west of the Blue Ridge mountains, some researchers believe that they were not very numerous in Virginia because their home was in the western North Carolina and eastern Tennessee area (McCary, 1987, 8). The Cherokee, contrary to some opinions of researchers, lived and hunted with their Iroquoian brothers, the Nottoway, and possibly the Meherrin (Minutes of the Colonial Council of Virginia., 1741, 62). The Colonial Council's Minutes recorded one incident in which the Cherokee murdered three Nottoway and "carried away three other Nottoway."

The Council of Colonial Virginia at Williamsburg had early contact with the Cherokee. The records of the Council proceedings have preserved the historical meetings and conferences that were conducted between the Cherokee and the Colony of Virginia. Some of the contacts have been compiled and summarized, and are as follows (Minutes of the Colonial Council):

MINUTES OF THE COLONIAL COUNCIL

Page   Date
Occasion/Event

Vol III

406   8/1715
Council expected great men of the Catawba and Cherokee to visit Williamsburg to treat for terms of peace.

Speaker requested passports be sent to the Catawba and Cherokee for their "safe going and returning."

554   10/23/1721

Great men of the Chickasaw with certain chiefs of the Cherokee visited Williamsburg with some proposals for their needs.

1   10/25/1721
Cherokee came to Williamsburg to request continuance of trade with Virginia.

Council presented Cherokee one trading gun and as much powder and shot as they shall have need in their journey home.

343   11/3/1721
Cherokee asked to be admitted to Council chambers with desire to settle on a branch of the Roanoke River so that they may enjoy convenience of free trade.

344
Council noted that this request did not seem convenient because Cherokee might disturb other Northern Indian hunting tribes.   The Governor promised to write to Northern Indians to set up peace conference with Cherokee.   Council ordered that interpreter who attended the Cherokee be paid five pistols for services.

398   6/1737
Governor informed Council that he wrote to Lt. Governor of New York and the President of Pennsylvania proposing meeting with deputies of Northern Indians to request that they go to Albany.

414   4/22/1738
President of Pennsylvania sent letter to Council with proposal to delay meeting of Cherokee and Catawba with Northern Indians until the beginning of August.   Governor sent message to the Cherokee and Catawba desiring them that they should postpone their journey to Albany until that time.

421   6/15/1738
Letters received from Pennsylvania and New York requesting that Virginia bear the expenses for maintaining the Cherokee and Catawba during their visit for the treaty with the Six Nations.

422
Council requested that interpreter be sent with Cherokee and Catawba to Conestogow, there to meet with the interpreter of Pennsylvania to set up conference with the deputies of the Six Nations and to assist them in settling terms of peace between them.

Vol V

62   6/11/1741

Robert Munford appeared before the Council to give account of his negotiation. He brought peace pipe from the Cherokee and a belt of wampum from the Catawba as token of their acceptance of said peace concluded at Albany on their behalf.

Robert Munford reported that he had heard that the Cherokee, while hunting together with the Nottoway Indians had murdered three Nottoways and had carried away three other Nottoway. The Nottoway representative who was present said that they suspected the Cherokee because they did not send the Nottoway prisoners back from Cherokee territory with Mr. Munford.

99   9/1742

Council proposed to give all assistance in their power to remove all jealousy that has been of late subsisting between the Nations of the Cherokee and Catawba Indians.

225   12/9/1746

The Governor communicated a letter to the Council from the Cherokee Indians dated October 26, 1746, in answer to the Governor's letter to them to stand firm and true to His Majesty King George and the interest of this government. They noted that they had sent presents to the Six Nations for a peace.

Ordered that sufficient quantity of blue cloth for a suit of clothes and six double breasted coats and scarlet for a suit and calico for gowns for a woman and two children be purchased. That the material be sent as a present from this government to the Cherokee Indians by next Spring.

237   6/10/1747

Ordered that the Receiver General pay Henry Morris the sum of forty pounds for going on express from the government to the Cherokee Nation of Indians.

349   8/9/1751

President of Council informed Council that he gave an audience to the Chiefs of the Cherokee. He noted that he said the following to the chiefs:

> I heartily congratulate you upon your safe arrival
> in Williamsburg and hope in your journey through the
> inhabitants of this Colony you have met with
> kind treatment and hospitable entertainment...I
> have appointed this meeting to give you an
> opportunity of communicating to me the important
> business that has brought you to this city through

such a vast extent of country.

To which the chief of the group returned the following answer:

> We set off from the Town of Choto, to visit you,
> and learn what you had to say to us; our Emperor
> Emperor sent us here to acquaint the Governor of
> Virginia that when his father (Chief's father) was
> in England, the King directed and advised him to
> apply to the Governor of Virginia or Carolina
> whenever the Cherokee were in want of anything...
> Upon these considerations, our Emperor has sent us
> to solicit a confirmation of your friendship and
> desire that you will be pleased to send white
> people amongst us, and establish a commerce
> between the King of Great Britain's subjects,
> inhabitants of this dominion, and the Indians of
> the Cherokee Nation.

351   8/10/1751
The President gave a second audience to the Cherokee and made the following statement:

> ...Assure you that the Government will always endeavor to
> cultivate a harmony and good correspondence between
> His Majesty's subjects and our friends the Cherokee
> and you may depend upon all due encouragement
> being given to the inhabitants that shall be inclined to
> trade with you for our mutual benefit, and as a pledge to
> our friendship and good wishes that a lasting
> peace and flourishing trade may be established
> between us...

352
To which the Chief answered:

> We have traveled through bushes and briers, to see
> our friends of Virginia, we have no cause to
> repent of our long and tedious journey, the pain
> and fatigue we have undergone..We have given our
> promise to make a good road for people of this
> country who shall be disposed to trade with us...

355-360
Communication from the Council of South Carolina regarding the Cherokee.

361-364 10/26/1751

Letter sent by Virginia Council to Governor Glenn of South Carolina regarding the Cherokee.

413-415 11/11/1752
The Emperor of the Cherokee, his Empress, son, two generals, and other attendants visited Williamsburg. They were welcomed and "promised they should be entertained with great civility during their residence in this city.."

418-419 4/12/1753
Letter from Col. James Patton signifying that the differences between the Emperor of the Cherokee and Samuel Stamaker was adjusted.

Vol. VI

8   6/1756
Council sent a messenger to the Cherokee to inquire into their conduct, and to know why their two boys had deserted the college.

23   12/15/56
Letter from Governor Lyttleton signifying he had many of the Cherokee with him at Charles Town and that he hopes the talk he had with them will produce good effects.

24   1/11/1757
Letter to the Council from Col. Read dated Lunenburg January 5th. Stated that Morris Griffith was taken prisoner by the Shawnee near Voss's Fort. That he saw five Cherokee near the town that runs into the Allegheny.

25   1/28/1757
Governor received several letters that he received from the Cherokee via a messenger that he had sent to the Cherokee Nation. A letter indicated that the Cherokee were doubtful with regard to the interest of the English. The Council ordered that men should be sent to the fort built by the English in the Cherokee Country.

40   4/1757
Governor communicated to the Council a letter from Col. Read dated Lunenburg the 5th of April, giving an account of the bad behavior of the Cherokee in that part of the country, and the good conduct of the Catawbas.

58   7/1757
Received intelligence by six Cherokee who scouted with Captain Spotswood toward Fort Du Quesne. That a large body of French and Indians with a train of artillery were actually marching from Fort Du Quesne with a design to march to Fort Cumberland.

The Governor indicated that they wanted to send for more Cherokee.

60   9/22/1757
The Governor communicated to Council a letter from the Emperor of the Cherokee and four of his chief warriors complaining of not having their fort garrisoned and trade according to the council's promise.

73   11/12/1757
Letter from Mr. Gist dated from Winchester, informing that thirty Cherokee were in Winchester from Chota and Tellico.

Letter from Col. Washington dated Fort Loudoun, November 5th, signifying the Cherokees demonstrated the sincerest disposition to support Virginia's cause and that they should be duly rewarded.

82   3/7/1758
Request from Loudoun requesting 800 of the best troops and requesting that a body of Cherokee be secured for this service.

114   10/14/1758
Letter mentioned an attack on the Cherokee.

120   11/11/1758
Information concerning the late murder of some Cherokee.

130   2/23/1759
Communication of minutes of conferences held with Cherokee deputies who arrived at Charles Town.

135   4/17/1759
Governor communicated to the Council the information he had just received from Qttocullocullo or the Little Carpenter signifying his people are well pleased to hear that all quarrels were amicably made up between them and Virginia--promising that they shall do no more mischief on the Virginia frontier.

144   9/3/1759
Communication regarding meetings between the heads of the Cherokee and four Creeks.

166   7/23/1760
Communication regarding the offensive against the Cherokee.

188   5/7/1761
Letter from John Chiswell and Thomas Walker to purchase the prisoners brought in by the Cherokee Indians.

199   10/26/1761
Letter from Col. Stephen that he had received a letter from Conocotocho, Emperor of the Cherokee, expressing great sorrow for the war that had occurred between him and Virginia.

208   3/11/1762
Letter from the head men and warriors in behalf of the whole Nation of Cherokee signifying their entire satisfaction with what passed at Big Island.

It was ordered that a proclamation be issued strictly requiring all people of the government to behave. That, in case any Cherokee shall be murdered by a subject of this Colony, a reward of two hundred pounds to any person who shall make information thereof on conviction of the offender.

214   4/22/1762
Skiagusta with four more of the chief warriors were received by the Council. They stated that they were again true friends to the English.

250   4/16/1763
Governor gave audience to Captain Dick, alias the Raven, a Cherokee, accompanied by four more of that Nation.

278   10/1765
Council advised to give notice to the Carpenter that some Shawnee were preparing to attack some of their towns.

279   9/8/1765
Communication regarding the drawing of the boundary line between Virginia and the lands reserved by the Cherokee for hunting grounds.

297   6/30/1768
Letter from Mr. Alexander Cameron signifying that he had assembled the Cherokee Chiefs concerning the boundary line between Virginia and the Cherokee lands.

298   7/29/1768
Communication from John Stuart regarding the agreement between him and the Cherokee respecting the boundary line.

306   11/5/1768
Communication regarding the conclusion of the treaty with the Cherokee, ratifying the cessions of land lying within the provinces of South Carolina, North Carolina, and Virginia.

Ordered that the goods that were meant to be compensation to the Cherokee for the murder of their relations be sent to the Cherokee.

310   12/19/1768
Communication regarding the boundary line.

10   2/13/1769
Communication regarding the boundary line.

314   4/25/1769
Discussion relative to the boundary line.

354   6/18/1770
Communication regarding the great uneasiness of the Cherokee on account of the delay in drawing the boundary line.

Mr. Stuart noted that the Cherokee have and still do claim the lands between the Kanawha and the Cherokee River, and that he is convinced that they will never relinquish their claims to the extent of the wishes of the House of Burgesses of Virginia.

360   8/6/1770
Mr. Stuart sent an express to Mr. Cameron, his Deputy, with directions to convene a conference with Cherokee chiefs at Lochaber, to treat about the land cessions on the frontier of this government.

381-82 12/12/1770
Letter from John Stuart to the Governor, on the subject of the said treaty. He mentioned that the Cherokee were willing to have given up large country but that they wanted to keep a small triangle of land for Mr. Paris.

600   5/26/1765
Proclamation:

"Whereas a party of Cherokee arrived at Staunton in Augusta, and intended to proceed from thence to Winchester, having obtained a pass from Col. Lewis for that purpose, where on their way thither by upward of twenty men, and their Chief and four more of the said Indians were killed, and two others of them wounded, in violation of the treaties subsisting between that Nation and us: That such villainies may not escape with impunity."

Lewis Preston Summers, in History of Southwest Virginia, 1746-1786, Washington County, 1777-1870, wrote extensively on the activities of the Cherokee in Southwest Virginia. A major battle between the Cherokees and Shawnees occurred near Rich Mountain, in Tazewell County, Virginia. Approximately two hundred Cherokee Indians and several hundred Shawnees were engaged in a contest that lasted for several days. At the end of the first day of combat, the Shawnees retreated

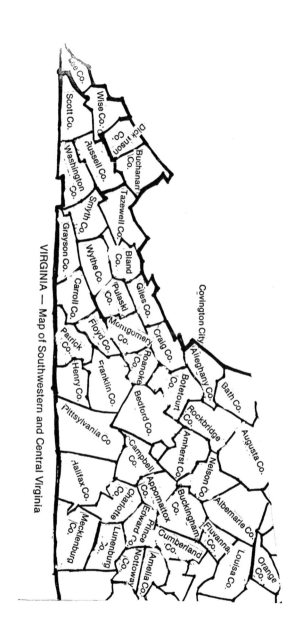

VIRGINIA — Map of Southwestern and Central Virginia

temporarily in order to regroup and returned the next day for another engagement with the Cherokee. Both groups were well armed and eager to fight. The battle continued on the second day. On the morning of the third day, the battle was renewed, but after a few hours, the Shawnees were forced to retreat. The losses of life were great for both groups (Summers, 1903, 26; Addington, 1956, 6).

Addington, in History of Wise County (1956, 6 & 7), stated that "Virginians always considered the Cherokees the original and rightful owners of the land of Southwestern Virginia." He noted that, in 1756, "the Governor of Virginia engaged 130 Cherokees to go with the Rangers west of Augusta under Major Lewis for the purpose of destroying the Shawnee towns of the Ohio River near the mouth of Big Sandy. This expedition proved to be a failure but the friendly relationship established with the Cherokees lasted, with but few exceptions, until the Revolutionary War" (7).

It is a well-known fact that Southwest Virginia had the distinction of having the route over which the Southern and Northern Virginia Indians used to "engage in peaceful intercourse or warlike expeditions, and by this same path they traveled when on the chase or their migrations." One of these trails was on the present McAdam Road near Roanoke, Virginia (Summers, 27).

Adair, an early trader with the Indians and historian, indicated that the Cherokee gave more trouble to the settlers in Virginia than all of the other tribes combined. He stated:

"I have known them to go a thousand miles for the purpose of revenge, in pathless woods, over hills and mountain, through large cane swamps full of grape-vines and briars, over broad   lakes, rapid rivers and deep creeks and all the way endangered by poisonous snakes, if not by the rambling and lurking enemy, while, at the same time, they were exposed to the extremities of heat and cold, the vicissitudes of the season, to hunger and thirst, both by chance and their religious scanty method of living when at war, to fatigue and other difficulties. Such is their revengeful temper that all these things they contemn as imaginary trifles, if   they are so happy as to get the scalp of their enemy" (Summers, 30 & 31).

The population of the Cherokee Nation in 1735 was numerous, and they had a fighting force of more than six-thousand warriors. For about thirty years after the arrival of the first settlers into the area, they "killed and scalped the inhabitants at every opportunity" (Summers, 32).

The Cherokee had a very good relationship with the Governor of Virginia in 1752. J.A. Osborne, in Williamsburg in Colonial Times (1936, 115-116), indicated that the Cherokee Nation's Emperor, Empress, and their young son, the Prince, came to Williamsburg on an official visit. They were accompanied by several of their warriors and great men and their ladies. The Governor had invited them to an evening of entertainment at the Hallam's theatre (Osborne, 16).

The Williamsburg's Virginia Gazette, November 17, 1752, reporting the visit of the Cherokee Indian Chief, and his delegation, noted that they were "received at the Palace by his Honour the Governor, attended by such of the Council as were in Town and several other gentlemen, on Thursday the 9th, instant, with all the marks of civility and friendship, and were entertained at the Theatre, with the play 'The Tragedy of Othello' and a Pantomime performance."

In a treaty with the Cherokees in 1756, Virginia sought the aid of the Indians in its struggle against the French and their Indian supporters. In the spring of 1757, when the "long promised aid arrived it was found to consist of but 400 warriors and of these only 180 remained at the fort at Winchester, the others immediately returning home. They had evidently become disaffected towards the Virginians through French influence, and now were bent upon mischief, for in their march back and forth through Virginia they committed many acts of violence upon the inhabitants" (Clement, 78). Governor Dinwiddie advised "reasoning with them in a mild way for fear of provoking them to open warfare, which he said `would prove of fatal consequences.."(Clement, 79).

Clement, in The History of Pittsylvania County, Virginia (1929, 78 and 79), noted the frustration of Colonel Fontaine in a letter to relatives in England, dated June 11, 1757:

"Those of the Indians that call themselves our friends do despise us, and in their march through our inhabited country, when going to our assistance, insult and annoy. It is not above a month ago since a party of about a hundred and twenty Cherokees, in passing through Lunenburg, insulted people of all ranks."

In 1757, the citizens of Bedford County asked for permission to kill the Indians and for soldier protection. The request was denied "in the hope of preventing open conflict" with the Indians and the citizens (Clement, 79). Bedford and Halifax Counties' citizens were experiencing violent acts of hostility by the Cherokees. Clement indicated the names of the citizens that were attacked, robbed, and harassed by the Indians as they traveled back and forth through the two counties (78-89).

The Cherokee also assisted Amelia and Prince Edward Counties during the French and Indian War. Bradshaw (1955, 45) noted that, in 1758, "Samuel Ewing presented to the Prince Edward Court a bill for seven shillings for goods furnished six Cherokee Indians." The bill was certified to the General Assembly. Some Cherokee passed through Prince

Edward County in March, 1829, and it was discovered that they had smallpox. The county health officials provided assistance to the Indians (Prince Edward County Order Book, 22:57).

Smith, in Colonial Days in the Land that Became Pulaski County (1975, 36 & 37), provided information about the confrontations of the Cherokees with the settlers. He noted that, in 1758, the settlers had the protection of militia patrols. As a result, the citizens felt secure from the harassment of the Indians. Smith stated that the Cherokees robbed houses, stole horses, and murdered settlers. He indicated that a company of 35 men commanded by Captain Robert Wade encountered some Indians who said that they were "Cherokee" in the Martinsville area, near Fort Mayo. The Cherokees traveled frequently through southwest and central Virginia during this period of time. Some of the counties recorded the more serious confrontation with the Cherokee in their official county history books. The fact that some counties were silent on the subject of the Cherokees may have resulted from the fact that serious atrocities that were committed by the Indians in some counties were not committed in others. It is obvious that the Cherokee had to pass through a large number of counties in Virginia to reach their destinations. The Governor of Virginia, after being advised of the Cherokees' behavior, cautioned the soldiers to reason with the Cherokees in a "mild way." He wanted to avoid open combat with the Indians.

In 1794, the Governor of Virginia, after receiving a gift from a militia officer on the southwestern frontier of Virginia. unwrapped the carefully wrapped package and was surprised to find in the package the scalp of a human (Journal of Cherokee Studies, Fall, 1976, 98). A letter, which had been enclosed, explained how the scalp had been acquired and named the militia lieutenant, Vincent Hobbs, as the hero. Bob Benge, a half-blood Cherokee, had been killed by Hobbs in the southwest Virginia mountains. Benge had become famous for his attacks on white settlers in southern and southwest Virginia and soon became a powerful leader among the Cherokee. His behavior made him so detestable that mothers throughout southwestern Virginia challenged their children to obey them by telling them that Captain Benge will get them. Virginia officials offered a large reward for him--"dead or alive" (Journal of Cherokee Studies, 100).

The Indian tribes in Virginia were reduced to one-third of their population between 1609 and 1669, as a result of spirituous liquors, war, the smallpox, and possession by whites of part of Indian territory (Jefferson, 1787). Almon W. Lauber, in Indian Slavery in Colonial Times Within the Present Limits of the United States, indicated that another reason for the reduction of the Indian population in Virginia was the close contact and marriage of the red and black slaves (1970, 287). It seemed that marriage between the red slaves and black slaves was not

27

restricted by the whites. Actually, the first slaves in Virginia were Indians, not Negroes, and the practice lasted for years (Forbes, 191).

The Cherokee in southwest Virginia are generally white today through intermarriage with European traders and settlers. Donald Wilson Read and Vivian Wilson Santini have researched the Cherokee in southwest Virginia and Donald Wilson Read wrote their findings in Brief History of and for Northern Tsalagi Tribe of Southwest Virginia (1989). He noted that "Through intermarriage with the whites and the passage of time, these Cherokee descendants have lost the historical link with their forebearers and are striving today to mend that link and regain some of that personal and individual dignity" (11). Their research also indicated that the Cherokee not only hunted in southwest Virginia but also lived in the area (11).

Martin "Walkingbear" Wilson, Chief of the Amonsoquath Tribe of Cherokee in Missouri, indicated that some of his ancestors once lived in Virginia. His narrative is as follows:

****

"The Treaty of Hopewell ceded or gave the Cherokee land to the British. The British passed a few trinkets to the Indians and took land. The very act, the Treaty of Hopewell, caused the Chickamauga Cherokee to split from the main body of the Cherokee. They went to Missouri and Arkansas with Chief Bowles. After the Treaty of Hopewell, they split off into many sections. Some are in Texas, Arkansas, Missouri, Tennessee, Mississippi, Alabama, Georgia, Florida, Kentucky, Louisiana, West Virginia, Indiana, Illinois, Ohio, New Mexico, Colorado, Oklahoma, Kansas, Iowa, Virginia, and other states.

A goodly part of the Amonsoquath Tribe left (Virginia and North Carolina) and went to Missouri in 1793. Some stayed in the southwestern Virginia area. They are in Cedar Bluff, Tazewell, and other cities in southwest Virginia. A large part of Cherokee who could pass themselves off as white did so. It was called survival. Our people are still in southwest Virginia today, on ancient grounds and will stay. They decided to learn the white man's ways and raise their children in traditional ways. They would live and multiply, and go as white, if necessary. If you can go for white and profit from it, then you will.

The Cherokee people are scattered in all fifty states. The fact that you have a clan or band here and there, and not part of the traditional Cherokee Nation in Oklahoma, the Keetoowah Band in Oklahoma, and the Cherokee Band in Cherokee, North Carolina, lets us know that they are scattered all over the area.

The clans and bands are one and the same. The clan or band would have a chief of the family or several families. Your in-laws' clan may have lost its chief and they didn't want to elect a new one. They would join your clan or

28

band.

The Cherokee Nation had divided opinions in 1861 when the Civil War broke out. Part went under the Confederate General Stand Waite, the only Cherokee to attain the rank of general. He was the last Confederate General to surrender. The muster rolls of his regiment include Cherokee soldiers from Webster, Christian, Greene, Taney, and other counties in Missouri. These rolls are in the History of Taney County, Missouri.

Some Cherokee fought for the Union with Generals Miles, Lyons, and others. Two battles where Cherokee fought Cherokee were the Battle of Wilson Creek in Greene County, Missouri, and the Battle of Pea Ridge, Arkansas.

The people in southwestern and central Virginia, western North Carolina, eastern Tennessee, eastern Kentucky, southern West Virginia, northeastern Alabama, the northern half of Georgia, and other states are Cherokee. Blood ties kept the people together. They had the independence from federal control, the free spirit, the freedom from being told what to do, when to do it, and how to do it. These people, those who retained their tribal bands, are truly a tribe, instinctively, with internal controls over their bands. They are not dependent on outside forces to maintain their survival."

* *

Chief Wilson indicated that his early ancestors, the Bollings and others, once lived in Virginia. He noted that a large number of his relatives in Missouri descended from and related to ancestors "on the Cherokee rolls" (Wilson, The Amonsoquath Tribe of Cherokee). Part of the history of the Amonsoquath Tribe of Cherokee, Ozark, Missouri, is recorded in The Amonsoquath Tribe of Cherokee, 1994. Wilson noted that there are 8,520 Cherokee in Missouri, according the 1990 census records (Bureau of the Census, Washington, DC) and that some of these Cherokees' ancestors came from Virginia. Missouri's total Native American population is 19,508 (Bureau of Census, Washington, DC).

Martin Wilson indicated that his relatives in Missouri can trace their ancestors back to Pocahontas and John Rolfe (married in 1614). The Amonsoquath Tribe --Heritage of a Proud Race, 1593--1993 and A Memoir of a Portion of The Bolling Family in England and Virginia, 1868, have been used as the Amonsoquath Tribe's referral sources. Wilson noted that some of the early Wilsons lived in Virginia (The Battle-Field of Chancellorsville, Virginia, 1867), in the Chesterfield, Virginia, area.

Vivian Wilson Santini, Chief of the Northern Tsalagi Tribe of Southwest Virginia, has conducted extensive research on the Cherokee of Southwest Virginia, Tennessee, and North Carolina. She made the following statement on August 23, 1994, in Burlington, North Carolina:

29

Vivian Santini

Amanda Richardson

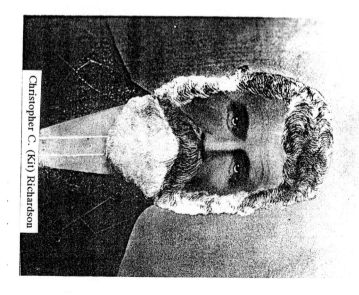

Christopher C. (Kit) Richardson

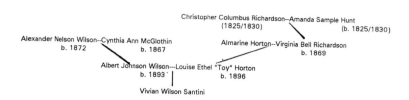

Christopher Columbus Richardson--Amanda Sample Hunt
(1825/1830)   (b. 1825/1830)

Alexander Nelson Wilson--Cynthia Ann McGlothin
b. 1872   b. 1867

Almarine Horton--Virginia Bell Richardson
b. 1869

Albert Johnson Wilson---Louise Ethel "Toy" Horton
b. 1893   b. 1896

Vivian Wilson Santini

I was born in or at the head of the Big Mill Creek, in the hunting grounds of Indians, in southwest, Russell County, Virginia, one of ten children. My father was Albert Johnson Wilson, of Cherokee blood. My mother was Louise Ethel "Toy" Horton. My father was born in Russell County, Virginia, in 1893, and my mother was born in 1896, in Russell County, also.

My father's father, Alexander Nelson Wilson, was born in Smyth County, near Saltville. He was born in 1872. He married Cynthia Ann McGlothin, from Swordscreek, Virginia. She was born in 1867.

My mother was of Cherokee blood also. Ethel Horton's mother was Virginia Bell Richardson, born 1869, in Russell County, Virginia. Her husband was Almarine Horton, of Cherokee descent. Virginia Bell Richardson's mother was Amanda Sample Hunt. She was born in Russell County, in 1865, in Pine Ridge. She was married to Christopher Columbus "Kit" Richardson. He fought in the Civil War with Gen. Robert E. Lee.

The Cherokee have always been in southwest Virginia. The Cherokee were free to go and come as were other tribes. The Cherokee lived on the outskirts of the hunting grounds, because of the plentiful game, berries, and other food sources. Anything you wanted was there. The Cherokee met there and were told by the Spirit that no man was to live in the hunting grounds because food was too plentiful and it would ruin them. They would not be worth anything. The Spirit told them to live away from the grounds. They lived in the outskirts of the boundaries of the hunting grounds of Virginia and Tennessee.

My people are in Kentucky. They are the Hortons, Wilsons, Jacksons, and Hunts. The Wilsons, Wards, and Johnsons are in Wilson, Tennessee. In Virginia, I have the whole southwest Virginia area as relatives--in Wytheville, Tazewell, Lebanon, Smyth County. They are Hortons, Wilsons, Hunts, Bowlings, Bollings, Samples, Hunters, all related to my (family) line. The McCoys are related to us through marriage. They are in the Kentucky, Virginia, and West Virginia area. The Beverlys are related by marriage. I have Wilson relatives in West Virginia.

I was delivered by a full blood Cherokee, a Cherokee midwife, who listed us as white. We would have been called "mulatto," "issue," "Indian," if she had not written in the "white." If the midwife listed us as Indian, we would not have been able to get jobs. We would have been treated like black people are treated today. The Neels in Wytheville worked in the lead mines in Wytheville as slaves, in the 1800s. They were really full blood Cherokee. My grandmother, my third great-grandmother, raised at Crab Orchard, was one of the Neels. She, Susan Neel, was listed on her marriage certificate, in the marriage book, as "black." They were Cherokee. Alexander M. and Susan Neel were listed as "black" when they got married. She was full blood and he was half blood Cherokee.

The Bollings in Virginia are related to the Pocahontas group but they are Cherokee in southwest Virginia. My family's ancestors are on the Cherokee Rolls. Virginia practiced genocide and they still say that the Cherokee don't exist (in Virginia).

Virginia needs to admit to their true history concerning the Cherokee in Virginia; that they have always been in Virginia. The Bowlings, Bollings line has kept the Cherokee connection. We have a Powhatan connection but we are actually Cherokee. All the Bowlings and my people are Cherokee.

I am the Chief of the Northern Tsalagi Tribe of Southwest Virginia. North Carolina, Virginia, West Virginia, and Kentucky have people who are Cherokee. My group is headquartered in southwest Virginia, in the Russell County area. We hold meetings all over the state and in Tennessee, where my elders live.

My husband's grandmother, Mabel Eldridge, is on the Cherokee rolls. He is part Cherokee. I can identify about twenty-one names in my line, not counting my husband's line, that are on the Cherokee rolls.

****

Vivian Wilson Santini's fourth Great-grandfather William Wilson, husband of full-blood Cherokee Rachel Wilson, participated in the action that burned and destroyed thirteen villages. The Cherokee village of Chota and others were destroyed (from sworn declaration of wife, Rachel Wilson, to obtain the benefits of the provisions made by the act of Congress, passed on the 2nd February 1848, War Records, Archives of Washington, D.C.; Barrett, Revolution and Despair, 1978). His wife provided the information in her application for a pension. She noted the action of her husband and other troops against the Cherokee under the command of Captain Nivian Hoskins and Colonels John Sevier and Authur Campbell, even though she, herself, was full-blood Cherokee. "William Wilson was born in 1759/60 in Amelia County, Virginia. His father sold his properties and took his family westward" (Barrett, Revolution and Despair, 1978,1)

William Pendleton (1920) indicated, in History of Tazewell County and

Southwest Virginia, 1748-1920, that "during the wide-spread frontier wars, a tribe of peaceful Cherokees and a few Shawnees found refuge on the headstream of Clinch River near the present town of Tazewell. At first, they lived in caves and improvised shelters. Some of them established trading posts and claimed squatter's rights. A few slaves who were ex-body servants of Revolutionary War officers covertly joined the Indians in their secluded retreat. A social relationship soon developed between the Indians and the settlers' slaves and a number of interracial marriages resulted. An unwritten law of the area was if an Indian man married a slave woman their children were considered slaves. When a male slave married an Indian woman the children were 'free born' because the children lived with their mothers" (119,120). This "unwritten law" was that, whether the father was Cherokee or not, the children of Cherokee mothers were Cherokee (Perdue, 1989, 30). This tradition might account for the fact that very few, if any, of the early Buffalo Ridge residents were slaves. While most of the residents looked Cherokee, traditional Cherokee, a very small number had Negroid and Cherokee features. These few residents, however, were not slaves. They were listed on the census records as free colored or mulatto citizens prior to the 1860s.

Henry Thompson Malone indicated that the early Cherokee during the early to mid 1700s were average to tall in height and were lighter than the "Southern Indians" (15). In the Cherokees' effort to adopt the white man's lifestyle, they became, in many ways, more like the white man than other area Native American tribes in their appearance and dress. They often progressed financially and socially to the point that they did not look like the "stereotype" of an Indian. The Buffalo Ridge Cherokee were generally light-skinned in appearance and dressed like their white neighbors during the early to late 1800s. Malone noted that, during the late 1700s, the Cherokee did not have "few clothes" but were "very well clad" (15). The women wore "skirts of buckskins," which came down to their knees.

Some of the early settlers were very fearful about hunting in areas inhabited by the Cherokee during the mid to late 1700s. Actually, some of these settlers were very friendly with the Cherokee and were able to venture into the unsettled areas. A few of the settlers were mixed with, or married, Cherokee and had a pass to travel without fear or restriction into the Indian hunting grounds. They were known as the "long hunters," or hunters who had the skill and will to go on these long hunting trips for game. The Blevins, known throughout the Cherokee Territory (at that time) in North Carolina, Virginia, and Tennessee as part-Cherokee (Jordan, Cherokee By Blood,), were skilled long hunters. The White Top Mountain Blevins were members of the White Top Mountain Cherokee band. Clement (1929) described some of these settlers as white people:

32

"In the year 1761, as soon as the state of affairs with the Cherokees and Catawbas would admit of hunting in the wilderness, Elisha Walden and a party of 18 men, made up of his friends and neighbors, formed themselves into a company for the purpose of taking a 'long hunt.' Walden lived on Smith River at the place called the 'Round-a-bout,' about two miles west of Martinsville; we have seen that in 1748 he was appointed constable of western Lunenburg, from Smith River to the Wart Mountains. He had married a Miss Blevin, the daughter of a neighbor, Will Blevin, a noted hunter, and in the hunting party were some members of the Blevin family, Henry Scags, Newman, Charles Cox, and others of western Halifax and Bedford.

'Long-hunting' is described by the old frontiersman, John Redd, in the following manner:

'The (long) hunter set out about the first of October, and each man carried two horses, traps, a large supply of powder, lead, and a small hand vise and bellows, files and screw plates for the purpose of fixing the guns if any of them should get out of fix, they returned about the last of March or the first of April***. In their hunts there rarely ever went more than two or three in a company, their reason for this was very obvious, they hunted in the western part of Virginia and Kentucky. The country they hunted in was roamed over by the Indians and if they happened to be discovered by the Indians two or three would not be so apt to excite their fears about having their game killed up, besides this small parties were more sucksesful in taking game than large ones.'

Long hunting was an occupation that required much hardihood, courage and endurance, but in return yielded a good profit..."(89).

These early hunters usually had trained Indian companions to assist them on the long hunts. These mixed Indians, usually of Cherokee and Irish, German, Scotch, or English descent, acted in many ways like the white man but had the hunting skills of the Native American. The Blevins were known to be a part of the White Top Mountain Band of Cherokee in southwestern Virginia and their descendants filed hundreds of applications in the U.S. Court of Claims in 1906 (Jordan, Cherokee By Blood). The Blevins still lived in the Halifax (central Virginia) area as late as 1906 when their descendants filed claims and their testimonies referred to "Halifax, Virginia" on numerous occasions (Miller, 41-46). The Blevins and their relatives during the 1800s were afraid to admit that they were Cherokee and managed to be recognized as "white" people (Guion Miller, 46). Leah M. Harris noted that she has "always passed as a white woman and my father as a white man"(43). William Blevins of Marion, Virginia, indicated in the Miller Report (Records Relating to Enrollment of Eastern Cherokee) that his father and brothers talked about the "enrollment of 1851" and that they were "afraid that they would be carried to the Territory and scattered on that account"

(Miller, 46). George Blevins indicated that his father lived in Grayson County, Virginia, and died in 1898, He stated, "My grandmother, father and I were considered white people, but when people got mad with us they would throw up 'Indian'" (Miller, 45). Mary Sullivan testified that her mother's Cherokee blood came through her mother, "Louise Baldwin, who was also born in Grayson County, Virginia "(45).

Guion Miller made the following statement regarding the claims (1):

"In the matter of the enrollment of the Eastern Cherokees for participation in the fund existing from the judgment of the Court of Claims of May 28, 1906, and under the supplemental order of April 29, 1907, I have the honor to report that 45,857 separate applications have been filed, which represented a total of about 90,000 individual claimants. Of these, I have enrolled 3, 203 of these residing east of the Mississippi River, and 27,051 residing west of the Mississippi River."

These persons would share the $1,000,000.00 fund that had been appropriated by the U.S. Government as a result of the Eastern Cherokees vs. the United States in the Court of Claims, number 23214. Miller summarized his reasons for rejecting the Sizemore claims, representing Sizemore relatives in southwestern Virginia, northwestern North Carolina, northeastern Tennessee, southern West Virginia, and northwestern and western Alabama (46):

"While it seems certain that there has been a tradition in this family that they had a certain degree of Indian blood, the testimony is entirely too indefinite to establish a connection with the Eastern Cherokee Indians at the time of the Treaty of 1835. The locality where these claimants and their ancestors are shown to have been living from a period considerably prior to 1800 up to the present time, is a territory that, during this time, has not been frequented by Cherokee Indians. It is a region much more likely to have been occupied by Indians from Virginia, North Carolina into Virginia. It is also significant that the name of Sizemore does not appear upon any of the Cherokee rolls. For the foregoing reasons, all of these Sizemore claims have been rejected" (46).

It seems that Miller used the (1) reduced Cherokee geographical boundary in 1835 and (2) the census rolls (Eastern Cherokee Roll of 1835 and the Chapman Roll of 1851 in the east and Drennen Roll in the west) of the people who lived within those geographical boundaries as his criteria on which to reject a large number of claimants from Virginia and other states. He excluded the Cherokees who lived in areas that were once a part of the Cherokee Nation, unless they could prove that they were related to approved claimants who lived within the limits of the present Cherokee geographical areas. This approved list of claimants and census rolls of Cherokee who lived within the reduced Cherokee geographical areas have become the basis for determining who is Cherokee today. Average citizens in central and southwestern Virginia viewed these documents, the financial claims settlement list, removal rolls, and census rolls, as proof or the reason that they give for believing that their Virginian neighbors, who claimed Cherokee ancestry, are not really Cherokee but "white" or "colored" people. True Cherokee history has been ignored or painted over (Native Americans called "mulatto," "black," or "white") in areas that were a part of the Cherokee Nation prior to 1835 but are now annexed within various state boundaries. Some Cherokee bands dissolved into white or colored residents. Others, like the Buffalo Ridge group and bands in Southwest Virginia, refused to let their bands break-up and their history torch go out.

Vivian Wilson Santini, in <u>My One Account</u> of the family, 1994, provided the following information about some of the family members:

Lewis Horton, half Cherokee, married Ruth Davis (or Rutha). All Hortons were large land owners. Most of the people of Cherokee blood seemed obsessed in owning as much land as they could in hopes of keeping the white man out of their area.

The story of the Neel and Thornton lines is a sad one to relate. They were in the area of the lead mines and living peaceful until the lead became something of money to the whites. They were killed by rifles as they sat at their evening meals, (others) captured and taken as slave labor to work in the mines. My father took me to Washington County, and there we came upon an old furnace still standing (last year), hidden by overgrowth. He said to me, "Your Grandparents were held prisoners here in Wythe County and made to work until they died." He then took us to Marion where some had been incarcerated as being crazy. Graves were evident of the deaths of the older ones. After he had driven a few more miles, we stopped in the Crab Orchard Village where, to my surprise, many (people) came forth calling to Albert. Little did we know how well he was known in that little town until we were invited into the homes. All of a sudden I realized that everyone was looking at me, smiling and shaking their heads. Yes. My hair was blue black, straight and fine, and hung to my waist. Moma had braided it that morning. I had the same skin tone as they had and my brown eyes sparkled with the attention I was being given. I felt so special that day. I came home with several gifts and a pair of knit gloves which were so pretty to me. I went back home in 1949 to have my child on the land of his ancestors. Each year we return for the reunions of each line. This is about three to four weeks in all. We are in the process of moving home, now that we are retired, to spend time with dear ones we love so much (Santini, 2).

Barrett, in <u>Russell County, A Confederate Breadbasket,</u> noted that Civil War Veteran Christopher C. "Kit" Richardson "became the largest land owner in the southeastern section of the country after the war" (1981, 93).

Barrett included pictures of both Christopher Richardson and his wife, Amanda Richardson (93, 54).

Vivian Santini noted that "Life and the settlers pushed the Indians deep into the Middle Ground, as survival became the first order of the life we had left to us. Cabins and camps were built in isolated areas of the Middle Ground and secret life was a new way of the Indian and some whites who chose to go with them. My mother was a Horton by birth, her lines were of the Richardsons, Hunts (Hunters), Davises, Jacksons, Wilsons, and Samples; all found on the Indian Rolls, east and west. These people are found still living and holding their land from the Blue Ridge into the Kentucky, North Carolina, and Ohio borders" (1).

Perdue supported this view, the marriage between Cherokee and settlers and traders. Perdue (1989) noted that by the early 1700s, traders were moving into Cherokee country and resided in the area throughout the year (30). Traders often married Cherokee women and thereby became a part of the community. The traders served the Cherokee in many ways other than buying and selling, they became military and political advisors. Men like James Adair and other traders left their mark on the Cherokee Nation, including their surnames (Malone, 14, 15).

There are many areas in the United States that have people who do not reside on reservation land or speak Indian language, yet their physical features are decidedly Indian. These people do not have tribal or Indian surnames, yet they often refer to their Cherokee ancestry as proof that they are Indian (Beale, 1957, 1958, 1972; Berry, 1963, 1972; Trigger, 1978, 290). The State of Virginia has a large number of citizens whose appearance is clearly Indian, traditional customs are Indian, and surnames are connected to the Cherokee.

George A. Townsend, in his book, Campaigns of A Non-Combatant, wrote about his travels in Virginia in 1861 (Townsend, 1866, 76). He noted the he "met some of the mixed Indians and Negroes from Indiantown Island" at White House near the Pamunkey River.

The number of Indian slaves in Virginia was small because of the large number of indentured servants and the introduction of Negroes in the colony (Lauber, 287); however, the regulations concerning the management of slaves in Virginia were essentially the same for Negroes and Indians (Bruce, 1910, 130).

Virginia further forced the decline of the Indian as a distinct group by the introduction of the term "mulatto." The law in 1705, provided that the offspring of "an Indian should be deemed, accounted, held and taken to be mulatto" (Hening, 1823, 252; Lauber, 254). Raleigh Pinn, Benjamin Evans, and other residents of Amherst County were listed as "mulattoes" on the 1790 U.S. Census. Although the census enumerators had instructions to list Indians as "I," they apparently did not follow the instructions. The classification of Indians as mulatto, or "M," was followed by census enumerators as late as the 1880 U.S. Census in Virginia. The census records in Amherst and surrounding counties did not utilize the "I" classification for Indians; only the "M" was used, which placed the Indians in the same category as black residents who were classified as mulatto because of their appearance as white as a result of a mixture of white ancestry (Humbles Penn, 1990).

Rev. Peter Fontaine recommended that marriage between whites and Indians be permitted as a means of promoting their conversion to Christianity and "civilization" (Meade, 1878, 82, 283-285). Early in the history of Virginia, it seems that marriage between whites and free Indians was encouraged. The term "mulatto," however, was applied to children of Indian ancestry.

Other states indicated "Indian" rather than the "mulatto" or "mu" term. The 1900 U.S. Census in Virginia referred to some members of Indian families as "b" or "black" instead of the term "mulatto." This is documented by the "b" notation on the 1900 census for many of the members of the Monacan Tribe in Amherst County, as well as the residents who have traditionally been known as Cherokee descendants.

In just twenty years, from 1880 to 1900, the Indians in Amherst County were systematically erased from the record books by the stroke of a pen. They were forced by law in 1705 to be called "mulatto" and then called "black" in 1900. Many of the Cherokee descendants of Amherst County accepted this term without resistance. In fact, by 1850, as "free inhabitants" of Amherst County, the Cherokee families lived in the communities with blacks and whites and many of the families "went" for black or white, depending on the racial community in which they lived and felt happy and secure.

Some of the Cherokee residents in the Stapleton area "went for black" even though they knew that their major ancestry was Indian, Indian/white, Indian/white/black, or Indian/black. The census enumerators classified some of them as black or colored, so many of them "went for black or colored." They attended the colored school, Fairmount, on Buffalo Ridge in the Stapleton area, even though a number of them were full, three-quarter, or half-blood Cherokee. Directly across the James River, in the Stonewall Mill area of Appomattox, near Turner Mountain, however, some of their bi-racial or tri-racial Cherokee relatives went to school with children of white residents, even though they themselves chose to be considered as colored in the community (John Ferguson, 1991).

Most of these Indian residents passively accepted the "black" designation. Actually, some of their ancestors are believed to have been on the run from the Removal to Oklahoma enforcers and were happy with the warm and supportive hideout of the Buffalo Ridge and Glades area of Amherst County. Other relatives came into the area as skilled Indian farmers and worked as tenant farmers in the 1700s, or earlier. Judith Ferguson insisted that her children be "colored" against the wishes of the white and Cherokee father, Dr. Frederick Isbell, who wanted them to pass as white (Carson, 1991). She was satisfied with the Indian/white/black background but felt secure with the black culture she had come to admire through exposure and interaction.

Of those who left the Buffalo Ridge/Glades/Stapleton area, most moved to Lynchburg, Eagle Rock, Covington, Clifton Forge, Beckley, and other locations to find work. Some of these people came to Amherst County initially in the late 1830s to early 1850s from other areas of the Allegheny and Blue Ridge Mountains. A large number of their relatives still reside in Eagle Rock, Indian Rock, Covington, Clifton Forge, Roanoke, Washington County, Beckley (West Virginia), and other areas. Some of their relatives are members of the United Cherokee Tribe of West Virginia (Humbles Penn, 1990). Some of the members of the United Cherokee Indian Tribe of West Virginia indicate that they are related to members of the United Cherokee Indian Tribe of Virginia, Inc. (Humbles Penn). Some of Buffalo Ridge Band's relatives acknowledge that they have "Cherokee Indian" in their blood but have not officially joined the Buffalo Ridge tribal group to keep in touch with their cultural heritage.

Montell noted that the "Coe Clan" of Kentucky, like the Cherokee members of Stapleton, have "always proudly proclaimed their Cherokee ancestry" while "freely" acknowledging their black and white ancestry as well (Montell, 1970, 1972; Trigger, 1978, 292). Some of members of the Virginia Cherokee Group, headquartered in Amherst County, admits Native American ancestral heritage while, at the same time, readily accepts the fact that they have black and/or white ancestors (S. Penn, 1991; F. Jordan, 1990; Harris, 1991). The Melungeons also acknowledge their multicultural heritage, including Cherokee ancestry (N.B. Kennedy, 20, 24, 91, & 93).

Whenever the times were hard in Amherst, the people of Stapleton/Buffalo Ridge returned to the Blue Ridge/Allegheny area or the general vicinity to work (F. Jordan, 1990). They did not leave the area to pass for Indian or white (C. Penn, 1990; F. Jordan, 1990). Only a few cases have been noted where the Stapleton Indian residents left the area because they did not want to be designated as "Negro" or "colored." M. O. Ferguson indicated that one of his grandfather's relatives left Appomattox County and passed for white in Lynchburg (M. Ferguson, 1985). Actually, most of the Buffalo Ridge Cherokee descendants are proud of their Indian-black-white American cultural connection.

The Cherokee traveled and hunted in this area frequently and were familiar with the beautiful topography and game-rich area of Stapleton. It is not surprising that they were attracted to Amherst County and vicinity, since the area was very much like their home territory in North Carolina, Tennessee, Georgia, Alabama, and other areas, including southwestern Virginia. The Cherokee traveled through Lynchburg and Amherst Counties on a regular basis. I.S. Moore remembered his mother's accounts of the Cherokee. He noted:

"I have often heard my mother tell of the Cherokee Indians who would come through Lynchburg from Western North Carolina on their way to Washington to collect their compensation or to arrange their transfer to the Indian Territory. They always camped in the wagon lot attached to the warehouse of which my grandfather was inspector. She said that the citizens would split sticks and place a copper cent in them for the Indian boys to shoot at with their bows and arrows. She said that they rarely missed the cent which was always the prize for their accurate shooting..."(Moore, 1923, 16).

A band of Cherokee was known to have settled in the Amherst County Blue Ridge Mountain area after the Revolution (Percy, 1952, 2). Many of Amherst County citizens have been informed by their ancestors that they have Cherokee ancestry. They have passed the information on to their children and grandchildren. Amherst County and surrounding counties have oral traditions that support the view that many of their citizens have Cherokee ancestry (O'Neill, 1969; Houck, 1984, 124; Tompkins and Davis, 1939, 82; McLeRoy and McLeRoy, 1977, 13). The oral tradition among a people about a particular tribe of Indian, if popular across a wide area, and without an opposing popular oral tradition concerning another tribe, must be accepted as having some merit. The oral tradition of Cherokee blood in the Lumbee Indians of South Carolina, for example, is also so strong that it is impossible to "dismiss the claim" (Dial and Eliades, 1975, 16).

Actually, Cherokee lived throughout Virginia and other southeastern states. A large number of applications was filed in the U.S. Court of Claims in 1906-1910 by people who indicated that their ancestors had Eastern Cherokee ancestry. These 2000 applications represented approximately 5000 claimants who resided chiefly in northwestern North Carolina, northeastern Tennessee, southwestern Virginia, southern West Virginia, and northwestern and western Alabama. Virginia submitted a large number of claims. The Sizemore cases represented individuals who were related in sections of several states, including southwestern Virginia and other sections of Virginia. W.H. Blevins, of Marion, Virginia, indicated that he was the chief of the principal Cherokee Indians living in the White Top Mountain area of southwestern Virginia. His application was dated April 11, 1908, and signed "W.H. Blevins, Marion, Virginia" (Jerry Wright Jordan, Vol. I, 169-172; Guion Miller).

Sarah A. Mashburn's application, Roll # 664, noted that her claimants were descended from Chief Donohoo. She indicated that Chief Donohoo was born in Virginia, probably near the James River. The evaluator of the application noted that there is a "well-recognized tradition in the family" that he was Cherokee and that he was from the James River "neighborhood" (Jordan, 237). The Buffalo Ridge Cherokee have a similar tradition about Cherokee living in the James River area.

The Buffalo Ridge ancestors were aware of--and present descendants have heard--legends about the Cherokee's attraction to the James River (Humbles Pinn). Although in the 1700s the James River separated the Appomattox County (then Buckingham County) clan--chiefly Fergusons, McCoys, Pin(n)s, Beverlys, Bankses, Evanses, and Tylers--from the Buffalo Ridge clan of Pinns, Beverlys, Redcrosses, and others, it also joined the two clans together at the James by the Stapleton Ferry and canoes for reunions, church services, work projects, and numerous other tribal activities. They valued the James River because of its rich source of game and fish, and for transportation. It is no wonder that the Donohoo family members kept the legend for more than two hundred years of "Cherokee on the James," just as the Buffalo Ridge Cherokee remember the stories about the James. One can only wonder if Chief Donohoo lived in or near the Stapleton area! One can only wonder if he lived with the Buffalo Ridge band. The James River was a source of travel for the Buffalo Ridge family members who were living in Covington, Clifton Forge, and other areas of Alleghany County and West Virginia as they visited their relatives on the James in Amherst and Appomattox Counties.

The Sizemore applications were rejected because the claimants' ancestors were not enrolled on the Cherokee rolls or on the official censuses of the Cherokee Nation as it existed when the census enumerations were taken. The Cherokee had ceded land--land in Virginia and sections of North Carolina and other southeastern states where the Sizemores lived--and therefore the Cherokee (1) were not enumerated and (2) could not document Cherokee ancestry according to the criteria of the Eastern Cherokee. It was not a question of being Cherokee; the real question was, "Were your ancestors documented as a part of the Cherokee Nation and living with those people in a tribal relationship?" (as the Nation existed geographically at the time of the census). The Sizemore claimants (cases 6088-6188), therefore, were rejected. These claimants were bold enough to submit their applications and therefore left written records to give later generations firm

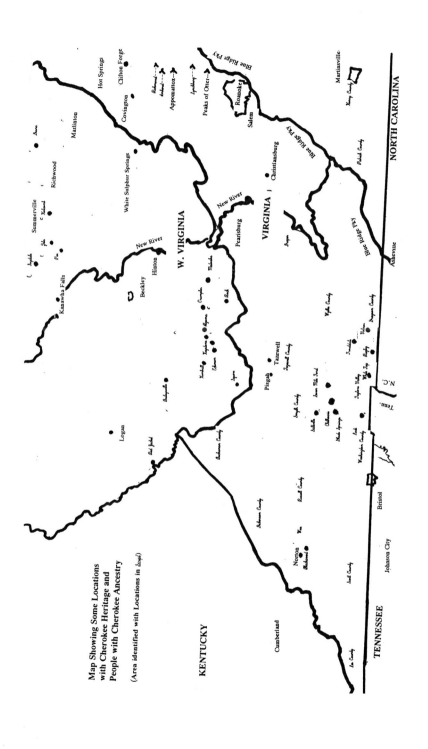

Map Showing Some Locations
with Cherokee Heritage and
People with Cherokee Ancestry

(Area identified with Locations in *detail*)

documentation that they were Cherokee. The people in central and southwestern Virginia knew that they were Cherokee and would not let a political land cession separate them from their true heritage (S. Penn; Vivian Wilson Santini). Some of the towns and cities in Virginia that represented residents who claimed Cherokee ancestry and submitted applications were, to name a few, Rugby, Grosses, Azen, Front Dale, Green Cove, Park, Saltville, Redjacket, Amherst, Lynchburg, Richmond, Damascus, Brighton, Blackwood, Seven Miles Ford, Taylors Valley, Lodi, Cale, Kipling, Chilhowie, Trot Dale, Grant, Fairwood, and Jeffersonville. These families were the Blevins, Hopkins, Osborns, Chambers, Carters, Miller, Hagas, Hughes, Rosses, Baldwins, Esteps, and others. Two families, the Hughes and Chambers families, were accepted as Cherokee because they were related to ancestors who were recorded in the Cherokee geographical area (Fanny Hughes, 712 Court Street, Lynchburg, vol. 5, 299, with two children, George and Jeanie Alexander; and Rosa Chambers, and son, William A., Jr., 417 West Grace Street, Richmond, Vol. 5, 296). Calvin Knuckles, whose ancestors were from Amherst, Virginia, lived in Johnson City, Tennessee, at the time he submitted his application. His application was rejected because his ancestors lived in Virginia (J.W. Jordan, 250), an area that had not been considered as a Cherokee area, even though a section of Virginia was once owned by the Cherokee Nation and that the Cherokee tradition in the area was strong and rich (Royce; Whitehead, 1896).

West Virginia, formerly a part of Virginia, seceded from Virginia and was admitted as a state on June 20, 1863. West Virginia has a very close relationship with the Cherokee of Virginia, and in particular, with Buffalo Ridge. Some of the cities and towns of West Virginia that were represented by Cherokee residents who filed applications were Moroco, Clay, Poe, Vaughan, Zela, Pierpoint, Saulsville, Jared, Jumbo, Baileysville, Cassaway, Hinton, Eckman, Kimball, Burke, Matoka, Joe Branch, Masseysville, White Sulphur Springs, Tue River, Holcomb, Redjacket, Crumpler, Briar, Dott, Serena McComas, Rock, Powhatan, Hallsville, Widemouth, Sizemore, Gladesprings, and Diana. Jerry Wright Jordan compiled the names and location of applicants and her work may be found in Cherokee By Blood (Vols. 1-8). The original report, The Report of Guion Miller, U. S. Court of Claims, 1906-1910, may be reviewed at the National Archives, Washington, D.C. (12 microfilm rolls, M685).

The Cherokee were famous for practicing a "slash-and-burn" method of agriculture. "They cleared the land by stripping the bark from trees and later burning the trees" (Encyclopedia Americana, 1972, 399). In the Glades area of Amherst County near Buffalo Ridge and beyond, oral tradition supports the fact that Cherokee Indians resided in and hunted throughout the area and frequently burned trees to keep the area grassy to attract deer and other game (Percy, 1961, 2). Many residents of the Rockbridge County and Amherst County areas believe that the local descendants of Indians have Cherokee ancestry as a result of their ancestors slipping away from the forced march to Oklahoma and hiding in the hills of the Blue Ridge and Allegheny Mountains (O'Neill). Others tell of different racial connections with the Cherokee who were forced to live in the mountains by the authorities of Rockbridge County because they were found to have smallpox (Tompkins and Davis, 1939, 82). There is strong documentation that confirms the fact that some of the Buffalo Ridge Band members, living in a tribal setting, were on the Ridge when the early settlers began to arrive in Central Virginia in the 1700s.

CHAPTER IV
Nv gi (Four)

AMHERST COUNTY AND VICINITY

The United States Census Records
and the Paper Genocide

Amherst County and the surrounding counties, including Appomattox, Bedford, Buckingham, Campbell, Nelson, and Rockbridge, have had Cherokee residents in their midst before or since the 1700s (Amherst County Marriage Register; Whitehead, 1896; Neblet, Hume, & McIvor, 3). Their domicile in the area may have occurred prior to the 1700s. Bob Benge, a half-blood Cherokee (Journal of Cherokee Studies, 96), created numerous problems for the settlers in southern and southwestern Virginia. He gained notoriety for his frequent raids on white residents and soon he rose to a high position of leadership among the Cherokee and Shawnee. He was killed in 1794 by a Virginia Militia lieutenant named Vincent Hobb. Samuel Benge, who is believed to have been Bob Benge's father, lived in Albemarle County, near Crozet, Virginia, at the base of the Blue Ridge Mountains.

Samuel Benge purchased land on October 6, 1766 on Beverdam Creek, off Route 250, in Crozet (Albemarle Land Record Book, page 317). There were several Samuel Benges on the Cherokee Rolls (Samuel H. Benge, Jr., age 29, 1/2 Cherokee, and Samuel Benge, age 4, 1/8 Cherokee, Roll # 1764, Indexed Final Rolls of the Cherokee). In 1766, at the time of the Crozet land purchase--just five years after Amherst County was created from Albemarle County--sections of Virginia were included in the Cherokee Nation. The Cherokee residents in Virginia maintained close contact with the Cherokee in other states of the southeast. Actually, the Blue Ridge Mountain range provided a direct route through much of the area populated by the Cherokee in several states to central and southwest Virginia. Indian and traders paths ran along and near the Blue Ridge and Allegheny Mountains. Bands of Cherokee lived on and at the base of the Blue Ridge Mountain. The Cherokee contacts with relatives in other areas continued long after the political land cessions (A. Thomas). Many of the Native American southwestern Virginia residents were related to residents in central Virginia, as far as the Cherokee Holston River area (Smoot, 174, 175; Jordan, Vol. 5, 296, 299). Jordan noted a large number of residents along the Blue Ridge who claimed Cherokee ancestry in her book, Cherokee By Blood. A band of Cherokee was known to have roamed the Blue Ridge in Amherst County in the 1700s, after the Revolution (Percy, 1952, 2).

The Virginia Colonists invited large numbers of Cherokee into Virginia to

Many of these Cherokee roamed the Old Dominion freely with weapons and passes granted by the government of Virginia (see Treaty with Virginia). They were in Virginia before the Revolution and remained in Virginia after the Revolution (Whitehead; Percy, 2).

Dr. W.A. Plecker, Director of the Virginia Department of Vital Statistics, stated that a "group of Cherokee were returning to North Carolina from Washington. They developed smallpox in Amherst and the three survivors decided to remain" (Withrow, 1924, 17). Dr. Plecker indicated that "these people overflowed the Blue Ridge and took possession of Irish Creek (area in Rockbridge County, near Amherst County). I do not know whether any of the original white people remained or not." The complete accuracy of these statements by Dr. Plecker may be questioned by researchers. It is, however, a well-known fact that Cherokee roamed on and lived in the Blue Ridge area, on both the Rockbridge County side and Amherst County side of the Blue Ridge prior to and after the Revolution. Actually, a traveler may find descendants of Cherokee scattered along the Blue Ridge in Bedford, Botetourt, Roanoke, Franklin, Montgomery, and Patrick Counties, Virginia, to name a few, and along the Blue Ridge as far as the Qualla or Cherokee Reservation in North Carolina. All of these counties had and have people with Cherokee oral histories (Jordan; G. Miller). Amherst and Bedford Counties have descendants of the Poindexters or Poingdextres (Ackerby and Parker, Our Kin; Amherst County Historical Museum, The Poindexter Papers. The Poindexters are descendants of the Poindexters of Louisa County, Virginia. Louisa County, which has a town named "Poindexter," has a Cherokee tradition (Jordan, Cherokee By Blood; Guion Miller, Miller Report).

It is believed that Cherokee lived as far as Central and Eastern Virginia, with many of the traditional eastern Native American tribes' surnames being included with the Cherokee Rolls. Guion Miller noted that many of the claimants said that their Cherokee ancestors lived in Virginia, along the "Rappahannock" and "James" Rivers (Jordan, 236). Eastern Native American surnames, Atkins or Adkins, for example, appear on the Removal Rolls (Bob Blankenship). It is believed that the Cherokee may have lived as far east as the Tidewater area, with the Tidewater Indians (Haywood, Report to the Bureau of Ethnology, 223), and that some of the Cherokee intermarried with them. It is a well-known fact that the Cherokee were "at peace" with the Powhatans. The Pocahontas and Cherokee tradition and connection are very strong among the Bollings, Fergusons, Blairs, Beverlys, and Megginsons of Amherst and Appomattox Counties. These surnames, however, are Cherokee surnames on the Removal Rolls; and Central and Southwestern Virginia Native Americans note today, and their ancestors have always stated, that they are "Cherokee,"

The Cherokee in Amherst County represented a high percentage of the early marriages, long before many early settlers populated the area. The early settlers and traders followed the same pattern as the white man followed in other areas (Clarke, 7). They married Cherokee women in Amherst County and vicinity. Official records during the 1800s as well as the oral histories, surnames, and racial classifications suggest that they had tribal connections that were similar to residents in southwestern Virginia and other states with heavy Cherokee populations. Their surnames matched names on Cherokee Tribal Rolls (Indexed Final Rolls of the Cherokee; V. Santini, 1994; Rice, 1991, 42-49, 186-187) and their descendants continued to proclaim their Cherokee heritage (V. White; B. Beverley; R. Carson; A. Thomas; M. Wilson). They usually married other Native Americans and therefore strengthened their tribal connections (Amherst Marriage Records; Appomattox Marriage Records; Huffer). Bailey F. Davis, a compiler of Amherst County marriage data, noted in 1965, "History tends to repeat itself as far as the marriages between various families in Amherst County." These families often permitted marriages between first cousins as well as distant relatives and other Cherokee residents to hold their tribal connections firmly in place (see Amherst County Marriages--Family Members).

EARLY AMHERST COUNTY MARRIAGES
(Families with Cherokee/Native American Surnames and/or Oral Histories)
(Book 1, Amherst County Marriage Book)

Date	Husband/Wife	Parents	Witnesses
11/8/1783	Powell, Benjamin Cooper (Cowper), Jane	Powell, Lucas Powell, Wm(Guard)	Powell, Nathaniel Wright, John
6/10/1784	Tiller(Tyler), John Hopper, Nancey	Tiller, Wm. Hopper, Thomas	Tiller, Larry; Hopper, Elizabeth; Hudson Josh
11/1/1784	Hudson, Joshua Banks, Elizabeth		Hudson, Joshua Sr.; Reid, J.
1/24/1786	Pendleton, John Banks, Salley	Banks, Linn	Wade, Ballinger; Banks, Reuben; Taliafarro, John
1/1/1787	Bowling, Wm. Mays, Sealey	Mays, Wm.	Bugg, Sherod; Hill, Ezek; Taliafarro, John
2/15/1787	Carter, Abraham Roberts, Mary	Roberts, Joshua	Roberts, Alexander; Davis, John
8/6/1787	Scott, Jacob Franklin, Milley		Franklin, Samuel; Franklin, Henry
9/8/1788	Cooper, Joseph (from Henry County) Dillard, Jane	Cooper, Thomas Dillard, James	Bell, Drew; Christian, Martha; Dillard, G.
10/6/1788	Christian, Turner Leek, Elizabeth	Penn, Phillip	Christian, J; Gayne, J. Stinchcomb, A.
2/2/1789	Tyler, John Dillard, Elizabeth	Tyler, Charles Dillard, William	Tyler, Daniel; Dillard, Mary
4/6/1791	Carter, John	Carter, Mary	Day, John; Hill,

	Day, Salley	Day, Samuel	Madison; Scott, Eleanor
9/17/1791	Dillard, John Penn, Salley	Penn, John	Watts, Charles; Murphy, James; Penn, Eliz.
2/4/1792	Jordan(ain), Wm. Watts, Susan	Watts, Stephen	Christian, James; Haskins, Thomas
5/7/1792	Martin, Edward Warwick, Polly	Warwick, Abraham	Warwick, Daniel; Haskins, Owen; Lewis, Char
6/1/1792	Peters, Elisha Tiller, Jane	Tiller, Wm.	Watts, Charles Haskins, Thomas
11/10/1792	Harris, Wm. Roberts, Sussana	Roberts, Elizabeth	Roberts, Nancey
11/29/1792	Beverley, Frances Williams, Mary	Williams, Nancey	Penn, Rolley
9/4/1793	Ferguson, Samuel Ball, Susannah	Ball, Wm.	Ferguson, David; Kidd, James; Ball, J.
6/7/1794	Pendleton, Wm. Cox, Patsey	Cox, Archer; Cox, M.	Cox, Melliden
10/20/1794	Carpenter, Enol Evans, Salley		Evans, Wm.; Crawford, Reuben
2/28/1795	Christian, James Watts, Cordelia	Nowell, Reuben Watts, Stephen	
5/18/1795	Scott, John Rose, Elizabeth	Rose, Charles	Rose, John; Rose, Patr.
10/7/1795	Scott, Alexander Williams, Ann		Clark, Wm.
11/2/1795	Evans, Thomas Pinn, Anna	Pinn, Rolly; Pinn, Sarah	Lonogen, John
3/13/1797	Cox, Milliner Bolling, Sadey	Bolling(Bowling, James	
8/27/1799	Pinn, James Redcross, Nancy	Redcross, John	Pinn, Rawley; Shrader, George
9/10/1799	Jackson, Burwell Evans, Alley		Lowing, John; Jordan, Benj.
9/25/1799	Spencer, John Clasby, Nancy		Clasby(Gillaspie), Wm.
2/17/1802	Scott, Issac Dillard, Martha		London, Laskin
2/18/1803	Nuckuls, Wm. Blair, Sally		Blair, Allen
3/9/1807	Gue, Rosemerry Hogg, Mary Ann		Gue, John; Byass, James
5/8/1807	Jinkins, John Embly, Hannah		
8/13/1807	Pinn, Turner		Sale, Wm.; Edwards,

		James	
	Humbles, Joyce		
3/31/1800	Sale, Wm.		Sale, Wm.; Duncan,
	Duncan, Viney	Duncan, John	John
2/3/1808	Bowman, Wm.		West, Frances
	Ferguson, Salley		Ferguson, James
2/17/1812	Jones, John	Jones, Thom	Sale, Samuel
		(Capt., Nelson Co.)	
	Sale, Martha	Sale, John	
8/31/1809	Wood, James Jr.	Wood, James	Duncan, Dadey;
	Duncan, Elizabeth	Duncan, John	Duncan, Wm.
10/6/1812	Pinn, James		Salle, Wm.; Cooper, John
	Cooper, Jane		
8/19/1811	Jenkins, John		
	Jenkins, Betsey		
9/10/1811	Robinson, John		Taylor, Samuel; Hill, Wm.
	Terry, Polly	Terry, Thomas	
12/11/1812	Cobbs, John , Dr.		Pendleton, Wm.;
	Garland, Jane	Garland, David	Pendleton, J.
6/21/1813	Scott, John		Pinn, James; Salle, Wm.
	Pinn, Jane		
12/2/1813	Tyler, Charles		
	Johns, Nancey		
9/7/1815	Nuckles, Obediah		
	Gue, Belinda	Gue, Marget	
1/22/1818	Carter, John		Carter, Wm.; Carter,
	Elliott, Elizabeth		Abram
2/22/1818	Scott, Wm.		Powell, Geo.; Pendleton,
	Pendleton, Eliz	Pendleton, Reuben	Wm.
8/10/1821	Cooper, John		Garvis, Joseph; Davis, B.
	Sorrells, Nancey		
2/15/1823	Toler (Tyler), Lem		Allcock, John
	Allcock, Elizabeth		
3/24/1823	Mays, Joel		Mays, Washington;
	Scott, Elizabeth	Scott, Isaac	Mundy, Jesse
11/17/1823	Dillard, Wm.		Staples, Joseph
	Christian, Sarah	Dillard, John	
12/10/1823	Christian, Charles		Christian, Samuel;
	Tiller, Frances		
6/3/1824	Ware, Mansfield		Allcock, J.; Ware, John;
	Franklin, Susan	Franklin, Peachy	Waugh, R.
2/5/1825	Scott, Benjamin		Jewell, Thomas, Scott,
	Evans, Annes		John
12/21/1826	Jewell, James		Jewell, Thomas
	Jewell, Harriett		
6/18/1827	Pinn, Rolla		Jewell, Thomas
	Scott, Susanna(h)	Scott, Samuel	

Date	Names		
7/16/1827	Bowling, Lewis Pinn, Frances	Coleman, Robert	Woodroof, Seth
12/18/1827	Sparrow, Bartlett Pinn, Maria	Pin(Pinn),Turner	Beverly, Jonathan; Jewell, T.
2/9/1828	Blair, Wm. Sale, Clara		Sale, Wm.
8/6/1828	Christian, Stephen Christian, Lucy	Christian, Mourning	Christian, Charles
8/7/1828	Christian, John Howl, Nancy	Christian, Elizabeth	Howl, Absolon; Howl, Mary
1/7/1829	Blair, Winston Lain, Nancey		Tinsley, Robert
8/14/1829	Tuppence, Richard Pinn, Polly	Pinn, Thomas	Jewell, Thomas; Pinn, John
3/10/1830	Berley(Berly),Uriah Jewell, Tracy		Christian, Daniel; Christian, P.
5/27/1831	Scott, John Franklin, Pocahontas	Franklin, Mary	Franklin, Fayette
2/21/1832	Franklin, Fayette Tyree, Mary	Franklin, Merry Tyree, Jane	Scott, John; Tyree, Jane
1/28/1832	Harris, Wm. Coleman, Lucy		Coleman, Robert; Penn, Lucy
9/22/1834	Hughes, Spotswood Jenkins, Paulina	Jenkins, Wm.	Burnett, John
9/12/1836	Christian, Wesley Christian, Evelina		Christian, Elijah
9/13/1838	Jewell, George Pinn(Pin), Martha	Pinn, Turner Pinn, Joicy	Sparrow, Bartlett
1/21/1839	Nuckles, Andrew Niceley, Emelina	Niceley, James	Niceley, James; Nuckles, Obediah
10/4/1839	Bevley(Bevly), Matt Bevley, Elizabeth	Beverly, Samuel	Powell, Paulus; Christian, Polly
11/9/1840	Jackson, Daniel Pinn, Sejus	Pinn, Turner	Sparrow, Bartlett;Staples, D.
5/12/1840	Scott, Samuel Davies, Ann Eliz	Davis, Henry	Scott, Charles
6/29/1843	Jordan, Edwin Penn, Jane		Brown, Hugh
12/7/1843	Sale, Wm. Carter, Sarah	Carter, Joseph	Franklin, Jeremiah
8/20/1844	Ross, Jefferson Beverley, Permelia		Duncan, Geo; Peters, Reuben
3/28/1845	Cooper, Wesley Peters, Julian		Peter, Reuben
3/26/1846	Gillaspie (Clasby), Wm Franklin, Elizabeth		Franklin, Benj.; Franklin, Henry

1/17/1848	Ware, John Sale, Hopseyann	Sale, Benj.	
6/5/1848	Blair, Francis Watts, Emely	Watts, Wm.	Turner, Stephen; Watts, America
3/6/1849	Sale, Alexander Hicks, Eliza	Hicks, Maria	Hicks, Madison
9/3/1849	Cooper, Alfred Hartless, Rebecca		Hartless, Peter; Curry, Peter
11/23/1849	Sale, George Carter, Melinda	Carter, Joseph	Hicks, Madison
11/24/1849	Davis, George Carter, Elizabeth	Carter, Joseph	Powell, Paulus

The 1810 U.S. Census, for example, has eight Penn (Pin) listings in Amherst County (U.S. Census). The Penn/Pin(n) family members married other Cherokee residents, and this trend continued in the 1900s (Amherst County Marriages--Family Members). Although the Creek Rolls included citizens with the Penn surname, the Cherokee Rolls in Oklahoma also included Penns (Panns). Like the surname list in the Irish Creek section of Rockbridge County (Huffer), Buffalo Ridge's surnames, as well as other Amherst County sections' surnames, look like a list taken from the Cherokee Rolls (B. Blankenship; J. Tyner; M. Wilson).

Amherst County, like other central and southwestern Virginia counties, has a very large population of residents with Cherokee ancestry. The owners of Cherokee surnames and oral histories continue to marry other residents with similar Cherokee surnames and Cherokee family oral histories (Settlers in Amherst County with Cherokee Surnames and Oral Histories; Amherst Count Marriage Register, 1798-1834). Cherokee residents of Appomattox followed this same pattern in their marriage preference. A review of records of the tribal members' ancestors also reveals a similar trend (Appomattox County Marriages, 1854-1890; Appomattox County Marriages).

In the early 1900s, many Appomattox residents believed that the Ferguson, McCoy, Tyler, and Beverly families, as well as other Cherokee-surnamed families in Appomattox and Amherst Counties, were trying to start a "third race" (Raymond Ferguson), when these people actually were already Native Americans (U.S. Census, Appomattox & Amherst; Rice, 1991) but had been denied the opportunity to proclaim their heritage. This "third race" belief was based on the fact that these people were light-skinned, Indian-looking" people who only married people who had Cherokee ancestry, "looked Indian" like themselves, and/or were at least distantly related to them.

It is a well-known fact that the Appomattox and Amherst county Fergusons, McCoys, Beverlys, and other relatives tended to marry each

49

It is a well-known fact that the Appomattox and Amherst county Fergusons, McCoys, Beverlys, and other relatives tended to marry each other from generation to generation. Although most of the United Cherokee Indian Tribe of Virginia, Inc. (UCITOVA) ancestors were listed as "mulatto" on the 1790, 1840 ("Free Colored"), 1860, 1870, and 1880 census records and were light-skinned Indians as a result of English, Irish, and Scottish ancestors, their race was changed to black in the 1900s because they did not choose to "go for white." Bernard Humbles Pinn, Chief of the United Cherokee Indian Tribe of West Virginia (UCITOWVA), has studied Cherokee history in Virginia and West Virginia extensively. He noted (1994) the following information about the Treaty of 1756 (Treaty Held with the Catawba and Cherokee Indians, at the Catawba Town and Broad River, February and March, 1756):

Robert Dinwiddie, the British Lieutenant-Governor,
and Commander in Chief of the Colony and Dominion
of Virginia, entered into a treaty in 1756 with
the Cherokee Nation. Peter Randolph and William
Byrd, a member of His Majesty's Council of
Virginia, met representatives of the Cherokee
Nation at Broad River, in North Carolina, March
13, 1756, to negotiate a treaty with the sachems
and warriors of the Cherokee. The representatives of Virginia
requested the assistance of the Cherokee to defend the colony
of Virginia and its settlers against the pending encroachment of
the French and their allies, the Delawares and Shawnees. The
colony was concerned about the "mischief" of the French in the
surrounding areas to subvert the peace of the Old Dominion.
The commissioners of the Virginia colony requested the
assistance of the Cherokee Nation with the approval of the
British. The commissioners addressed the Cherokee
representatives at Broad River and stated:

"You have undoubted heard that many skulking parties of Indians,
prompted thereto by our treacherous and most
perfidious enemies the French, have made incursions upon our
Frontiers, murdering and captivating all the men, women, and
children, who were so unhappy as to fall into their way. The
Indians principally concerned in this bloodshed
are the Shawnee and Delawares, who
delighting in blood, and not observing the most
solemn treaties, at which they have always had a
large share of the Royal Bounty, have by the cunning and artifice
of the French, been withdrawn from their allegiance to the Great
King, the Father of us all, and prevailed on (to) take up
the murdering hatchet against his children.." (The Treaty of

The treaty confirmed the following points:

1. That the ancient alliance be renewed, and the old chain brightened between the English and Cherokee.

2. That if the French King shall at any time wage war against the King of Englind, the Cherokee shall wage war with all their power against the French King, and all his allies.

3. That Virginia shall assist in contributing their proportion toward building a strong fort, in such part of the Cherokee country as the sachems and warriors of the Nation shall direct, for (the protection of the wives and children of the Cherokee warriors).

4. That as soon as the said fort shall be built, the Cherokee shall within forty days notice, march into Virginia, four hundred able warriors to such fort or place as the Governor of that place shall order or appoint, to be employed in the service of the said colony as soldiers, in defending the inhabitants thereof against the encroachments of the French and Indians in their alliance.

5. That if the French shall at any time, directly or indirectly make use of any means, either by coming into the Nation themselves, or sending their Indians with belts of wampum, or by any other way whatsoever, endeavor to prevail on the Cherokee to infringe this treaty, the Cherokee shall forthwith dispatch a messenger, in whom they can confide, to the Governor of Virginia, to acquaint him with the same, and the particular measures so taken.

6. That if the Cherokee at any time shall know, or

be informed of any schemes that the French or their Indians may plan, to the prejudice of the English, they shall give immediate intelligence thereof to the Governor of Virginia.

7. That the warriors which shall be employed in the service of the English, in the Colony of Virginia, be found and provided at the expense of that colony, with all necessary cloaths, victuals, arms, and ammunition.

8. That neither the Cherokee nor Virginians shall protect the disobedient subjects of the other, or entertain rebels, traitors or fugitives, but within twenty days after due requisition made, shall deliver them up.

9. That the Cherokee not suffer or permit the French to build any fort or fortification, on any of their land, on the waters of the Mississippi or elsewhere, that may annoy the English, if in their power to prevent it.

10. That if any subject belonging to the King of Great Britain, residing in Virginia, or any other Cherokee belonging to the Cherokee Nation, shall offend against this treaty, they shall be punished, without the treaty being any way therefore infringed.

The Cherokee reminded the commissioners that they could not send their warriors to Virginia until they, the British representatives, had built a fort for the defense of their citizens while their warriors were away in Virginia. The treaty considered that fact and included a condition that the fort will be built first and then the warriors will come to Virginia to help the settlers and the British.

The Cherokee knew the area of Virginia very well. Part of Virginia at this time was connected to the Cherokee Nation. Cherokee had traveled throughout Virginia and knew where each hill or creek was situated. They had moved freely throughout Virginia long before the arrival of the first settlers. Cherokee bands lived in various areas of Virginia and the present areas of West Virginia, especially in areas along the Blue Ridge and Allegheny Mountains and locations near the mountain ranges. In Virginia, these people were living and their descendants are still residing, for example, on Buffalo Ridge in Amherst County. One of

Ridge Band of Cherokee, selling land on Buffalo Ridge to Indians and white settlers (1761-1807 Amherst County Deed Book). It is believed that Rawley Pinn acquired the land as a gift for services to the British, either as a warrior himself or a leader or advisor to the warriors (B. Humbles Pinn). If this theory is not the case, the only other conclusion, since the county records do not show him purchasing all of his land, is that he and his ancestors had been in possession of the land from earlier real estate awards or transactions. The Executive Journals provide excellent information about early land grants in Virginia in the 1700s. Joshua Fry received "1,000 acres in Albemarle on the Branches of Stovall and Porridge Creeks" on November 8, 1748 (near the present Buffalo Ridge in Amherst County, Executive Journal, page 264). Joshua Fry, William Cabell, and James Christian received "6,000 acres on Wreck Island Creek and Branches adjacent and the Fluvanna in Albemarle..." (Fluvanna River later named the James River and this section of Albemarle County became Amherst and Appomattox Counties; October 26, 1751, page 368). William Megginson, distant ancestor of the Megginsons of Appomattox County, appointed Justice of Peace for Albemarle County (page 344) and received land grants (Executive Journal, 15, 51, 85, 136, 315, and 446). It is a mystery how Raleigh Pinn first acquired his land. The Amherst County Courthouse has numerous records of his land transactions during the late 1700s.

Many soldiers in the Revolutionary War were from Amherst County and vicinity. Rawley or Rolly Pinn, an ancestor of the Buffalo Ridge Band of Cherokee, was a soldier in the Revolutionary War (Percy, 1961, 49). It is believed that he was awarded some of his land as a result of his service during the Revolutionary War (DiProsperis, 1995). Percy noted other Amherst County Revolutionary War soldiers that are or are believed to be related to Band members, including John Redcross, Thomas Hopper, Captain John Christian, Pendleton Isbell, Ben Megginson, Samuel Megginson, William Evans, William Megginson, Reuben Jordan, and Thomas Elliott. Saffell (1969) listed some of the soldiers whose descendants are possibly residing in Central Virginia. Some of the soldiers named in his list included John Hopper, William Harris, and Thomas Howl (Owl or Howell).

Many of the Amherst County soldiers who served in the Revolutionary War were skilled Cherokee or mixed-Cherokee soldiers. The rifle company soldier was issued a rifle and a tomahawk (Percy, 1961, 42). These soldiers used their military-issue tomahawks with the natural skill that was expected of Cherokee. They scouted and protected the areas of Stonewall Mill, Buffalo Ridge, and other areas with the precision that has always been a tradition for Native American warriors.

In Stonewall Mill (formerly Buckingham County and now a part of the County of Appomattox), on the James River, three or four miles from the top of Buffalo Ridge, Rawley Pinn is listed on the tax rolls in 1773

(Woodson, 83). The Pinns had tribal pockets in Stonewall and on Buffalo Ridge. They intermarried within and between the two tribal groups. John Fields, an ancestor of the Buffalo Ridge Cherokee, is listed in 1774 as "mulatto" in Buckingham County (Woodson, 39). Other names listed on the tax rolls of Buckingham County were Robert Evans, 1773 and 1774, 38; Edward, Joel, John, Moses, and William Ferguson, 1773 38; and Edward and Joseph Jenkins, 1773.

Amherst County tradition holds that Buffalo Ridge (Leonard Tyree) and the areas between the Ridge and Stonewall Mill are Cherokee territory; it is and has always been occupied principally by Cherokee. Leonard Robert Tyree (1992) made the following statement regarding Buffalo Ridge, the ridge that runs along Amherst and Nelson counties:

I have lived on this mountain for sixty-three years, over there in that house. My older son and I used to go each Sunday and look for them (arrowheads) for a couple hours. We found them all the way over to Buffalo Ridge in Nelson County.

I work for the Kynite Corporation. I drove a bulldozer. Kynite used to own all of the mountain for approximately five miles. I drove the bulldozer to clean off the area. I waited until it rained and then went back to look for them (Indian artifacts).

I know that the people that were on this mountain were Cherokee. That is all that I have heard from the people in this area. I found two places that appeared to be settlements. One of my bosses, Frank Webb, owned this area. He said that the people were Cherokee. People who come to view my rocks recognize them as Cherokee.

I have two eagle rocks, that were buried with the owner or chief. These are two of the three known eagles in Virginia. My daddy is a Tyree and my mother is a Goins. All Tyrees and Goins are related.

We found two campsites. I plowed in the area with the bulldozer. There was one campsite with ashes. I believe that it was a campsite or settlement because there were thousands of arrowheads. Rev. Covington got about 600 arrowheads from one of the sites. I find arrowheads all over my land. I found the two eagles stones at the foot of Buffalo Ridge in Nelson County.

* *

Cherokee did not meet the traditional stereotype for Native Americans; they were not dependent on missionary organizations to assist them in maintaining their tribal identity. They had a standard of living much like that of the white settlers and, therefore, were following the prosperous lifestyle of Cherokee throughout the southeast (Malone, 1956, xi). While land-seeking settlers were forcing Native Americans from their homes and farms, the Buffalo Ridge people generally kept their farms and refused to leave their property. They owned land and supported themselves and their families with the revenues and products of their farms. They maintained a strong tribal connection without Bureau of Indian Affairs' supervision or missionary societies' assistance. They were not forced to retreat into isolated areas because the settlers forcefully confiscated their homes and land. They were known as Indians (Sandidge, 1995) but acted like "white" people; they had their own houses and operated successful farms. They wore traditional frontier (or Stapleton/Buffalo Ridge) clothes, not traditional Native American dress (Malone, xi). The Buffalo Ridge people did not fit the stereotype of "Native American" or "loin-cloth-attired" warriors. Even the Cherokee warriors from Buffalo Ridge and Amherst County who were soldiers in the American Revolution, including the mulatto Raleigh Pin(n) (Percy, 49), were not allowed to wear long, Native American-appearing hair; they did not look "Indian," because they were required "to wear their hair short and as near alike" other soldiers as possible (Percy, 42).

Ann Megginson, for example, an ancestor of the Buffalo Ridge/Stonewall Mill clans, was a very successful farmer. "She had 100 hands (workers) who worked on her farm" (William Clifford Megginson). Some of the Indian people on the Ridge owned slaves (Rice, 1991, 24; McLeRoy and McLeRoy, 189, 190, 192, 193, 198).

William E. Sandidge, clerk of the Amherst County Court for more than fifty years, noted that "the Indians on the east side of Amherst County did not specify what tribe they were but the Indians on the west side claimed to be Cherokee. The records at the courthouse were not segregated by race. They were mixed up like they are today. My father was clerk of the court for thirty-three years and his father was the clerk for seven years. I was born in 1904. I have lived in Amherst all my life. My grandfather was clerk from 1893-1900. My father was clerk from 1900 until 1933. I started in 1933 and worked until 1983."

The Buffalo Ridge Band, like many Cherokee (Cherokee Phoenix, 1829), were successful in assimilating into the general culture but yet they maintained their tribal identity by marrying other Cherokee from generation to generation, by instinctual or family understanding. Generally, they only revealed their Cherokee heritage to family and friends. While each generation since the mid-1700s kept up the tribal tradition (Hibbert, Nov. 25, 1993, B2), it is only by taking a longitudinal view of the 235-240 year period that we can see the consistent, continuous pattern of tribal marriages, family customs, medical and pharmaceutical practices, and other traditions that were Native

American (Rice, 1991).

The Buffalo Ridge Band resided on the east side of Amherst County and in the Stonewall Mill area of Appomattox County, east of the James River. The Band has always proclaimed their Cherokee ancestry. The Buffalo Ridge Band members have retained their Cherokee heritage and have not taken the route of some Native Americans on the west side of Amherst County who began to identify with the Monacan tribe in the 1980s.

Raleigh Pinn served as the first recorded tribal leader. He frequently attended weddings of the tribal members, assisted in real estate transactions for the members (Beverly/Williams, Nov. 29, 1792; Evans/Pinn, Nov 2, 1795; Pinn/Redcross, Aug. 27, 1799), and served as the mentor for the groups, both on the Ridge and at Stonewall Mill, from the mid-1700s through the early 1800s. Like Abraham and Sarah in the Old Testament (Gen. 12: 7), Raleigh and Sarah became trusted early leaders of the Ridge and Stonewall Mill groups. B.F. Davis compiled a large list of land transactions in Amherst County, including the Buffalo Ridge area. Raleigh Pinn (330, 1797; 341, 1798; 363, 1800, and other land transactions), Alexander Jewell and trustee Samuel Scott (116; 1832), and other Native American residents of the Ridge were respected citizens and acted like "white" people," rather than Native Americans, or "mulattoes," as they were called. They were on the Ridge, as B.F. Davis' compilation documents, long before many of the European settlers arrived in the area. The Isbells were also land owners on the Ridge.

Polly Beverly--who lived in Buckingham County (Appomattox Stonewall Mill area) but moved to the Ridge, across the James River--served as the Beloved Mother of the tribe until the mid-1800 (Cherokee Indian Women, Pennsylvania Archives, 1787). Turner Pinn, a prosperous farmer, served as a leader for the Ridge Band while his daughter, Polly Pinn Two Pins or Two Pence, later served at the Beloved Mother of the group. Her son, John Turner Pinn, Turner Pinn's grandson, was the tribal leader on the Ridge until Willis West, Betsey Beverly's son, came of age to lead the band (Amherst County Deed Book # 61, p. 570--to Deacon Willis West, church official, 1909). Willis West was a deacon and Sunday School superintendent at Fairmount Baptist Church, on the Ridge. M.O. Ferguson was a strong leader of the group between 1940s and 1980s, serving as Chairman of the Deacon Board and Sunday School superintendent. Samuel Pinn, Chief of the Buffalo Ridge Band (UCITOVA), which includes the Stonewall Mill Band, presently serves as the leader of a very formal organization. He presides over monthly meetings of the members, executive officers, and clan leaders. Membership is maintained on computerized membership rolls. These rolls also include members in West Virginia and other states, descendants of the Buffalo Ridge and Stonewall Mill ancestors.

William Beverly, Anthony McCoy, and Stephen Ferguson served as the first recorded leaders of the Stonewall Mill Band and, between 1850-1870s, Albert McCoy served as a leader of the band. Sometime between 1880 and 1900, Joseph Peter Ferguson, son of Judith Ferguson and grandson of Stephen Ferguson, became one of the major leaders of the Stonewall Mill group. His wife, Margaret Isabell Megginson Ferguson, became the Beloved Mother of the group, and bonded the Megginson family with the Fergusons, McCoys, Beverly, and Tylers. The relationship between these people on the Ridge and Stonewall Mill, both of whom have Cherokee and some Pocahontas heritage, and the large number of people in Virginia and other states whose ancestors had a Pocahontas connection and were registered on Cherokee rolls support or give some credence to the assertion by Haywood (1823, 223) that the "Powhatans were said by their descendants to have been once a part of this (Cherokee) nation..."

Amherst County tradition holds that Buffalo Ridge and the area between the Ridge and Stonewall Mill are Cherokee territory, that it is and has always been occupied principally by Cherokee (L. Tyree). The older tribal members have heard stories about Buffalo Ridge being a point of security as their members retreated to the area in battle (B. Beverly). Some members believe that the Ridge was a haven for Native Americans during the "genocide of Indians" by Virginia colonists in the 1600s, and that the "flight to the Ridge" legend may be related to the "genocide" period rather than the "Removal " period.

It has been suggested that the Ridge was a place where the Cherokee warriors, who were employed for the British treaty to defend the colony, resided between their security missions on the James River (Treaty Article # 4). The mountains on the Stonewall Mill side of the James River would have been an ideal area from which to monitor enemy travel on the river. The James River was a source of travel for settlers and soldiers, both friends and foes, to points between the Blue Ridge and Williamsburg. The Williamsburg commissioners had requested that the Cherokee help protect Virginia, and it has been suggested (Humbles Pinn) that sentry duty on the Ridge and in Stonewall Mill would have been the logical and strategic positions from which to spot enemy travelers on the river or on the trails near the river, and to dispatch warriors to flank the intruders where the river bends. Rawley Pinn, Stephen Ferguson, and other Cherokee may have provided security and shelter to the hired Cherokee warriors.

The warriors knew where the pockets of sympathetic Cherokee bands were and, when the "talk started" about "Cherokee removal to the West," they came into southwest Virginia, southern West Virginia, and other locations, including the Ridge/Stonewall Mill area and other areas of Amherst County. They and their descendants, who were familiar with this area of Virginia, (see Council of Colonial Virginia records) returned to these areas in Virginia (and West Virginia) when the pressure of the "Removal" reached its peak. They knew the area well; they were familiar with the locations and/or had been told about the Cherokee villages by their ancestors. The treaty had provided the permission to have modern weapons and therefore they were in possession of the state-of-the-art tools to hunt and to defend themselves (Treaty Article # VII).

Today, West Virginia has citizens who are related to and/or have the same surnames as people in Virginia and other Cherokee-inhabited states. Some of the sections and surnames, to name a few, are as follows:

Location	Surnames
Beckley	Penn, Pinn, Bolling, Boling, Bowling, Banks, Ferguson
Kanawha County, Charleston	Ferguson, Wilson, Beverly, (Bevert, Bevly, Blevin, Bevins)
Hamlin	Adkins, Rodgers, Rogers, Branham
Marion County	Blevins, Terry

Many of the Cherokee people have been called "free issues." The Treaty of 1744 (page 37) suggested that the Indians who passed through Virginia and present-day West Virginia be given safe passage or passes. The Cherokee and other Indians who received these passes for safe passage were called "free issues" or travelers who were not to be mistaken for enemies or slaves but had approval of the Colony and the Crown to travel freely through Virginia (Humbles Pinn). It is strange that the original inhabitants or citizens, who lived in Virginia before the arrival of the British settlers, had to get passes to travel through Virginia in the years following the early settlements.

The Pin(n), Penn, and Redcross descendants in West Virginia and Virginia are believed to have been people who identified themselves as permanent Cherokee residents of the area by displaying crosses made from pins on their lapel, which could be easily seen by travelers. Although the Treaty of 1757 (page X) requested that the commissioners "agree on some definition or signal whereby the Catawbas and Cherokees may be distinguished from other Indians when they come into our inhabitants," it is believed that the Redcrosses displayed a red Christian cross on a white background. This method provided sufficient time for and space from the observer to recognize the Redcross Cherokee as a Christian friend, a member of one of the five civilized or Christian tribes and not a member of the Six Nations, or the Delaware or Shawnee tribes. The Catawbas also used a method to distinguish their people (Humbles Pinn).

The Pin(n)s also wore the "cross"and have a tradition of being connected with the Keetoowah Band of Cherokee (who were pure blood Cherokee), and may have worn the cross for a different reason or for an additional purpose. Bernard Humbles Pinn--in a conversation with John Ross, the present Chief of the Keetoowah Band of Cherokee or "Pin" Indians in Oklahoma--learned that the Keetoowah Band of Cherokee believed in keeping the Cherokee culture, laws, and sacred objects "from the beginning of time" (B. Humbles Pinn, 1992). Although the Pin(n)s and Redcrosses have been identified with the Keetoowah section of Cherokee, they received other Cherokee into their homes and community. The Cherokee in West Virginia and southwestern Virginia carry the same surnames as the people in Amherst County and other areas of Virginia. Some of the residents of Amherst County are related to Cherokee in West Virginia (Whitehead), southwestern Virginia, and Tennessee (Jordan, 258, 259)

The Beverly family, for example, has a rich place in history with the Ridge Band and other Virginia inhabitants. The 1810 U.S. Census (Virginia) presented the following breakdown of Beverly/Beverley families in the state of Virginia (all were listed as mulatto):

County	Number of Families
Augusta	One
Buckingham (later Appomattox/ Stonewall Mill area)	Seven
Caroline	One
Culpeper	One
Franklin	Two
Rockbridge	One
Spotsylvania	One

Buckingham County or the present Stonewall Mill area and vicinity of Appomattox County had half of all of the Beverly/Beverley families that were listed as mulatto in the state. Most of the central Virginia Beverly families descended from the Appomattox Beverly clans and it is believed that all of the Beverly families in Virginia--many listed as "free colored" or "mulatto" were Native Americans and were related to each other. The southwestern Virginia Beverlys are possibly related to the central Virginia Beverlys and some of the Blevins/Bevins/Bivins are believed to be related to the Beverlys/Beverleys/Bevleys. Today, there is a large number of Beverlys and Blevins in southwestern Virginia. Most of the

Beverlys/Blevins are white residents who claim Cherokee ancestry. The ancestors of the Buffalo Ridge and Stonewall Mill Bands of Cherokee were the Beverlys, Fergusons, Goins (Goings, Gowens, Gowans), Megginsons, McCoys, Pinn/Pins/Penns, Rogers, and others. Some of the Beverlys moved from Buckingham County (Appomattox/Stonewall Mill) area to Amherst County (McLeRoy and McLeRoy, Strangers in Their Midst; U.S. Census, Buckingham, 1810; U.S. Census, Amherst, 1840). These family members have continued to marry each other from generation to generation, in central and southwestern Virginia (Index of Virginia Marriages: for example, Ferguson/Fields, July 4, 1867, Russell County; Beverly/Beverly, May 10, 1860, Wise County; Beverly/Murphy, October 28, 1873, Montgomery County).

There was a time when all of the Beverlys claimed to be related but as they united with different clans in Amherst and Rockbridge, they went in different directions, some marrying as "white," "Indian," "colored," and "black." Most of the Beverly families came from the Stonewall Mill area (U.S. Census, Buckingham, 1810). In fact, two census records have been found in central Virginia with the classification of "I" (Indian) beside the names of residents who were Native Americans. This classification was noted next to two Beverly families of Amherst County. The census enumerators were generally successful in keeping "I" or "Indian" from the racial designation except for these two cases (U.S. Census, Amherst County, 1870, p. 64, lines 4-12 & 19-21; Frederick Beverly and family and Richard Beverly and family). The enumerator listed all nine members of Frederick Beverly's family with a "B" for race and changed the classification to "I." Richard Beverly and his son's classification was noted with an "I" but the enumerator wrote a "B" above the "I." Court clerks continued to follow this procedure, putting the "B" designation on records, the paper genocide of Native Americans, as late as 1940. Houston Robert Beverly and Lee Anna Clark's marriage record was changed from "Indian" to "Mixed Indian." The word "Mixed" was written above the word Indian (Amherst County Marriage Register 5, page 205).

The Ridge people often kept their in-breeding to a minimum by seeking Cherokee brides in other sections of Amherst County or in other counties (Gus Ferguson's Marriage Certificate; Amherst County Marriage Register). Gus Ferguson, a resident of Stonewall Mill, Appomattox County, dated and married Nannie West, a Buffalo Ridge, Amherst County resident. As a result of this marriage custom, there is a strong Cherokee heritage in Amherst and surrounding counties (Buffalo Ridge Band of United Cherokee Indian Tribe of Virginia Registrations; L. Smith; Some Common Cherokee Surnames in Amherst County and Vicinity; O'Neill; Whitehead; Amherst County Marriages; Appomattox County Marriages). Cherokee residents of Pedlar Mills in Amherst County and the adjoining Irish Creek area of Rockbridge County married across counties between the 1700s and 1900 (V. White; Plecker in County News; Rockbridge County;

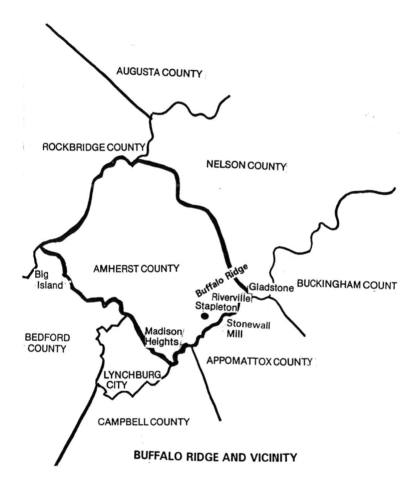

AUGUSTA COUNTY

ROCKBRIDGE COUNTY

NELSON COUNTY

Big
Island

AMHERST COUNTY

Buffalo Ridge

Gladstone BUCKINGHAM COUNT

Riverville

Stapleton

BEDFORD
COUNTY

Madison
Heights

Stonewall
Mill

LYNCHBURG
CITY

APPOMATTOX COUNTY

CAMPBELL COUNTY

BUFFALO RIDGE AND VICINITY

Huffer).

Most people with Cherokee ancestry are proud to reveal their Indian connection while others are more secretive with the facts, often only admitting the information to friends whom they really trust or to people who respect Native Americans (L. Smith, Director, Amherst Historical Museum). Dr. Plecker became one of the forces behind Indian people in Virginia renouncing or being ashamed of their Cherokee heritage in preference for a "white" connection (Plecker's Letter). Descendants of the Cherokee did not want people to think they had black ancestors (Rice, 1991; McLeRoy and McLeroy, 1993), since most of the Indian people who had been listed as "Mu" on the census as late as 1880 were changed to "B" on the 1900 census, including most of the ancestors of the Buffalo Ridge and Monacan Tribes (U.S. Census, Appomattox, Amherst, Nelson, and Rockbridge Counties).

Today, most of the residents with Cherokee ancestry and those who were listed as "free colored" and "mulatto" in the 1840 and 1850 census records in central Virginia and southwestern Virginia, prefer the "white" racial designation while others are classed in the "colored" or "black" category. During the 1700s and early 1800s, Cherokee people did not think "color," but they knew that they were related regardless of the colors of skin. Today, as a result of the Racial Integrity Laws and its proponents (Dr. Plecker's Letter; Racial Integrity Laws), many older residents of Amherst County with Cherokee or other Native American ancestry, who classify themselves and/or are known to neighbors as "white" do not want to mention their racial background.

The McCoys, who were in Appomattox County prior to 1850 (U.S. Census, Appomattox), were skilled Cherokee tenant farmers (M. McCoy; R. Carson). The Tylers, Tolers, or Tillers, cousins to the Fergusons and McCoys of Appomattox and Amherst Counties (see (Thomas) Ferguson Birth Certificate, son of Judith Ferguson, Appomattox County, p. 46, line # 17; Kitty A. Ferguson McCoy Birth Certificate, daughter of Albert McCoy, 1/1/ 1858, Appomattox County, p. 46, line # 18), were first recorded in the Amherst area as early as 1784. Lemuel "Sim" Tyler was listed as the "name of the informant" for the Ferguson and McCoys births. He married Elizabeth Allcock,, daughter of John Allcock, on February 15, 1823, in Amherst County. He is believed to be related to Charles Tyler (who married Nancy Johns, a relative of Lawson Tyler, on December 2, 1813 in Amherst County. John Tiller (Tyler), son of William Tiller (Tyler), married Nancey Hopper (possibly from Cherokee name "Grasshopper"), daughter of Thomas Hopper, on June 10, 1784. The Tylers, Lemuel's son and others (see U.S. Census, Appomattox, 1850, 1860), lived in a tribal setting with the Beverlys, McCoys, and Fergusons (U.S. Census, Buckingham, 1840; Appomattox, 1850, 1860). "Sim" Lemuel, Sr., or "Sim," Jr. informed the Appomattox Court clerk when tribal births occurred in the Stonewall area. Some Tylers, relatives of the Appomattox Tylers, lived in Fluvanna County. Cumberland County has several residents with the "Hopper" surname. The Hopper name has generally disappeared from Amherst and Appomattox Counties for several reasons. Most of the Hopper residents during the 1700s were females and lost the name in marriage, while others possibly allowed the name to be converted, altered, or transposed into "Harper" and, to a lesser degree, into "Hooper."

Albert McCoy's family and other Cherokee residents (Fergusons, Tylers, Beverlys, Megginsons) indicated that they were born in Virginia. This fact would place their presence in central Virginia long before 1800. It is not known how many of these related families' ancestors, on both sides of the James River, lived in the area before 1700 and how many came into the area prior to and during the American Revolution and "Removal Period." All families indicated in the 1850 census that they were born in Virginia. The descendants of these early Indian inhabitants remain proud of their Cherokee heritage and continue to honor the oral history and traditions of the past.

Gus Ferguson was the son of Peter Ferguson and grandson of Dr. Frederick Isbell. Although Dr. Isbell went for white, he, like many central and southwestern Virginia Cherokee, was both European and Cherokee ancestry. The Isbells in Appomattox, Oklahoma, and North Carolina have Cherokee family traditions. The Isbell surname is a traditional Cherokee family name (Starr). Gus Ferguson purchased a 200-acre farm in Amherst County after marrying Nannie West, his Cherokee bride. He used his Indian agricultural skills to support his young family (M.Ferguson). The Gus Ferguson estate has an Indian burial ground over which he cautioned his descendants never to plow (I. Fields; G. Sparrow). This information had been passed down from generation to generation. Gus Ferguson and other members of the Buffalo Ridge Band of Cherokee were descendants of Peter Ferguson (son of Dr. Frederick Isbell and Judith Ferguson). The Isbell family members were progressive businessmen in Appomattox and Lynchburg. Peter Ferguson, Gus' father, married Margaret Isabelle Megginson (daughter of Ann Megginson). The Megginsons were descended from the Pocahontas clans of Appomattox--the Beverlys, Bollings, Fergusons, Blairs, and McCoys--and have both a Pocahontas and Cherokee heritage. Some of the Wilsons, Beverlys, McCoys, Blairs, and other Appomattox and Amherst County band members are distantly related to some members of the Tsalagi Cherokee Tribe of Southwest Virginia via the Pocahontas lineage (Santini; V.; Wilson, M.; Robertson and R.A. Brock, Pocahontas and Her Descendants; U.S. Census, Appomattox. 1850. 1860).

Amherst County marriage records since 1798 have provided documentation of marriages between people who have Cherokee oral histories and surnames (Amherst County Register of Marriages--1798-1834). These people were often listed as white and on other occasions were listed as free colored. The 1850 through 1880 censuses in Amherst, Appomattox, Buckingham, Nelson, and Rockbridge listed them as "mulatto." These marriages included the surnames of Pinn, Beverly, Palmore (now Palmer), Childress, Peters, Evans, Carter, Clark, Christian, Taylor, Blair, Tyler, Hill, Sneed (Snead), Allen, and many more (Settlers in Amherst County with Cherokee Surnames and/or Oral Histories, 1798-1834). Many of the residents were light-skinned enough to pass for white, even though they may have been related to residents who were classified as "mulatto" or "free colored."

The Buffalo Ridge people were mixed with European ancestry. Abraham Pendleton, an immigrant from Germany, married Alice West, daughter of Willis West. William Pendleton married Floretine Isbell on July 30, 1821. The Isbells have a strong Cherokee heritage. This pattern, Native Americans marrying Europeans, has been followed in other counties as well as in Amherst County. William Pendleton was a witness with the bride's father, Reuben Pendleton, at the marriage of Eliza Pendleton to William Scott in Amherst County, on February 22, 1818. The Scotts were known as and to have married Cherokee residents for generations in Amherst County (see Sam Scott's interview). They were listed on some of the early 1800s census records as "Scoot."

The Ailstocks in the Alleghany County area have a Cherokee tradition and are descended from German ancestors. Several Persinger families were listed on the Alleghany County Census (U.S. Census, Alleghany County, 1850, Gabriel Persinger, Rebecca, Mary, & Peter). It is believed that the Ailstocks, who married Amherst County Native American residents (for example, Absolom Peters, February 6, 1840) and other residents with Native American heritage, were of German descent and acquired the Native American connection through marriage with local citizens. It is interesting to note that the Cherokee intermarried with European settlers in the area and acquired European surnames. Some of the Ailstocks are related to people in other areas with heavy Native American populations. During a recent interview with Tim Ailstock, in Asheville, North Carolina, he noted that some of his relatives live in the Potts Creek area of Alleghany County, Virginia. His Cherokee connection is as follows:

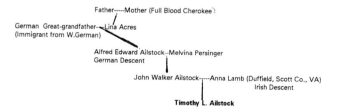

Father-----Mother (Full Blood Cherokee)

German Great-grandfather--Lina Acres
(Immigrant from W.German)

Alfred Edward Ailstock--Melvina Persinger
German Descent

John Walker Ailstock-----Anna Lamb (Duffield, Scott Co., VA)
                                        Irish Descent

Timothy L. Ailstock

Tim Ailstock
Asheville, North Carolina

August 14, 1994

"My father retired from the Navy in Charleston, South Carolina. He was trained in electrical and hydroelectrical engineering. He moved to the Asheville, North Carolina, area in 1983. I moved to Asheville with him from Charleston. My relatives are in the Covington area. My father owns property that belonged to Grandmother Persinger in the Potts Creek area."(Alleghany County).
****

During the early to mid-1800s, the families started clustering together in geographical and/or religious groups. "Pinn Park," one of the first official church/tribal burial grounds in Amherst County, is believed to have been an interment site as far back as 1750 (Land Survey of Fairmount Baptist Church/"Penn Park Cherokee Grounds," Amherst County). By the 1840s, Turner Pinn, Samuel Scott, Madison Beverly, Anthony Beverly, Bartlett Sparrow, Polly Beverly, George Jewell, and others were living in the same tribal setting (clustered together in a residential clan connection) and listed as "free colored" individuals (U.S. Census, Amherst County, 1840). It was only later that white settlers began to purchase land from these Native Americans and build dwellings between them. Census records show these families clustered together in 1840 and earlier. The later census records show a progressively larger number of non-family members settling in these previously "closed" areas. They were prosperous farmers on the Ridge. Turner Pinn--one of the descendants of Raleigh Pin(n), the chief or leader of the Buffalo Ridge Band--owned two slaves during the 1840 census period. He owned four slaves in 1829 (McLeRoy and McLeRoy, 1993, 32; Jackson, 1942, 70; Rice, 1991, 24). These people and others, those wealthy enough, followed the slave-owning customs of Cherokee in other areas of the Southeast. These band members became very serious about assimilating into the general environment and acting like wealthy white people.

The threat of Removal to Oklahoma resulted in three accompanying factors that further alienated and divided Native Americans. First, many Indians could claim exemption from the removal process if they were Christians and met two other requirements. Second, if they spoke English, instead of their native language, and were Christians, they would have a stronger case against removal. Third, if they had removed themselves to an isolated area of residence, in the Appalachian area, for example, and formed isolated groups, their case against removal would be even stronger. Although these three factors helped to exempt them from the removal process, the same factors contributed to their alienation as Native Americans. Cherokee residents' attire was usually the same as the white residents. These people have been placed in an "Indianless" group; "Because they are not fierce, feather-covered warriors," they must not be real Indians (McElwain, 1981, 24, 25).

Many of these Indians wanted to hide away and not be recognized out of fear of removal. They would often inform their children through oral information and traditions to maintain their connections with their Cherokee ancestry. The Cherokee connection is very strong in Amherst County. You need only to ask many of the residents who have Indian-white, Indian-white-black, and Indian-black racial background their tribal association and they will -- usually without further questions -- respond that they are Cherokee. Some of the residents now indicate that they are Cherokee and/or Monacan, after having read the book, Indian Island in Amherst County, (1984).

The Echota Cherokee Tribe followed a similar pattern. During the Removal Period some of their ancestors moved into the hills and areas beyond the heavily populated locations. Some of the members denied being Indians and slowly assimilated into the general population (The Echota Cherokee Tribe, Alabama).

The Cherokee were very successful in their attempt to hide out in the Buffalo Ridge/Glades/Stonewall areas. Many of these people went unnoticed because they were not the traditional "Indian on a reservation." They were successful farmers. Their family names, customs, and oral traditions still remain to support their Cherokee connection. Virginia's use of "free colored," as a official category on the census, made it appear that "freed slaves and Indians were not legally differentiated" (McElwain, 25; C. White, 299).

Contrary to the common belief that all Negroes and other free coloreds, or Indians, were slaves in Virginia prior to the end of the Civil War, there were in fact a large number of "free colored" inhabitants in Amherst County (McLeRoy & McLeRoy, 1977, 52). Free colored inhabitants comprised approximately two to three percent of the county's population between 1810 and 1860 (McLeRoy & McLeroy, 52). It is believed that the major portion of these residents were, in fact, Native Americans. While some of the free colored persons were former or freed slaves, the other residents were Native Americans, descendants of full or mixed blood ancestors. The children of Native American mothers were born free while the children of slave mothers and Native American fathers were not free because the children usually lived with their mothers. If their mothers were included in the institution of slavery, they were born in bondage. This fact partly accounted for the large number of slaves that had Native American features.

The 1840 Census listed a number of categories on the census report. Some of the categories included:

1. Free White Persons, Including Heads of Families

2. Free Colored Persons

3. Slaves

4. Number of Persons in Each Family Employed in:
   A. Mining
   B. Agriculture
   C. Commerce
   D. Manufactures and Trades
   E. Navigation of Ocean
   F. Navigation of Canals, Lakes, and Rivers
   G. Learned Professions and Engineers

5. Pensioners for Revolutionary or Military Services, Included in the Forgoing-Name

The 1840 United States Census (Amherst County, Eastern District, Microfilm # 704, Roll 550) included a number of names of "Free Colored" individuals (Indian and/or Negro). It listed the name of the head of the household and the number of family members. Some of the names of individuals that were included on the census are as follows:

Polly Evans	page 198
John Redcross	page 204
Nathan Johns	page 205
Jona. Beverly	page 208
Joel Brannum	page 213
Madison Beverly	page 213
Albert Terry	page 213
Samuel Beverly	page 213
Richard John	page 213
John Johns	page 213
Samuel Scott	page 222
William Harris	page 222
George Jewell	page 222
Artis Beverly	page 222
Bartlett Sparrow	page 222
Turner Pinn	page 225
Polly Beverly	page 225
Seth Woodroof	page 228
Joseph Pinn	page 231

This is not a complete list of the free Indian and black residents on the 1840 U.S. Census in Amherst County. Turner Pinn (page 225), for example, at this time, was the head of a family that was composed of ten members:

One male, under 10
One male, 10 and under 24
One male, 24 and under 36
One male, 55 and under 100
Two females, 10 and under 24
One female, 24 and under 36
One female, 36 and under 55
Two Slaves, 24 and under 36

Four persons in the family were employed in "Navigation of Canals, Lakes, and Rivers."

Polly Beverly's thirteen family members were as follows (page 225):

Four males, under 10
Two males, 10 and under 24
Three females, 10 and under 24
Two females, 24 and under 36
One female, 36 and under 55
One female, 55 and under 100

Seven persons in the family were employed in "Agriculture" and two were employed in "Navigation of Canals, Lakes, and Rivers."

The 1860 Census (Microfilm # 653, Roll # 1332, p. 144, line 10- 17), of Free Inhabitants of Amherst, shows Polly Beverly as an Indian or "M" (mulatto), age 55, and other members of the family: Eliza, age 25, female, "M"; Huran, age 7, male, "M"; Aldridge, age 30, male, "M"; Henry, age 16, male, "M"; and Lucy, age 35, female, "M." Bartlett Sparrow (p. 145, line 24-28) is listed as "B"(black), age 60, with Martha, his wife, and three children, ages 18, 15, and 11. All were listed with a "B" racial classification. "Cooper" is listed as his occupation. His personal estate was valued at $700.00. William Scott (p. 145, line 29 & 30), age 30, his wife Mary, age 30, and his family members are listed as mulatto. Thomas Johns (Court House District, p. 7, line 5), a farmer, and his wife and child are listed as Mulatto. Family Heads (Court House District) Paulus Redcross (p. 7, line 38), John Redcross (CH District, p. 26, line 14), William Johns (line 3), Tarlton Johns (line 5), and Richard Branham (line 16) are listed as Mulatto, including all of their family members. John Beverly (1860 Census, p. 144, lines 4-6), age 35, Leanah Pinn, age 7, and Mary Beverly, age 30, are listed as mulatto.

John Fields (p. 146, lines 4-6) and family members Betsey and Susanna are classified as Mulatto. Bailey Beverly (p. 146, lines 7-22), a neighbor, had the following family members: The 1860 Census (15th Amherst District, Microfilm # T9, Roll # 1353) classified the following families as mulatto:

Bailey Beverly	Age 45	Male	Mulatto
Delilah	48	Female	Mulatto
Aldridge	30	Male	Mulatto
Lucy	27	Female	Mulatto
Betsey	23	Female	Mulatto
Henry	14	Female	Mulatto
Aderson	7	Male	Mulatto
Marcellus	3	Male	Mulatto
William E.	1	Male	Mulatto
Willis (West)	6	Male	Mulatto
Ben	3	Male	Mulatto
Mary	29	Female	Mulatto
Addison	5	Male	Mulatto
Spencer	3	Male	Mulatto
George	2	Male	Mulatto
William	1	Male	Mulatto

Samuel Beverly (Amherst Court House District, p. 190, line 34), Samuel Beverly Jr. (p. 191, line 20), Reubin Terry (p. 191, line 38), and Betsey Johnson (p. 190, line 31) are listed as family heads and, along with their family members, were classified as mulatto. James Sparrow (p. 195, line 23), the head of a family of four, was classified as "M" but the enumerator changed the "M" to a "B"(wrote over the "M").

The 1880 Census (15th District, Microfilm # T9, Roll # 1353) classified the following families, for example, as Indian or mulatto (this is not a complete list of families classified as "M"):

Henry Beverly	35	p. 114	line 24
Georganna	30		line 25
Lucy	48		line 26
Howard	10		line 27
Martha A.Pinn	18	p. 114	line 28
Reubin	1		line 29
Martha	1/2		line 30
Willis West	24	p. 114	line 31
Martha Pinn	21		line 32
Otis West	3		line 33
Mary West	2		line 34
Ann E.	2/12		line 35
Betsey Beverly	43	p. 114	line 36
Benj.	22		line 27

George Pinn	25	p. 114	line 47
Marcella	24		line 48

William Pinn	34	p. 114	line 49
Leanna	28		line 50
Holcombe	11	p. 115	line 1
William J.	8		line 2
Orianna	5		line 3
Samuel	4		line 4
Wilton	7/12		line 5

John Turner Pinn	54	p. 115	line 6
Martha	59		line 7
Ellison	23		line 8
Charles Beverly	15	Cousin	line 9
Judy A.	11	Cousin	line 10

Robert Pinn	26	p. 115	line 11
Lelia A.	23		line 12
Serena	3		line 13
Birdie	1		line 14

Sam Braxton	23	p. 115	line 6
Mandy	21		line 7
Mary	4/12		line 8

William Jordan	47	p. 119	line 7
Winy	47		line 8
Leannie	19		line 9
Alice	16		line 10
Tommie	13		line 11
Johnie	9		line 12
Sidney	7		line 13
Sallie	5		line 14
Dillard	3		line 15
Eddie	2		line 16
Augustine	8/12		line 17
Ester Broadstreet (B)	75	Mother-in-law	line 18

Frankie Jackson	50	p. 119	line 39
Easter Christian	24		line 40
Jack Jackson	20		line 41
Charlie Jackson	16		line 42
Ellen Jackson	8		line 43
Solomon Jackson	7		line 44

Eli Johnson	26	p. 119	line 45
Anna	22		line 46
Kate	1		line 47
Beverly Carpenter	34	p. 120	line 17
Fannie	25		line 18
Mary L.	8		line 19
Martha J.	4		line 20
Nannie	1		line 21
Jim Green	63	p. 120	line 22
Aldophus	15		line 23
Lucy J.	14		line 24
Peter McCoy	33		line 25
Bettie McCoy	18		line 26
Robert J.	1		line 27
Frank Banks	35	p. 120	line 28
Louisa	35		line 29
William A.	12		line 30
Bertie C.	8		line 31
Anna L.	6		line 32
Sarah M.	4		line 33
James R.	6/12		line 34
Paulus Rose	40	p. 125	line 32
Mary J.	25		line 33
Samuel	12		line 34
Eddie	9		line 35
Porter	6		line 36
Alice	4		line 37
Powell	1		line 38
Jarvis	2/12		line 39
Matilda Hutcherson	49	p. 127	line 21
Charles	19		line 22
William	16		line 23
Joshua	24		line 24
Fannie	10		line 25
Jack	8		line 26
Thomas	7		line 27
Jesse	5		line 28
Thomas Bibby	80	p. 127	line 35
Hannah	70		line 36
Ealy	21		line 37
Thomas	19		line 38

In Appomattox County/Bent Creek Area (Microfilm # 653, Roll # 1332), the following family, for example, was listed in the 1860 U.S. Census (p. 74, lines 7-13):

Andrew J. Burks	Age 38	Male	(Race not noted, denotes white)
Louisa McCoy	45	Female	Mulatto
Rosella McCoy	8	Female	Mulatto
General McCoy	6	Male	Mulatto
John McCoy	25	Male	Mulatto
Nancy Furguson	23	Female	Mulatto
Anthony Furguson	6	Male	Mulatto

In the Oakville District of Appomattox (1860, p. 71, lines 15-22), we find a Beverly family, for example, listed:

America Beverly	41	Male	Mulatto
Panulia Beverly	30	Female	Mulatto
Chalman Beverly	13	Male	Mulatto
Georgianna Beverly	9	Female	Mulatto
Calvin Beverly	7	Male	Mulatto
Paul Beverly	2	Male	Mulatto
Leanna Beverly	5	Female	Mulatto
Peter Beverly	1	Male	Mulatto

In the Stonewall Mill District of Appomattox (1860, p. 88, lines 39 & 40), we find, for example, the following families:

Frederick Isbell	44	M	White	Real EstateValue-	$5,000
	Personal Estate			Value-$6,000	
	Occupation-			Physician	
Lucy Isbell (w)	67	F	White		

Other family members in the Stonewall Mill District included:

Albert McCoy	24	M	Mulatto p. 94, lines 2-15
Mary J. McCoy	35	F	Mulatto
M. McCoy	20	F	Mulatto
Mary McCoy	16	F	Mulatto
Charles McCoy	14	M	Mulatto
Peter McCoy	12	M	Mulatto
Benjamin McCoy	11	M	Mulatto
Sallie McCoy	9	F	Mulatto
Wm D. McCoy	8	M	Mulatto
John McCoy	6	M	Mulatto
Elizabeth M. McCoy	4	F	Mulatto
Catharine McCoy	2	F	Mulatto
James McCoy	5/12	M	Mulatto
Judy McCoy	5/12	F	Mulatto

Stephen Furguson	72 M	Mulatto p. 92, lines 16-27
Susan Furguson	67 F	Mulatto
Judy Furguson	25 F	Mulatto
Susan Furguson	22 F	Mulatto
Stephen Furguson	5 M	Mulatto
Joseph Furguson	3 M	Mulatto
Sam Furguson	7 M	Mulatto
Nancy Furguson	5 F	Mulatto
Lucy Furguson	7 F	Mulatto
Peter Furguson	6 M	Mulatto
Hudson Furguson	5 M	Mulatto
Thomas Furguson	3 M	Mulatto
Richard Furguson	62 M	Mulatto p. 92, lines 3-6
Lucy Green	36 F	Mulatto
Bellie Green	7 F	Mulatto

The 1880 United States Census (Microfilm # T9, Roll # 1353, the 16th District, Amherst County) included a large number of "mulatto" residents. Some of these residents are as follows:

Moses McGuire	p. 140, line 4
Washington Gibson	p. 140, line 20
Patricia Shrader	p. 141, line 6
Harvey Patterson	p. 143, line 40
Ida North	p. 143, line 1
Ella Lee	p. 144, line 19
Calvin Ferguson	p. 144, line 18
Lucy Johnson	p. 144, line 31
Dolly Paxton	p. 144, line 48
John Wesley	p. 144, line 49
William Adcock	p. 145, line 8
Richard Brannon(am)	p. 145, line 33
Wilson Harlow	p. 147, line 5
Wilson Tinsley	p. 147, line 46
Rosa Perrow	p. 148, line 1
Ann Parrish	p. 150, line 10
Peter Higginbotham	p. 150, line 48
Elvira Beverly	p. 150, line 31
Geo Wash. Shrader	p. 150, line 39
Ambrose Clark	p. 151, line 42
Austin Watson	p. 152, line 18
Louisa Davis	p. 152, line 48
Samuel Beverly	p. 162, line 2
John Hamilton	p. 162, line 11
Daniel Tyree	p. 162, line 16
James Tyree	p. 162, line 19

Albert Terry	p. 162, line 22
William Adcock	p. 163, line 35

The 15th District of Amherst (1880 United States Census, Microfilm # T9, Roll # 1353) included, for example, the following residents who were classified as "mulatto":

Oscar Blair	p. 111, line 29
Charles Jordan	p. 114, line 7
Horace Day	p. 116, line 34
Peter Payne	p. 116, line 37
Henry Beverly	p. 115, line 24
Milly Woodson	p. 116, line 45
Martha A. Pinn	p. 115, line 28
Willis West	p. 115, line 31
Martha Pinn West	p. 115, line 32
Betsey Beverly	p. 115, line 36
John T. Pinn	p. 115, line 6
Henry Blair	p. 115, line 25
Wilson Scott	p. 114, line 18
Preston Chambers	p. 112, line 16
Thomas Brown	p. 112, line 10
Sam Braxton	p. 115, line 6
Maggie Hutcherson	p. 117, line 9
Ella Crawford	p. 117, line 28
Mary Evans	p. 119, line 10
Patsy Mundy	p. 120, line 3
Fannie Carpenter	p. 120, line 18
Jim Green	p. 120, line 22

Peter McCoy	p. 120, line 25
Frank Banks	p. 120, line 28
Emily Spencer	p. 120, line 44
Sarah Pendleton	p. 121, line 6
Charles Scott	p. 123, line 14
Margaret Wilson	p. 124, line 25
Preston Peters	p. 125, line 40
John Blair	p. 125, line 1
Harriet Liggon	p. 127, line 4
Thomas Bibby	p. 127, line 35
Ambrose Scott	p. 128, line 36
Paul Watkins	p. 128, line 14
Edward Yuille	p. 130, line 49
Mary Carter	p. 133, line 36
Lizzie Branham	p. 133, line 9
Sam Hicks	p. 134, line 3
Mary Johnson	p. 135, line 2
Wyatt Reynolds	p. 136, line 18

Louis McDaniels	p. 136, line 42
John Johns	p. 137, line 9
George Mantiply	p. 137, line 47
Harvey Taylor	p. 138, line 37
Laura Hawkins	p. 138, line 39

The enumerators experienced some difficulty in classifying individuals by race. Bernard Humbles Penn, Chief of the United Cherokees of West Virginia, noted that the time of the year had an impact on the classification; he indicated, "The enumerator might classify a person as 'mulatto' in June but the same individual could be classified as 'black' in August. The reason for this discrepancy stems from the fact that some residents tan easily and would be much darker if the enumerator came around later in the summer."

It is very difficult to identify Native Americans. They may look like other residents in a community. Harlan (1987, 120) discussed the difficulty of identifying Indians. He used the example of a Cherokee woman who resided on a Cherokee reservation and had a half Cherokee daughter with brunette hair and one-quarter Cherokee grandchildren with blond hair.

There are many families in other neighboring locations with the same composition of surnames as the surnames of Amherst County and vicinity families. The Covington Township Census (1880), for example, included Benjamin Jenkins, Maria Jenkins, Mary Jenkins, William Jenkins, Echolds Jenkins, Grace Jenkins, and Clay Jenkins. All were listed as mulatto.

In 1900, the Appomattox Census included Hudson, Joseph, and William Ferguson as "Black." They were, by this time, listed as heads of their respective households. Their family members were also listed as "Black" by the census enumerator. These Indian families were erased from a Native Indian status to "Black" within a period of forty years. Hudson, Joseph, and William Ferguson were listed as mulatto in 1860, 1870, and 1880. Did these people change racially or did the societal racial categorization or political procedures change within the twenty to forty-year period?

In the 1860 U.S. Census, Covington (page # 138), there was a large number of residents who had the same last names as Amherst residents. The following names, for example, are noted:

Henry Redcross	Age 76	Male	Mulatto	line # 2
James Merchant	45	Male	Mulatto	line # 4
William Liggins	62	Male	Mulatto	line # 7

A large number of residents in Amherst County is related to families in the Rockbridge, Clifton Forge, Covington, Eagle Rock, Indian Rock, and Lexington areas. Many of the residents indicate that their ancestors migrated to Amherst County from the Allegheny and Blue Ridge Mountains locations. Some Amherst residents moved back to the Allegheny area on different occasions. The Clifton Forge- Covington, Iron Gate, Potts Creek, Virginia Telephone Directory (August, 1990), for example, lists fourteen McCoys, forty-five Carters, fifty-two Clarks, six Clarkes, thirty-six Crawfords, thirteen Hickses, twenty-one Higginses, seven Jenkinses, six Murphys, twenty-two Lees, seventeen Reeds, twenty Robinsons, thirty-three Roses, eighteen Rosses, forty-six Reynoldses, twenty-eight Sneads, eight Sorrel(l)(s) (*Squirrels), one Sparrow, fifteen Terrys and one Turpin (*Terrapins), seven Wests, and three Yanceys. These names are also popular names in Amherst, Appomattox, Campbell, and Bedford counties and the City of Lynchburg. They are also Cherokee surnames.

The 1860 Nelson County Census, Elk Creek District (microfilm # M653, Roll # 1365), included, for example, the following free inhabitants:

Name	Age	Sex	Race	Page	Line
Thos Carter	36	M	Mu	102	21
Sally Sparrow	55	F	Mu	102	22
Jos Farrar	40	M	Mu	102	23
Martha Sparrow	45	F	Mu	102	24
Washington Sparrow	35	M	Mu	102	25
Robert Sparrow	25	M	Mu	102	26
James Sparrow	35	M	Mu	102	27
Amanda Sparrow	25	F	Mu	102	28
Mary Sparrow	25	F	Mu	102	29
Lena Sparrow	5	F	Mu	102	30
Frances Sparrow	31	F	Mu	102	31
Felix Sparrow	11	M	Mu	102	32
Elizabeth Sparrow	9	M	Mu	102	33
George Sparrow	8	M	Mu	102	34
Adaline Farrar	15	F	Mu	102	35

The 1880 Census, Lovingston District (microfilm # T9, Roll # 1379), Nelson County, included, for example, the following residents:

Sarah Robinson	Page 189	Line 11
Emily Robinson		Line 12
Lilly Robinson		Line 15
Lucophus Robinson		Line 16
Moses Loving		Line 27-34

Emily Goins   Page 85   Line 18

Nelson County Census, 1880, Massies Mill District, page 269:

Elviny Harris   Line 11-16

Nelson County Census, 1880, Rockfish District:

Susan Harris	Page 295	Lines 8-10
David Powell	Page 297	Lines 21-23
Zachariah Cosby	Page 298	Lines 17-28
John Ware	Page 310	Lines 42-50
James Richerson	Page 319	Lines 33-40
Lewis Spears	Page 322	Lines36,38-43
William Johnson	Page 209	Lines 23-30
James Beverly	Page 210	Lines 2-7
Maria Christian	Page 211	Lines 5-8
Crealy Jackson		Line 20
O. H.Coleman		Line 24
Andrew McCoy		Line 33
Elizabeth Johnson	Page 212	Line 15
Ned Beverly		Line 20
George Carter		Line 28
James Pendleton	Page 213	Line 25
Alfrca Davis		Line 33,35-41
John Patterson		Line 31
Eliza Banks	Page 222	Lines 20 & 21
Peyton Thomas	Page 224	Lines 36-42
Sandy Rucker	Page 233	Lines 31-35
Edith Rose		Lines 6-9

Massies Mill District:

William Epps	Page 235	Lines 23,25-28
John Liggon		Lines 42-45
Winston Giles	Page 257	Lines11,13-19
John Key		Lines11,13-20
Wilson Brown	Page 260	Lines 16-27
Samuel Woods	Page 324	Lines 11-20

The Lovingston District, 1880 (microfilm # T9, Roll # 1379), included, for example, the following residents:

Felix Jenkins	Page 206	Lines 20-25
Davy Jordan		Lines 34-37
John Pinn		Lines 40-45
Robert Sparrow		Lines 46-50
Henry Spencer		Lines 8-11
George Lucas		Lines 42-47

Cumberland County, Virginia, has a number of residents with Cherokee ancestry. The Hoppers and Hambys, for example, are residents who have Cherokee ancestors (L. M. Hopper; M.E. Hamby). Some of the Haislips of Cumberland and Fluvanna Counties have Cherokee ancestry and are "related to General Stonewall Jackson" (A.W. Haislip, Sr.). A.W. Haislip's mother, Virginia Poe Haislip, is "related to Edgar Allan Poe," the famous writer and poet (A. W. Haislip, Sr.).

Charles White, in the Hidden and Forgotten(1985), noted that Henry Parson, born circa 1794, was the ancestor of the Parsons of Buckingham County. "He was a pure Cherokee Indian slave; however, he was later freed and became a landowner before the Civil War. Parson also protected several members of his family by purchasing their freedom, but kept them in that particular institution called slavery. Henry Parson fathered three pure Cherokee children..." (299). The Cosby family descended from the Parson family, including "Bill Cosby, the well-known comedian." White indicated that one of Henry Parson's children operated boats on the James River Canal. As already noted, a large number of Cherokee from the Buffalo Ridge Band was navigators for the James River Canal (see Polly Beverly's census information, 1840).

A large number of Amherst County ancestors migrated from areas in the Cherokee Nation to Covington, Clifton Forge, Buchanan, Rockbridge County, and Amherst County. The Covington and Clifton Forge areas have always had a large number of Cherokee families within their geographical locations (Jordan, Cherokee By Blood, Vol. 7, 84, 85).

Willis West, Sr., father of Willis West, is believed to have migrated from the Etowah River area of Floyd County, Georgia, to Stapleton, in Amherst County, Virginia. He fathered one son, Willis West, by Betsy Beverly, and may have been a descendant of Jacob West (Tyner, Those Who Cried, 1974, p. 60; Blankenship, B., Cherokee Roots p. 26.). Tyner notes that Jacob West's family included:

> "One halfbreed and five quarterbloods. One white intermarriage. Owned thirteen slaves. Two farmers. Two mechanics. Seven readers of English. One weaver and one spinner" (p. 60).

Oral traditions support the belief that many of the ancestors of residents of Amherst County and vicinity came from the Cherokee Nation. It is possible that, for example, the Fields family of Amherst County and Harris family of Amherst and Nelson Counties are descendants of John Fields and Nancy Harris, of Etowah River, Floyd County, Georgia (Tyner, 59) The Fields have a very strong Cherokee heritage in central Virginia.

John Fields' family included:

> "Ten fullbloods. One slave. Two farmers. Two readers of Cherokee and two of English. Two weavers and two spinners" (p. 60).

Nancy Harris' family had the following members:

> "Ten fullbloods. Two farmers. Two weavers and three spinners" (p. 60).

The Redcross Family, which has roots in Amherst County and vicinity, has members as far away as the Yorktown/Hayes area. Evelyn Stokes Wright, the family historian for the Redcross family in that area, noted the following in a letter to Redcross descendants (E. S. Wright, 1989):

"During my researching, I have discovered that all of the Redcross families in this area are descendants from one John Redcross, born September 27, 1768, son of Lucy Redcross (St.. Peter's Church Register, p. 598), christened and baptized in St. Peters' Parish, New Kent. John was the son of Lucy Redcross, an American Indian, from Amherst County of Virginia near Lynchburg or from Henrico. I have arrived at these conclusions from entries in the parish book at New Kent and the 1800s American Census..."

Evelyn Wright has conducted extensive research on the Redcross family. Some of her findings are as follows (The Redcross Report):

CENSUS DATA
Index

Virginia--1787 Census

County	Name	Taxable	Page
York	John Redcross	1 White Male over 16	1338
Amherst	John Redcross	1 White Male over 16	190

County	Name	Reference #

Virginia--1810 Census

County	Name	Reference #
York	John Redcross, Jr.	882
York	John Redcross	882
Amherst	John Recross	917

Virginia--1820 Census

Bot	Henry Redcross	69A
York	Molly Redcross	159A

Virginia--1830 Census

York	George Redcross	434
York	Henry Redcross	428
York	John Redcross	431
York	Meade Redcross	428
Alleg	Elizabeth Redcross	124
Alleg	Henry Redcross	124
Amher	John Redcross	496

Virginia--1830 Census

York	George Redcross	434
York	Henry Redcross	328
York	John Redcross	431
York	Meade Redcross	428
Alleg	Elizabeth Redcross	124
Alleg	Henry Redcross	124
Amher	John Redcross	496

Virginia--1850 Census

Amher	John Redcross	194	Eastern District
Lync	Amanda Redcross	089	Lynchburg
Hn	Ann Redcross	435	Richmond
Lync	Catherine Redcross	077	Lynchburg
York	George Redcross	363	
York	Henry Redcross	358	
Alleg	Henry Redcross	029	1st District
York	James Redcross	358	
Hn	John Redcross	259	Richmond
Amher	Mahala Redcross	088	Eastern District
York	Mead Redcross	365	
Camp	Ritty Redcross	111	Lynchburg
Amher	William Redcross	152	Eastern District

Virginia--1860 Census

Rockbridge	Alexdr Redcross	087	Glenwd P.O.
York	Cary Redcross	1037	Halfway House P.O.
Amher	Eliza Redcross	254	Amherst C.H. P.O.
Campbell	Fannie Redcross	376	Lynchburg
York	George Redcross	1042	Halfway House P.O.
Alleg	Henry Redcross	138	Covington P.O.

York	Henry Redcross	1047	Halfway House P.O.
York	James Redcross	1047	Halfway House P.O.
Amher	John Redcross	254	Amherst C.H. P.O.
Henrico	Nancy Redcross	385	Richmond
Amher	Paul Redcross	235	Amherst C.H. P.O.
York	Robert Redcross	1037	Halfway House P.O.
Amher	Varland Redcross	236	Amherst C.H. P.O.
York	W.H. Redcross	V043	Halfway House P.O.

Her mother, Mabel Patterson, grandfather, George Redcross, Jr., and great-grandfather, George Redcross, Sr., are listed as Cherokee Indians on the Tribal Roll (United Cherokee Indian Tribe of Virginia, Inc.). The Redcross Cherokee connection has been noted in a number of other writings (Houck, 1984; Carson, 19). Evelyn Wright, a member of the United Cherokee Indian Tribe of Virginia, has been actively researching her family roots and eagerly passing the information on to her descendants.

Throughout the Appalachian and Blue Ridge Mountains and surrounding areas, you will find the same family names as the common names in Amherst County. Many of the ancestors indicated that they were related to many of citizens in these areas and in West Virginia (Humbles Penn, 1990).

How did these names originate and what meaning did they have to the bearers? Let us examine the Christian and Cherokee surnames to determine their origin and meaning.

CHAPTER V
Hi s gi (Five)

CHEROKEE NAMES

A Link to a Former Great Nation

It has been estimated that there are approximately "a hundred thousand current surnames of British origin" (Matthews, 1966, 15). Almost half of all recorded men around A.D. 1100 had second names. The surname was not in popular use prior to the twelfth century. Matthews, in English Surnames(1967), indicated that there are basically four principal types of surnames. His book explores the whole area of surnames and provides an excellent base from which to understand the origin of surnames in America. The Cherokee appeared to have made frequent use of occupational names and nicknames. Location names also were and are popular with Native Americans. Some of the Cherokee surnames are as follows:

Principal Types of Names	Cherokee Surnames
Occupational Names	Cooper,Gardner, Hogshooter,Taylor, Hunter, Carter.
Nicknames:	Beaver, Cheater, Going up Stream or Going Snake (Goin, Going), Pence, Sparrow, Owl (Howell, Howl,), Sharp, Crow, Coffey, Hartless, Hopper, Kidd.
Names of Relationship:	Hopkins, Hawkins, Littlejohn, Jackson, Higgins.
Location Names:	Bank(s),Hill, Park, West.

Elsdon C. Smith, in The Story of our Names (1970), noted that the Indian

81

surnames developed out of the requirements of the English-influenced society. As European settlers and traders made contact with Native Americans, the new visitors encouraged Native Americans to identify themselves with simple or English names, names that could be written or pronounced with ease. The new settlers and traders in the 1770s obviously had difficulty pronouncing, for example, the name of the Cherokee leader, Chief Attakullakulla. As Native Americans sought employment from the European immigrants, they gladly accepted first and/or last names. Many of the Cherokee adopted the names of these newcomers, whether they acquired the surnames as a result of marriage to or being an offspring of settlers (for example, Adair or Hilderbrand) or just coming into contact with the new visitors.

Crispus Attucks, the first Revolutionary War soldier to fall in battle, was both black and Indian. His Indian name was "Red Deer." Leonard Ashley, in his book What's in a Name? (1989, 98 & 99), in mentioning Crispus Attuck as an example of a man who was both Indian and black, indicated that a third of all African-Americans have some Native American ancestry. Ashley further noted that a "great many white Americans" have some Indian blood.

Many of the indian names originated in a manner similar to the development of surnames in England. Since the early settlers were British, the Cherokee had contact with these names and likely added surnames to their first or Christian names. Some of these first names may have become last names. There are many Americans who sided with the "cowboys" in "cowboy and Indian" movies without any knowledge that they had Native American blood running in their veins. What side would they have taken, if they had known the truth? The truth was often hidden by parents and historians from descendants of mixed-blood Native Americans because of the social pressures that accompanied this knowledge and lifestyle.

Basil Cottle, in the book The Penguin Dictionary of Surnames(1967, 47). noted that the English name "Beverley" means "beaver stream." "Beverly," "Beverley," or "Bevley" seems to have originated from the word "beaver." "Beaver" was used as a surname by the Western Delaware Indians (Trigger, 1978, 228), Cherokee on the Henderson Roll, and the Buffalo Ridge Cherokee ("Beverley" and "Beverly").

John McGill, in The Beverley Family of Virginia--Descendants of Major Robert Beverley (1641-1687), indicated that Robert Beverley came from the town of Beverley, Yorkshire England (1641-1687). Robert Beverley emigrated to Virginia about 1663 and settled in Jamestown, Middlesex County. He was known as Major Robert Beverley, married twice, and fathered nine children. McGill noted that Major Robert Beverley was Clerk of the House of Burgesses and the first person with the Beverley name in Virginia. He was the father of Col. Robert Beverley.

McGill indicated that Col. Robert Beverley, the historian, was the son of Major Robert Beverley, the House of Burgesses' Clerk, and Katherine Hone. Col. Beverley was probably a very wealthy man in the area (308).

Jennings Cropper Wise, in Col. John Wise of England and Virginia (1617–1695)--His Ancestors and Descendants, indicated that the Beverley family was connected with town of Beverley from the days of King John. Wise provided the names of his nine children by his first wife, Mary Keeble, Catherine Hone (7).

Other traditionally Cherokee names may be found in the Amherst area. There is, for example, a large number of "Eagle" or "Eagles," twenty-three "Eagle(s)," a Cherokee name, in the Lynchburg, Virginia Telephone Directory (C&P Telephone Directory, 1986); nine in the Charlottesville area (Charlottesville Centel Telephone Directory, December, 1987); and two the in Madison Heights area (Dominion Directory, 1989).

During an interview, Principal Chief Jonathan L. Taylor, Eastern Band of Cherokee Indians, Cherokee, North Carolina, noted that a number of local surnames in Amherst and vicinity are the same surnames as those owned by Cherokees in Cherokee, North Carolina (J. Taylor, 1991). He indicated that "before the removal, our people were in Virginia, Alabama, Kentucky, Tennessee, North Carolina, South Carolina, Georgia, and part of West Virginia."

Some of the surnames of Cherokee in Virginia (Evans, Bollings, Chambers, Ferguson, Hartless, Goins, Isbell, McCoy, Branham, Fields, Jenkins, Hopper, Blevins, and many others) are the same as those owned by Cherokee on the reservations. It is believed that these Virginians are descendants of or related to some of the Cherokee who were removed to Oklahoma or escaped from the "Trail of Tears." Some Cherokee surnames--for example, Beverly, Redcross, Persinger, Poindexter, Pin(n), Sizemore-- are not popular Cherokee names on Cherokee reservations but have strong Cherokee traditions in Virginia. Very few, if any, Virginia residents were included in the "Trail of Tears," (unless they were, for example, visiting relatives in the Cherokee Nation at the time of the Removal), even though a large section of Virginia was a part of the Cherokee Nation at a time prior to the Removal. Therefore, some Virginia Cherokee names are not as popular as those owned by Cherokee who were removed from the southeast and moved to the west. Other states, likewise, have unique Cherokee surnames that are surrounded with Cherokee history and traditions but are not the same surnames as those traditional surnames owned by Cherokee on the reservations.

Bob Blankenship's book, Cherokee Roots, provides essential information for persons who are interested in "checking to see if any of one's ancestors was in fact of Cherokee descent" (Blankenship). The book includes the rolls of the Cherokee Nation prior to the removal to Oklahoma of most of the Cherokee. It also has the names of Cherokee and their descendants who were successful in evading the removal and remained in the Eastern United States.

The 1835 Henderson Census was conducted three years before the Oklahoma Removal (National Archives of the United States, 1934, 1835 Census Roll of the Cherokee Indians East of the Mississippi, w/Index; Bob Blankenship). The census or Rolls after 1835 include those Cherokee who avoided the removal and their descendants.

Henderson Roll 1835
(Examples of the names on the roll-not a complete list)
Arrow Totater
Big Dollar
Beaver Toater
Bridgemaker
Brannon (possibly changed to and/or pronounced as Brannam(ham)
Big Field
Bull Frog
Benge, Martin
Betsey
Blair, George
Beaver Tail
Beaver Carrier
Bever Carrie
Bag John and Two Sons
Beavers, Washington
Benge, John
Benge, Martin
Chickleece
Colson Daniel (possibly Cousin)
Culsutte (doctor)
Cheah (otter)
Coulson, Henry
Eagle on the Roost
Elliot, John
Field, Willis
Field, Turtle
Going Wolf
Going
Gone Under
Gone By
Grasshopper

Thank you for visiting the
Allen County Public Library

Title: The Buffalo Ridge Chero...
Type: BOOK
Due: 11/4/2010,23:59
Item: 31833059671971

Total items checked out: 1

Telephone Renewal: 421-1240
Website Renewal: www.acpl.info

Green Gardner
Groath
Guts
Harriss, Charles
Head in the water
Hicks
Hopkins
Hopper
Hog John
Jackson
John Towie
Josiah
Lowen
McCoy A.
McDaniel, Watt
McCoy, Daniel
Nanny
Nicholson John
Peter
Read Bird
Red Bird
Rogers, William
Rogers Robert
Sharp
Standing Waters
Squirrel
Sweet Water
Spears, Archy
Spears James
Spencer Daniel
Spannish Peter
Stand
Scott, Samuel
Scott, Dick
Scott, Samuel
Standing Buffalo
Turtle
Turtle Fields
The Eagle
Terrapin Hean
Terapin
Terrapin Strikeron
Terapin Head
The Eagle
Watts, Capt.
Watts, Thomas
West John
Willson

West Betsey
West Jacob
Wison
Young Beaver
Woodward

Mulloy Roll 1848
(Partial list)
Lewis Cowhee
Woodpecker, Ji
Oo yous kih
ar chee
al kin neh
Betsy
Benjamin Beaver or Taw yih
Bank of Chooa lookih
Catharine
Cul sow neh
Elijah
Ezekiel
Ellick
Otter Jim or Tail Sticking Out
Peter or Queeta
Peter or Queetah
Raper, Lewis
Stephen
Standing or Ka to ga
Sa ti geh
Sparrow or Chees quoh
Tin neh
Tow ih, John
Tut ti eh
Ward, Charles

Siler Roll 1851
(Partial list)

Coleman, Elizabeth
Coleman, Robert M.
Coleman, Mary E.
Davis, Thomas
Ben Tow nan ih
Elliot
Fields, Riley
Fields
Garland, James
Garland, Fellius
Harris, Susan

Harris James
Hudson, Lewis Blackburn
Johnson, Catherine
Langly, Sarah
Langly, Lock
Langly, John Jr.
McCoy, Eveline
McCoy, Muzedore
Wee lih
West, Nancy
West, Sarah

Chapman Roll 1852
(Partial list-Some of the more familiar names related to the family names in Amherst County and vicinity)

Betsy
Carns
Coleman
Davis
Garland
Harris
John
John or Cun tees kih
Langley
Lewis Cow lih
Lessih
Johnson Lo ish
Louis
Lu ih
Rogers
Ta hah nih (Terrapin- possibly Terry)
Terrapin (Te kah nuh)
Ward, Charles
Ward, Cherokee
West, James W.
Willis, Catharine
Willis, Sarah

Hester Roll 1883
(Partial list)

Anderson
Benjamin
Battle
Coleman
Christian
Davis

Day
Fields
Garland
Green
Going
Green
Hensley
Hester
Hamilton
Hale
Henry
Jackson
Jones
Jordan
Le sih (Possibly Lewis)
Lee
Lu sih
Ledford
Langley
Lewis
Murphy
McDaniel
Maroney
McCoy
Mathis
Peter
Reed
Rogers
Robinson
Robertson
Tucker
Thomas West
Will West
Willis

**Churchill Roll 1908
(Partial list)**

Conseen (possibly Cousin)
Davis
Clark
Garland
Green
Johnson
Jordan
Lee
Lossie
Lossiah

McCoy
Meroney
Mathews
Murphy
Otter
Reed
Robinson
Rogers
Rose
West
Yance

**Baker Roll 1924
(Partial list)**

Beavers
Burgess
Carter
Clark
Conseen
Crawford
Foster
Garland
Green
Hamby
Harris
Hogan
Jackson
Jones
Johnson
Kidd
Lee
Lossih
McCoy
McDaniel
Meroney
Moore
Patterson
Payne
Reed
Rose
Reynolds
Robinson
Nichols (Possibly Nuckles)
Taylor
West
Whip-poor-will Manley
Wright

Yance

The Index and Final Rolls of Citizens and Freedmen of the Cherokee Tribe in Indian Territory (June 21, 1906) listed many of the surnames of residents in central and southwestern Virginia, including the residents in Amherst, Appomattox, Buckingham, Campbell, Nelson, and Rockbridge Counties and the city of Lynchburg. Some of these names are as follows:

NAME	NUMBER LIST
ALLEN	18
ANDERSON	19
AUSTIN	3
BEAVERT	9
BEAVERS	7
BECK	7
BIVIN	3
BIVINS	3
BLAIR	19
BOLIN	9
BOLEN	2
BOWLIN	2
BOWLYN	1
BONHAM	5
BRANDON	1
BRANHAM	2
BRANNON	4
CAMPBELL	33
CARNES	14
CARTER	26
CARPENTER	10
CASH	4
CHAMBERS	5
CHILDERS	6
CHRISTIAN	8
CLARK	81
CLARKE	3
CLASBY	6
COBB	48
COCKRAN	126
COCKRUM	10
COCKRELL	5
COCKRAM	1
COFFEE	4
COLEMAN	8
COOPER	3
COPELAND	5

CROW	12	
CURREY	8	
DANIEL	2	
DAVIS	172	
DUNCAN	73	
DUFF (Delph)	4	
EAGLE	21	
EDMONDS	9	
ELLIS	4	
ELLIOTT	4	
EVANS	3	
FERGUSON	7	
FIELDS	106	
FROG	6	
FRY	2	
FRYE	21	
GOINS	1	
GRAVES	6	
GREEN	40	
HALE	5	
HAMILTON	8	
HILDERBRAND	5	
HARLESS	10	
HARRIS	92	
HARTNESS	10	
HAWKINS	57	
HASTINGS	7	
HICKEY	11	
HICKS	99	
HIGGINS	6	
HILL	48	
HOGG	2	
HOPKINS	3	
HOPPER	10	
HORSEFLY	4	
HOUSLEY	7	
HOWE	4	
HOWELL	16	(often written in this area as Howl, may refer to Owl)
HUGHES	43	
HUTCHENS	1	
HUTCHING	1	
HUTCHINS	7	
HUTCHINSON	2	
ISBELL	6	
JACKSON	78	
JENKINS	13	
JIMISON	2	

JOHNS	6	
JOHNSON	240	
JOHNSTON	35	
JOHNSTONE	2	
JONES	140	
JORDON	70	
JUSTICE	7	
JUSTIS	3	
KEYS	83	
KIDD	12	
KING	58	
KNIGHT	29	
LEE	80	
LAYNE	5	
LEE	80	
LEECH	37	
LEIGH	5	
LEWIS	24	
MARTIN	26	
MATHIS	6	
MAYES	67	
MAYS	7	
MEEK	7	
MCCOY	76	
MERCHANT	3	
MILLER	276	
MOORE	72	
MORGAN	31	
MORRIS	138	
MURPHY	71	
MURPHEY	1	
OWL	8	(often written in this area as Howl or Howell)
PAINTER	7	
PALMOUR	12	
PANTER	8	
PANTHER	12	
PANN	9	
PAN	2	(often written in this area as Pin,Pinn)
PARRIS	14	(often written in this area as Paris)
PATTERSON	10	
PAYNE	60	
PEMBLETON	6	
PENDLETON	4	
PENNINGTON	4	
PETERS	25	
PENN	5	
PHILLIPS	25	

POWELL	9	
PRICE	5	
REDMOND	1	
REED	37	
REID	9	
RICE	10	
RICHARDS	14	
RICHARDSON	10	
RICHIE	3	
RIGSBY	4	
ROBERTSON	30	
ROBERTS	44	
ROBINSON	42	
ROBISON	13	
ROBBINS	7	
ROBINS	8	
ROBERSON	15	
ROBIN	4	
RODGERS	4	
ROGERS	230	
ROSS	235	
ROSE	9	
SCALES	7	
SCOTT	87	
SOUTHER	1	
SOUTHERLAND	1	
SOUTHERLIN	2	
SQUIRREL	39	(often written in this area as Sorrell, Sorel, Sorell, Sorrell (s))
SPARROWHAWK	8	(often written in this area as Sparrow or Hawks, Hawkins)
SPEARS	26	
STEWART	5	
TERRELL	6	
TONEY	8	
TOWER	2	
TOWERS	4	
TOWIE	5	(often written as Tyree, Terry)
TOWRY	1	
TUCKER	71	
TULLY	1	
TURNER	32	
TURLEY	3	
TURTLE	16	
TWITTY	1	
TWILLEY	3	
TYLER	7	
TYNER	82	

WALLIS	5	
WALLS	5	
WARD	71	
WARE	8	
WASHBOURNE	10	(often written as Washburn)
WASHINGTON	41	
WARWICK	9	
WATT	2	
WILSON	8	
WINN	5	
WOLF	21	
WOLFE	97	
WOOD	73	
WOODS	18	
WOODALL	82	
WOODARD	35	
WOODS	18	
WEST	89	

Emmet Starr, in Old Cherokee Families--Old Families and Their Genealogy, 1968, included the names of prominent Cherokee family members who resided within the limits of the Qualla Boundary. Some of the surnames that correspond to the surnames in central and southwestern Virginia, including Amherst and vicinity. He listed a large number of surnames that were the same surnames that are common in Amherst County and in the Stonewall Mill/Buffalo Ridge area:

Banks, Blair, Bolin, Carter, Chambers, Clark, Cozens, Eagle, Elliott, Evans, Ferguson, Fields, Goings, Goin, Hicks, Hopkins, Hopper, Hughes, Isbell, Jenkins, McCoy, McDaniel, and Jordan.

The Western North Carolina Telephone Book, 1992-93, covers the names of residents within the counties of Jackson, Macon, Swain, Cherokee, Graham, and Haywood. Four of the six counties were within the "Eastern Cherokee domain" in 1835 (Guion Miller, 1906, Introduction, The Eastern Cherokees vs. the United States, Report of Guion Miller). Some of the names that are included in the first part of the directory are as follows:

NAME	NUMBER	PAGE
Adcock	3	1
Adkins	2	1
Atkins	4	4
Banks	19	4
Beasley	26	5
Bevis	3	6
Blevins	4	7

94

Bolin	6	7
Bolinger	2	7
Bolden	12	7
Branham	3	8
Branhan	2	8
Brannon	4	8
Chambers	73	15
Clarke	5	17
Clarks	141	16, 17
Cox	4	20
Evans	44	27, 28
Ferguson	97	27, 28
Hartness	2	37
Jenkins	55	45, 46
Johns	3	46

The Southern Bell Telephone Book (Asheville)--including listings for Arden-Skyland, Fletcher, Enka-Candler, Fairview, Leicester, Swannanoa Valley--listed a large number of surnames that are common to Amherst County and vicinity. This area has a very heavy population of Cherokee residents. Some of the names are as follows:

NAME   **NUMBER**

Name	Number
Adcock	4
Adkins	14
Atkins	26
Ailstock	1
Banks	114
Beverly	7
Blair	24
Blevins	14
Branam	2
Branham	4
Brannam	5
Brannon	3
Brandon	12
Carpenter	36
Carter	159
Causby	3
Causey	2
Chambers	41`
Childress	15
Clark	236
Clarke	26
Cooper	72
Eagles	7
Elliott	62

Evans	99
Ferguson	60
Field	6
Fields	21
Fox	126
Foxx	7
Going	2
Goings	2
Goin	5
Hamilton	44
Hare	27
Harris	186
Hicks	31
Hoppers	16
Hughes	88
Hutcheson	2
Hutchins	30
Hutchison	30
Isbell	2
Isbill	1
Jenkins	92
Jewel	1
Jewell	3
Jewett	4
Jordan	58
McCoy	39
Reed	81
Roberson	50
Robert	9
Roberts	271
Robertson	43
Robinson	347
Robison	9
Rodgers	18
Rogers	226
Sale	3
Sales	32
Sayles	18
Scott	80
Sharp	33
Sharpe	46
Sorrel	1
Sorrells	29
Sorrels	1
Southard	3
Souther	20
Stewart	113
West	102

A list has been compiled from some of the old Cherokee surnames on the <u>Index and Final Rolls of Citizens and Freedmen of the Cherokee Tribe in Indian Territory</u>, on the <u>1835 Census Roll of the Cherokee Indians East of the Mississippi</u>, in Emmet Starr's <u>Old Cherokee Families--Old Families and Their Genealogy</u>, in Bob Blankenship's <u>Cherokee Roots</u>,, in Jerry W. Jordan's <u>Cherokee By Blood</u>, in Whitehead's article (1896), and in James Tyner's <u>Those Who Cried</u>. The list of names has been placed below (in left column) and a list of some common Cherokee surnames in Amherst County and vicinity (surnames of residents who have Cherokee ancestry/oral histories and/or Cherokee surnames (in right column):

CHEROKEE SURNAMES	LOCAL CHEROKEE SURNAMES
ADKINS, ATKINS	Adkins, Atkins, Atkinson
ADAMS	Adams
AA GA, AA GY	Agee
AH YA STAH	Alcock
AILSTOCK	Ailstock
ALLEN, AH LIN	Allen
ALLISON	Allison
ANDERSON	Anderson
AUSTIN	Austin
BAKER	Baker
BALDWIN	Baldwin
BANK	Banks
BEAVER CARRIER, BEAVER, BEAVER TOTER, BREVERT	Beverly, Beverley, Bevly, Bevely Blevins, Blivins, Beverts, Bevins
BELL	Bell
BENGE	Benge
BIRD	Bird, Byrd

97

BLAIR	Blair
BLANKENSHIP	Blankenship
BLEVINS, BLIVINS, BIVINS, BEVINS, BELVINS	Blevins, Blivins, Bivins, Bevins, Belvins
BOLLINGER, BOWLING	Bollinger, Boling, Bowling, Bolden, Bolling
BOWMAN	Bowman, Bow
BRADLEY, BRADY	Bradley, Brady
BRANCH	Branch
BRANNON, BRANNON, BRANHAM	Branham, Brannam, Brannom, Brannum, Branom, Brannon
BROWN	Brown
BRYANT	Bryant
BURGESS	Burgess
BURRELL	Burrell
BYARS	Byers
CALAWAY	Callaway
CAMPBELL	Campbell
CARNS	Carn, Carns, Carnes, Karnes
CARTER	Carter
CARVER	Carver
CHAMBERS	Chambers
CHEATER, EL CHAU GAH CHIEF EAGLE	Cheagle
CHILDRESS	Childress, Childers
CHRISTIAN	Christian

CALARKSAW, CLARK	Clark, Clarke
CLAUSBY, CLASB(E)Y, CAUSEH E LAH	Clausby, Causby, Cosby Gillespie
COBB	Cobb
COCKRUM	Cockran, Cochrum
COFFEY	Coffey
COLE	Cole
COLEMAN	Coleman
COMPTON, CUMPTON	Compton
COOK	Cook
COOPER	Cooper
COTTRELL	Cottrell, Cantrell
COOKSON, COLSON, COKSON	Cousin, Cozen, Colson
COX	Cox
CRAIG, CRAIGG	Craig
CRAWLER	Crawley
CROWE	Crow, Crowe, Grow, Groah
DANIEL	Daniel
DAVIS	Davis
DAY	Day
DEAL	Deal
DEAN	Dean
DENNIS	Dennis

DENTON	Denton
DILLARD	Dillard
DOBSON	Dobson, Dodson
DUNCAN	Duncan
DUNLOP, DUNLAP	Dunlap
DOWNING, DROWNING BEAR, DOWNING DAVID	Dunning
EAGLE,	Eagle, Cheagle
EATON	Taton
ELDRIDGE	Eldridge
ELLER	Elders, Elder
ELLIS	Ellis
ELLIOTT, ELLICK, ELLIS	Elliott
ELY	Elly
EVANS	Evans
EWERS	Ewers
FALL	Falls
FERGUSON, FARGUSON FURGUSON	Ferguson
FIELD, LYING IN THE FIELD	Field(s)
FLOYD	Floyd
FOSTER	Foster
FOX	Fox, Foxx
FRENCH	French
GAINS	Gaines

GARDNER	Gardner, Garner
GARLAND	Garland
GARRETT	Garrett
GEORGE	George
GILLIS	Gillis
GILLISPIE, CLAUSBY	Gillispie, Causby, Cosby
GUESS	Gist
GOING UP STREAM, GOING INTO THE WATER, GOING SNAKE, GOING PANTHER, GOIN, GOING WOLF	Goin, Goin(s), Gowen, Gowan, Gowin, Going
GRAVES	Graves
GREEN	Green
GROATH	Groath, Groah, Grohs, Grow
HAIR, HARE	Hair, Hare, Harris, Harriss
HALE	Hale
HALL	Hall
HALSLEY, HULSEY	Halsley
HAMBY	Hamby, Handy
HAMILTON	Hamilton
HARRIS	Harris
HARRISON	Harrison
HARTLESS	Hartless, Hartness
HARTNESS	Hartness

HASS	Hass, Hess
HAWK	Hawk(s)
HAWKINS	Hawkins
HAYS, HAYES	Hays, Hayes, Haynes, Haines
HENDRICK	Hendrick, Hendricks
HENRY	Henry
HENSLEY	Hensley, Henley
HICKS, HIX	Hicks, Hickey, Hix
HIGGINS	Higgins
HILL	Hill
HOGSHOOTER	Hogg(s)
HOLCOMB	Holcomb
HOLMES	Holmes
HOPKINS	Hopkins
HOPPER, GRASS HOPPER, ASH HOPPER	Hopper
HORSEFLY, HORSLY	Horsley
HOWELL, OWL, OWELL	Howl, Howell, Owl, Howard
HOWARD	Howard
HUDSON	Hudson
HUGHES, HUGH	Hughes
HUNTER	Hunter
HUTCHERSON	Hutcherson
ISBELL	Isbell, Isbill, Isabel
JACKSON	Jackson

JAMES	James
JEFFREYS	Jeffries, Jeffrey, Jeffreys
JENK, JENKINS, JEKEY, JEH KEH	Jenkins, Jinkins
JOHNSON	Johnson
JOHN	Johns
JORDAN	Jordan, Jordon
JUSTICE	Justice, Justis
KEITH	Keith
KENNY, KE NAH	Kenny
KEY, CO YEA KEE, AU QUE TA KEE, AU QUITA KEE, CHU QUA LOF KEY, TAR KEY TU SKI A KEY	Key(s)
KING	King
KNIGHT KELLER	Knight
LEE	Lee
LEWIS	Lewis
LITTLEJOHN	Littlejohn
LONG	Long
LOVE, LOW WIN NOO KUH	Loving, Lowe
LOWE, LOWEN, LOWIN	Lowe, Lowen, Lowin, Lawing
LOWRY, LOWREY	Lowry, Lowrey
McCOY	McCoy, Coy
McDANIEL	McDaniel, McDaniels
McGINNIS	McGinnis, McGinness, McGillis

McLAUGHLIN	McLaughlin
MANLEY	Manley
MARTIN	Martin
MATHIS, MATTHEWS	Matthis, Mattis, Matthews
MAY(S)	Mays, May, Mayes
MEGGINSON	Megginson
MIX IT	Maxey
MILLER	Miller
MOON	Moon
MORGAN	Morgan
MOORE, MORRIS, MOSS, MOORE, MOSES, MOUSE	Morse, Moore, Moss, Morris,
MORSE	Morse
MURPHY, MURPHEY	Murphy
NEAL, NEEL	Neal, Neel
NELSON	Nelson
NEWTON	Newton
NICEY, NICCY	Nicely
NICHOLS, NICKEH, NICHOLSON, NICK IH	Nichols, Nuckol, Nuckles, Knuckles
OO TIE, OO TA TIE, OO TI EE, OTTER, UTIH, OYA TY	Otey
OWL, OWELL	Owl, Howl, Howell, Owell
OWEN(s)	Owen(s)
OWNESBY, OWENBY	Ownby

PATHER, GOING PANTHER	Painter, Going, Gowen, Goin
PARK, PARKS	Park
PARKER	Parker
PARROTT, PARRY	Parrish, Perry, Parrets
PATTERSON	Patterson
PAYNE, PAIN, PAN	Payne, Pin
PENN	Penn, Pinn, Pinn
PERRY	Perry
PERSINGER	Persinger
PETERS	Peters
PENCE	Pence, Pin, Penn, Pinn
PINN, PIN	Penn, Pin, Pence, Two Pins, Two Pence Tuppence
POINDEXTER	Poindexter
POWELL	Powell
PRICE	Price
PRINCE	Prince
PULLING, PULLIUM	Pullen(s)
QUAL LA	Qual la, Quarles
RACKLEY, RATLIFF	Rackley, Ratcliff, Ratliff
RAMSEY	Ramsey
REAVIES, REAVES	Reavley
REED	Reed
REYNOLDS	Reynolds

ROBERTS	Roberts
ROBERSON	Roberson, Robertson, Robeson
ROBINSON	Robinson, Robison
ROGERS, RODGERS	Rogers, Rodgers
RUNION	Runyon
ROSE, ROSS	Rose, Ross
RUSSELL	Russell
SANDERS	Sanders, Saunders
SATTERFIELD	Satterfield
SAWYER	Sawyer
SCOTT WILL, SCOTT ELIC, SAMUEL SCOTT, DICK SCOTT	Scott
SCUDDER	Scudder
SHARP	Sharp, Sharpe
CHEKELELEE, CHICKLEECH	Shifflett, Shifflet, Shiflet, Chilfet
SAMPSON, SIMPSON	Sampson, Simpson
SIZEMORE	Sizemore
SMITH	Smith
SNEAD, SNEED	Snead, Sneed
SQUIRREL, GROUND SQUIRREL	Sorrell(s), Sorell(s), Sorrel(s)
SOUTHER	Souther, Southers, Southards, Southherd, Suthards
SPARROW, SPARROW HAWK SPERROE	Sparrow, Hawk, Hawkins

SPENCER	Spencer
SPEARS	Spears
STACY, STACEY	Stacy
STAMPER	Stamper, Stamps
STE WIH, STE WIH STEPHEN	Steward, Stewart, Stuart, Steuart
STRATTON	Stratton
SUTTON	Sutton
SWAYNEY, SQUAIN CIH	Swain
TAH LIH	Talley, Tally
TAYLOR	Taylor
TEAGUE	Teague
TERRELL, TERRAPIN HEAD TERRAPIN STRIKER, TEE RIE, TA HAH HIH	Terry, Terrell, Terrill, Turley
THOMAS	Thomas
THOMPSON	Thompson
TAWNEY, TONEY, TOO NIE, TOR NEY, TOONI, TURN IT OVER	Toney
TUCKER, TU KI KEE, TA KIH	Tucker
TURNER, TURN OVER, THE TURNER TAH HIH	Turner
TEE RIE, TOWIE, TA WEE	Tyree
TWITTY	Twitty, Twiddy
TWO PENCE	Tuppence, Turpin, Two Pin, Pin(n)
TYLER, TILLER	Tyler, Tiller

VAUGHT	Vaughter
WALKER, WAL KIH	Walker
WALLUSIH	Wallace
WARD	Ward
WARE	Ware
WARRICK	Warrick, Warwick
WASHINGTON	Washington
WAT SON NIH	Watson
WATTS, WATT	Watts
WAYNE	Wayne
WEBB	Webb
WEBSTER	Webster
WELCH	Welch
WESLEY, WES LIH	Wesley
WEST	West
WE LIH	Wheeler
WHITE	White
WILLEY, WALLEY, WILEY, WAH LEY	Wiley
WILKEY, WAL KIH, WILKINSON	Wilkins, Wilkinson
WILL, WILLIS	Will(s), Willis
WILLIAMS	Williams
WILSON	Wilson
WINNIH, WIN NIH, WINN	Winn, Wynn

WOLFE, WOLF	Wolf, Wolff
WOOD LARK, WOODCOCK, WOODWARD, WOODALL WOY A HUT LEH	Wood(s), Woodall, Woodward, Woodard Worley, Whorley, Worrell
WRIGHT	Wright
YANCE, YA CHIN	Yancey, Yancy
YOUNG	Young, Youngue

There are thousands of English surnames that exist in most areas of the United States; however, in the Stapleton Area and vicinity, including the Lexington/Covington/Clifton Forge/Alleghany County area (where a large number of Buffalo Ridge Band's relatives resides), a very large number or percentage of Cherokee names prevails among the populations. Coincidence? The odds of this large a number of Cherokee names existing in this area due solely to chance are extremely small. Add to this fact the Cherokee oral traditions that prevail among the families of the name-bearers and we cannot deny that these people are descendants of Cherokee.

The Cherokee adopted a large number of Bible names as first names as well as surnames. Some of the names that they and their descendants in Amherst County and its vicinity owned are as follows:

Daniel
Issac
James
John
Elijah
Elizabeth or Betsy, Bitsy, Betsey
Martha
Mary
Joseph
Hanna(h)
Benjamin
Sarah
Thomas
Ester
David or Davis
Stephen
Rebecca
Peter
Delilah
Caleb

Zachariah
Josiah
Samuel
Christian

The Indians adopted names of locations:

Americus
Park
Standing Waters
Fields

They frequently chose names from animals:
Squirrel (possibly Sorrell)
Sparrow
Turtle, Terrapin (Terry)
Eagle
Crow

It is very interesting that the oral Cherokee tradition remained because of the secrecy of the mission to hide out in Amherst County and vicinity to avoid the Oklahoma Removal. McElwain noted that Cherokee in Chesnut Ridge, in West Virginia, kept their Cherokee ancestry secret (McElwain, 1981, 39).

Often, the local Cherokee who avoided the Removal would leave a hint that they were Indian by taking a name like Cherokee Jim or Delaware George or Pocahontas Beverly. This technique had the effect of preserving the Indian connection without admitting to this relationship. Later, after the threat of removal passed, the Indian admitted that they were "Indian" but Virginia did not allow this title to be placed on birth and marriage certificates The Indian people were systematically and purposefully erased from existence in Amherst County and vicinity.

Let us take a closer look at a few of these Indian families. They left their names and more.

CHAPTER VI
Su da li (Six)

CHEROKEE IN BUFFALO RIDGE AND VICINITY

A Remnant of a Great Nation Divided

When you see a turtle sitting
on the top of a tree stump,
you can only imagine the interesting
history behind that present scene!

(A common saying on the Ridge)

How did the turtle get on the stump? Who put him there? How long
has he been there? Does he want to get down? What history exists on
the situation? The same questions have been asked about the Buffalo
Ridge Band by family members and residents of Central Virginia. How
did they get here in central Virginia? They are different from their white
and black neighbors; for example, the leiotrichous hair of the yellow-red
race, skin color, shape of eyes and nose. (Rice, 1991, 66; Malone, 15).
The 1850 and 1860 Appomattox and Amherst census data show them
as standing out from the rest of the population like a turtle on a stump.
As a child would ask for information when he sees a turtle on a stump,
Central Virginians are seeking information about the Buffalo Ridge
Cherokee.

Fairmount Baptist Church's Centennial Bulletin (1976) was the first
publication with any specific history about the people near Buffalo Ridge
in Amherst County. It was first believed that the church for these
people was started "during the years 1860-67." Later data has revealed
that the people were on the Ridge before the mid 1700s. It is now
recognized that the early residents were interred in "Penn Park Cherokee
Grounds," the first known cemetery at Fairmount Baptist Church, and
that the people may have held informal worship services during that
period of time. Although most of the residents of the Ridge were listed
as "free colored," and had always been free Native Americans, a few
were slaves during the early part of this period and therefore these
residents had to have church services in secrecy. "Some of the older
members remember being told by grandparents of religious services
being held in their homes during 'slavery time'" (Fairmount Centennial
Bulletin,1). Some of the slaves had Cherokee ancestry. They sang
songs and prayed but kept the noise down so that their masters would
not hear them. Isabell Ferguson Fields remembers her ancestors telling
her what they had heard about early worship services. They "built a

111

grapevine covering in the woods and had church under it. Most of the people up there were related. A chairback preacher, a minister who stood behind a chair that he used for a podium, would stand under the bush covering and deliver the sermon" (Fields, 1991).

"The two years between 1865-67, Reverend Willie Murphy, Sr., was the shepherd of the flock, holding services first in the homes of the members. These members were the Morgans, Jacksons, Penns, Boldings (Bowlings), Beverlys, Franklins, Blairs, Strattons, Revelys, Pollards, Fitchs, Turners and Booths" (Fairmount Centennial Bulletin, 1976, 1). Although the bulletin only listed some of the names of families near Buffalo Ridge, most of these family names were listed in the 1860 Amherst County census as "Mu"(Indian) while the Cherokee Rolls also documented similar names, including Murphy, the pastor's name (Blankenship, Bob, 114 & 115; R.C. Chambers, 1992).

"It should be noted further that this period following the War Between the States was a very hard time. Business had stopped in the towns and in the cities. There were no goods to sell in the stores, and the people had no money to spend. The citizens of Virginia, Stapleton included, often went hungry. They were poor and they were sad, but their hearts were brave" (Fairmount Centennial Bulletin, 1). During this time, a few miles across the James River from Stapleton, General Lee entered a farmhouse at Appomattox Courthouse and signed the surrender before General Grant" (Fairmount Centennial Bulletin, 1).

Although many of the people were poor, they loved and valued the Buffalo Ridge area for its beauty and rich natural resources. The following Cherokee names could be used to describe the beauty of area on and around Buffalo Ridge (Salomon, The Book of Indian Crafts and Indian Lore, 1928):

Ga li'la hi	Amiable; gentle; attractive
Tsun ga'ni	Excels All Others
Ga ti'tla	They Run to Her

"They run to her" fits the tradition that says that Indians ran to the mountains to hide during the Revolution and Removal periods, including the Buffalo Ridge and Glades area of Amherst County.

They named their church "Fairmount" because of its appearance and the location of Buffalo Ridge (Fairmount Centennial Bulletin). The church became the focal point of the community; people from as far as ten miles away came to worship on Sunday.

Who were some of these families? What were their customs?

The first Fairmount Baptist Church has a very old and historic church

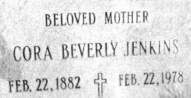

BELOVED MOTHER

CORA BEVERLY JENKINS

FEB. 22, 1882 ✝ FEB. 22, 1978

FATHER
WALKER DAVID
WEST

JAN. 16, 1883
SEPT. 19, 1963

BEVERLY

FATHER
JAKE A.
1893   1978

MOTHER
ETTA G.
1897   1988

FIRST CHURCH   SECOND CHURCH

PRESENT CHURCH
From <u>Fairmount Centennial Bulletin</u>, 1976.
Drawings by H.R.Rice

cemetery ("Penn (Pin) Park Cherokee Grounds"). Penn Park is believed to date back to the early-to-mid-1700s. Raleigh Pinn, who lived and owned real estate in this area of the Ridge in the mid-to-late-1700s is interred in Penn Park. This historic cemetery is near the church and the second cemetery is located near the second Fairmount Church. Some stones remain where the church once stood. The second church was located close to the main road on Buffalo Ridge.

J.W. Powell, in the First Annual Report of the Bureau of Ethnology to the Secretary of the Smithsonian Institute--1879-80(1881), reported that "the Cherokees of Tennessee 'seldom buried their dead, but threw them in the river.'"(180). The Indian people in Amherst County during the 1700s and 1800s generally followed the Christian custom of burying their dead with a Christian funeral service. The members have not heard of any aquatic burial legends.

The first Fairmount Church was located behind the second Fairmont Church. Penn Park, the church's cemetery, is in the area where the first church stood.

Some of the inscriptions on the markers are noted as follows:

Ada Hull
Born April 16, 1882
Died November 2, 1941

William Beverly
Peter Beverly
Died Aug 5, 1938

Sallie Ann Hull
Born July 2, 1859
Died March 23, 1918

Betsey Beverly
Born 1833
Died 1916

David Milton Beverly
Born April 23, 1889
Died December 19, 1899

Anne Wax
Born 1883
Died 1913

Ann Wax's marker was located between the markers of Betsey Beverly and David Milton Beverly. The family members do not have any knowledge of this lady. She seems to be a mystery person in the Penn Park. She may have been a member of the West family and the tombstone engraver may have misunderstood the pronunciation of the name "West" and engraved the name "Wax."

Husezell West
Infant of
Walker and Adell West

Blair Pendleton
Willie A. Pendleton
Wife of A. Pendleton
Born 1886
Died 1918

Albert Sparrow
Born June 28, 1916
Died Jan 17, 1919
Son of Ernest Sparrow

Ben Beverly
Born Jan 30, 1835
Died Aug 30, 1926
Age 69

Taylor Beverly
Born 18_?5
Died 1928

Penn
George Penn
Aurcelous Penn
1861-1928

Catherine Beverly
Died March 4
Buried Mar 6, 190_?

Analiza Jenkings
Died 1908

Walker Beverly
Born May 18, 1895
Died Jan 22, 1912

In Memory of
Ben Willis West
Born April 18, 1890

Martha J. West
Born Feb 6, 1860
Died Feb 27, 1890

Some of the members interred in the second cemetery are as follows:

Mary Lou Scott
Beverly
January 1, 1878-August 27, 1951

Nanny West Ferguson

Adell West
Born 1902-Died August 25, 1952

Maynard OK
Vaughter
October 21, 1921-November 19, 1945

John Bowling

Phil Bowling

Harris Hull

_____in Franklin, Jr.

The third Fairmount Baptist Church, located on Route 622, in Stapleton, has a cemetery within twenty-five yards of the church. Many of Stapleton's residents, as well as residents from other localities but descendents of the Buffalo Ridge clans, have been interred in this cemetery. Some of the members who have been interred in the third Fairmount Baptist Church cemetery are as follows:

Walker West
Jan 16, 1883-September 19, 1963

Maloney O. Ferguson-November 22, 1915
December 24, 1987

James G. Ferguson, Jr.
July 17, 1917-February 8, 1992

Elis Stratton
September 26, 1898-April 9, 1976

Bernard Jackson
March 15, 1888-March 25, 1966
Louise Jackson
1891-1981

Raymond B. Ferguson
1906-1973

Andrea Sue Vaughter
July 3, 1965-February 15, 1966

Ada M. Vaughter
March 4, 1881-July 25, 1964

James Gus. Ferguson, Sr.
January 9, 1880-January 10, 1969

Eddie Ferguson
April 10,1 912-June 22, 1958

Levelt Ferguson
September 12, 1904-December 31, 1963

Ledwell Jack Ferguson
November 21, 1909-November 6, 1968

Langley Junius Ferguson
September 15, 1914-September 19, 1985

Clarence O. Ferguson
January 9, 1919-April 17, 1989

Kathy Sue Franklin
July 20, 1959-November 5, 1959

Flossie H. Beverly
September 10, 1924-September 11, 1986

Jake A. Beverly
1893-1978
Etta Green Beverly
1897-1988

Henry Beverly
June 6, 1895-July 30, 1968
Peter Beverly
June 18, 1898-November 22, 1982

Roy Clifton Elliott
December 16, 1928-August 12, 1989

Marguerite Elliott
April 9, 1911-December 15, 1986

James Wesley Moore
June 1, 1871-April 24, 1959

Cora Beverly Jenkins
February 22, 1882-February 22, 1978

Arthur West
1911-1983

Dorothy Bowling Ware
1949-1986

John William Bowling
November 27, 1947-June 8, 1991

Beatrice Bowling York
1959-1985

Minnie Bowling
1979

Lloyd Elliott
September, 1876-June 8, 1967

Mary Franklin Scott
February 10, 1885-January 31, 1961

Ruth Harris
1895-1970

James Edward Scott
October 16, 1931-March 9, 1972

Nellie R. Franklin
1897-1981

Lillian Franklin Gilbert
July 24, 1909-October 27, 1987

Ruby Hester Scott
March 14, 1913-September 21, 1988

Samuel Scott
1904-1991

Mary Franklin Sparrow
October 9, 1936-May 22, 1991

Sylvester (Buck) Mason
April 1, 1908-October 6, 1981

Frank Hull

William C. Elliott, Sr.
1902-1968

Lewis H. Woodson
September 3,1 932-February 9, 1983

Robert Ernest Sparrow
December 14, 1909-January 13, 1989

Marion Sparrow
1910-1976

Jonathan Moore
1977-1977

Martha Rebecca Franklin Sparrow
December 24, 1903-January 7, 1978

Joseph Maurice Sparrow
1961-1962

Casey Woodson
1966-1990

Rossie Lewis Sparrow, Sr.
January 12, 1918-December 10, 1965

John Winston Sparrow
October 28, 1951-May 14, 1990

Doretha Lula Woodson
March 8, 1936-June 6, 1967

Lizzie B. Pennix
January 5, 1908-October 13, 1982

Mary Trent

1903-1972

Fannie L. Bowling
1905-1974

Baby Girl Williams
1972-1972

Alfred L. Bowling
1912-1976

William Daniel Franklin
March 7, 1894-February 7, 1979

William D. Franklin, III
December 26, 1952-July 14, 1975

Linda Coleman
1934-1994

Walter Lee Coleman
1929-1994

George Pennix
April 16, 1943-December 1, 1990

Gravestone Inscriptions in Amherst County, Virginia(1986, 290), compiled by Mary Frances Boxley, listed some of the gravestones inscriptions at Graveyard number 202A, Fairmont Baptist Church, on "top of Buffalo Ridge, south side of Rt. #624, 1\2 miles from Earley's place." The following inscriptions were listed:

Allen, Edward, November 14, 1965 age 2 yrs.
Beverly, Annie, Dec. 29, 1952, age 61 yrs. 4 mo. 8 das
Mary Lue   Scott, Jan. 1, 1878-Aug. 27, 1951
Brown, Viola, 1931-1982.
Ferguson, Nannie E. Jan. 28, 19___, age 66 yrs. 4 mo. 29 das.
Franklin, Baby Boy
Mays, Samuel Glover, May 25, 1914-Oct. 22, 1982.
Vaughter, Maynard O.K., Oct. 21, 1921-Nov. 19, 1945, WWII.
West, Odell M., Aug. 29, 1952 age 50 yrs.
Recorded by Scott Vail

It seemed that some of the people huddled together and married the residents within their particular settlement. The Buffalo Ridge Cherokee people have kept themselves as a sovereign Indian group since or before the mid 1700s. It has been suggested that the Ridge group and the

119

Bear Mountain Monacans have intermarried (Hantman). While there are some family members who have direct connections to the Bear Mountain group or "Monacans" via those Bear Mountain ancestors who proclaimed that they were Cherokee (B. Beverly's ancestors and others), the Buffalo Ridge members have generally intermarried with Buffalo Ridge, Stonewall Mill, and other Cherokee descendants since the mid to late 1700s. The early marriage records in Amherst County show marriages with some other families with Cherokee surnames and/or oral histories. The Beverlys of Virginia have always claimed that they have Cherokee ancestry. They married other Cherokee on the Ridge. Obadiah Knuckles once lived on the Ridge and his daughter, Roqueen "Rosa," married Benjamin Beverly, the son of Betsy Beverly. Rosa Knuckles' brother, Calvin, indicated in Cherokee By Blood (J. Wright Jordan) that he was Cherokee and was descended from the Redcross line via his mother, Susan. Two other daughters of Obadiah Knuckles married into the Beverly family. Benjamin Beverley's grandson, Ben Alton Beverley, holds the tribal office of Advisor for the Buffalo Ridge Band. The southwest Virginia Beverlys (Santini) and other Virginia Beverlys have Cherokee heritage.

Buffalo Ridge families included the Banks, Blairs, Beverlys (Beverleys), Bollings (Bowlings, Boldens), Carters, Chamberses, Davises, McCoys, Fergusons (Fargusons), Wests, Pinns (Penns, Pins), Jordans, Christians, Jenkinses, Jewells, Johnsons, Banks, Greens, Coopers, Sparrows, Warricks (Warwicks), Woods, and others. These people had Cherokee surnames and a rich Cherokee heritage. They attracted Cherokee from other areas to their band--the Sorrells, Cousins, Umbles (Humbles), and Tylers.

Dr. Plecker, State Registrar of Vital Statistics, preserved, unintentionally, the names of people who were trying to assert their Indian heritage by listing their surnames in his letter dated January, 1943 (Dr. Plecker's letter). Many of the names included in his letter match the surnames of Cherokee people. Dr. Plecker's letter requested that the clerks of the counties in Virginia list these people as "black," not white or Indian. He reminded the clerks that those who are guilty of this "fraud," claiming to be Indian, should be warned that they could face a one-year sentence in the state penitentiary.

The Buffalo Ridge residents, most of whom have always been free Indian people, and whose ancestors were never slaves (1790, 1800, 1810, 1840, 1850, and 1860 census records of Amherst and Appomattox/Buckingham counties), were listed as "free colored" and "Mu" until the 1900 census. In 1900, the Buffalo Ridge group, their relatives in Amherst and other counties, as well as members of the Monacan tribe, were all listed as "B." The Buffalo Ridge residents, who have been a peaceful and God-fearing people (Centennial Bulletin), quietly accepted Dr. Plecker's "illegal" order to make their Indian people "black," even though they had been classified as "Mu," "free colored," "I," and "W" (Dr. Plecker's Letter; S. Penn.; C. Penn). By accepting Dr. Plecker's order and the "colored" classification, they believed that they were obeying the law and were keeping themselves out of jail, and free from legal entanglements and controversy.

Dock Jenkins' parents, Ivanhoe Jenkins and Cora Beverly Jenkins (both have Cherokee surnames and oral histories), resisted the organized efforts to erase "Indian" from official forms by insisting that their race be listed as "Indian/white." They risked their freedom to maintain the tribal connection. Thirty-six years later, however, their race had been changed to "colored." (D. Jenkins' Birth Certificate; D. Jenkins' Marriage Record). An "Indian" classification was still eluding residents as late as 1940, so some Indians were only allowed to have "Mixed Indian" on certificates (Beverly/Clark Marriage Certificate).

While many of their distant relatives in Madison Heights, and the Town of Amherst gradually became "white" by marrying early white settlers' descendants, the Buffalo Ridge Band drew closer to their members on the Ridge (Fairmount Baptist Church Membership Roll; Fairmount Baptist Church Centennial Bulletin; Fairmount School Rolls). They gradually moved from a people of color or Indian ("Mu") to "colored." As a result of their obeying what they thought at the time was the "law," a "legal" order, and not challenging the classification, they became "colored." They maintained a tight tribal identity without the stereotypical supervision of the Bureau of Indian Affairs or missionary groups. They were not forced to "be Indians," to live in small, cramped settlements due to conditions of poverty. Some of the people were poor and some were prosperous--yet they worked together and survived in spite of hard economic times.

Although some of these people worked for their large land-owning relatives and were poor, most of the Buffalo Ridge tribal members during this agrarian period owned land, and some were very successful farmers. Ann Megginson (mother of Margaret Isabelle Megginson, wife of Peter Ferguson) is listed as a farmer, with nine children and one servant, on the 1880 U.S. Census (Stonewall Mill, page 1, line 33), Appomattox County. She was a successful farmer. These people did not have the usual, stereotypical situations to keep them huddled together as a tribe. The Megginsons and Fergusons have a Pocahontas and Cherokee tradition and made every effort to live up to the traditional expectations of descendants of Cherokee. They were expected to be hardworking and successful farmers. She employed more than one hundred farmworkers and had a servant in her home to assist with the house chores. Ann Megginson's daughter, Margaret Isabelle "Bell," a beautiful, princess-like lady (see cover page), taught her children to follow the same tradition of her mother. Augustus Ferguson and his siblings, the children of Peter and Bell, were hardworking farmers, like parents and grandmother.

This has been one of the problems for the Buffalo Ridge Band in being recognized as a true Native American Band. They "did not fit the stereotype." Although they were spread out, with the James River seeming to divide them into the Stonewall Mill Band and the Buffalo Ridge Band, they kept their tribal connections, by instinct and family tradition, and continued to marry their close and distant kin from generation to generation. It was only in the later years, when family members started leaving the area of Fairmount Church and the Buffalo Ridge area as they sought occupations other than farming, that the elders of the families suggested that an energetic leader should be selected to set up state tribal incorporation to maintain the Buffalo Ridge Band in history.

As some of the more recent ancestors and families left Fairmount Baptist Church and the Ridge area, they joined Scott Zion Baptist, Union Hill Baptist, First Baptist (Coolwell), First Baptist (South Lynchburg), Galilee Baptist, Rose Chapel Baptist, and other churches. This pattern was followed in the Stonewall Mill area, as many of the members joined churches beyond the Mount Zion Baptist and the Stonewall Mill area of Appomattox County, including Springfield Baptist, Mount Airy Baptist, Galilee Baptist, and other churches.

As the people became more prosperous and moved out from the ancestral farming areas, it is obvious that it required a stronger force than just kinship to keep the Native American band together as a unit. Their kinship, spiritual faith, and Cherokee heritage bonded all the relatives together, the Ridge and Stonewall groups. The same transformation was occurring in the Buffalo Ridge area. The band members were moving out and settling in new areas, as a result of financial upward mobility and/or a desire to be successful by moving closer to the jobs in the City of Lynchburg and vicinity. It has been said that it would take a miracle to keep these people together, to keep the kinship connection, to respect their ancestral heritage, to pass on the oral and religious traditions, and to band together in an official organization to replace the informal, natural one that existed for more than two hundred years. Yet, these people have a strong sense of their genealogical background, their noble heritage, their proud past. Actually, the average Buffalo Ridge band member today has more or at least as much knowledge about his/her relatives, the kinship structure, and ancestors than those ancestors who lived fifty to one hundred years earlier. This resurgence in pride of and interest in UCITOVA's history is due, in large degree, to the history lessons, both written and oral, both formal and informal, that families and the Buffalo Ridge Band members are passing on their their children today.

The Stonewall Mill members have intermarried for more than two hundred years. Both groups have intermarried with each other over the same period of time (see marriage records). They desired a formal tribal group to replace the natural, family, religious connection that had existed under respected elders for more than two hundred and forty years, since the first records (Woodson & Woodson, Virginia Tithables from Burned Record Counties--Buckingham, 1773-1774, 1970 (Fergusons, Pinns, Evans, Jenkins, Murphey,Fields)). Raleigh Pinn was a land owner in Amherst (Buffalo Ridge) and Buckingham (Stonewall Mill area, later to become Appomattox County) Counties (Deeds of Amherst County, Virginia, 1761-1807, B. F. Davis, 330, 341, 363; Woodson & Woodson, 38, 83; Appomattox County, Virginia, Tax Lists, 1845, H. Chilton, 1975, 4, 7; Pocahontas and Her Descendants, Robertson & Brock, 44, 52).

The elders/representatives--from the clan of the Fergusons, Beverlys, McCoys, Pinns/Penns, Chamberses, Cheagles, Wests, Woods, and others--met in 1990 and formed the structure for the corporation. The Band was formally incorporated in 1991, after more than two hundred and forty years of recorded tribal history. Samuel Penn was elected the tribal chief or leader and representatives from several families serve as pillars or members of the executive council.

Although some of the United Cherokee Indian Tribe of Virginia (UCITOVA) members are white residents with Cherokee ancestry, most of the descendants of the original Buffalo Ridge/Stonewall Mill Bands are considered "colored," even though they look more "Indian" than some Native Americans on federal reservations. UCITOVA is now placed in a position of proving that its people are "Cherokee." The descendants of ancestors who experienced more than two centuries of paper genocide (on census records, marriage records, tax records) have to document that the Buffalo Ridge Band is a remnant of the broken and divided Cherokee Nation. They kept their "Indian" appearance by controlling the members. It was easier to maintain group cohesion on Buffalo Ridge by "going for colored" (S. Penn; John Ferguson). The "rush off and marry white residents" mentality had been discouraged by the elders for generations (B. Beverley, M.O. Ferguson), although many of the members were often classed as "white." Reverend Lucas, in 1888, a new minister at Fairmount Baptist Church on the Ridge at the time, returned a marriage certificate to the courthouse for an Amherst County band member who married an Appomattox County band member (Wm. L. McCoy and Belle Banks, 2/20/1888, Book 3, 177). The court clerk assumed that the couple was white, since he could not determine the color of the new minister. Their marriage record listed them as white, even though the Ridge members were generally considered "colored." Some of these people, whose ancestors were originally Native American, did not really look "colored" (Malone, 15), but were forced, at every opportunity, to have colored placed on their legal documents. Some residents objected to this paper genocide (D. Jenkins).

Reverend R. D. Merchant served as pastor of Fairmount Baptist Church until 1935. He died on Sunday, January 6, 1935, at 9:00 P.M. Reverend Merchant was a leader among the Buffalo Ridge Band as well as the Amherst church community at large. He served for nine years as the Moderator of the Rockfish Baptist Association of Virginia, during the years between 1912 and 1921 (The Rockfish Baptist Association of Virginia,, 1991, 47). He had been a faithful and dedicated pastor as documented at the Amherst County Courthouse. The official marriage documents--a large number of which was tribal members--that were returned by Reverend Merchant support the fact that he was "faithful" and "dedicated." Some of these tribal/Native American marriages between 1900 and 1918, are as follows (Amherst County Marriage Register, Book 4):

Page	Year	Names	Parents
62	1918	Frank Johnson	Andr & Ann Johnson
		Bertha West	Otis & Betty West
63	1918	George T. Penn	George & Areolous Penn
		Carnolia Johnson	Andrew & Annie B. Johnson
124	1919	John Bolling	Cyrus Bolling
		Mary Catherine Johnson	
2	1913	Anderson Johnson	Benj. & Maria Johnson
		Mary Catherine Beverly	Mary Lou Beverly
69	1913	Charles McCoy	Albert & Polly McCoy
		Berta Ferguson McCoy	S & S. Ferguson
80	1900	Wm. Tyler	Jim & Lucy Tyler
		Mary Jones	____ & Edith Jones
105	1900	David Scott	Lucy Ann Scott
		Mary Franklin	Charles & Sarah Franklin
67	1901	Otis West	Willis & Martha Jane (Pinn) West
		Betty McCoy	Kitty Cousins
165	1902	Henry Johns	Phil & Sallie Johns
		Sallie Rose	Chas. & Emily Rose
128	1904	Samuel Sorrells	Sam & Martha Sorrells

		Martha Hylton	Sue Hylton
53	1905	Walker West	Willis West
		Rosa Moore	Wesley & Margaret Moore
76	1906	Jesse Hutcherson	J.J. & Matilda Hutcherson
		Fannie M Ferguson	Pauline Anderson
98	1906	Winston Bowling	Morris & Mary Bowling
		Susianna Turner	M. Turner
41	1907	Charles Beverly	Lucy Beverly
		Cora Lee Jackson	Andrew & Lucinda Jackson
145	1907	Wm. Pollard	Ad & Coraca Pollard
		Kate Mason	John & Eliza Mason
74	1908	Wm. Davis	George & Emaline Davis
		Fannie Jordan	C. & G. Jordan
95	1908	George T. Mays	W.R. & Maria Mays
		Mattie Hamilton	S.D. & Mollie Hamilton
61	1910	Isaac Ferguson	T. & Amer Ferguson
		Pearly Ferguson	Charles & Martha Ferguson
76	1910	Aubrey Martin	D. & R. Martin
		Cora Sparrow J. & E. Sparrow	
90	1910	George Robinson	Scott & Mary Robinson
		Liza Fitch	York & Liza Fitch
89	1910	Andrew Cooper	Wm. & Lucy Cooper
		Clara Pollard	A. & M. Pollard
19	1913	Charles Carter	G. & S. Carter
		Rosa N. Beverley	Ben & Rosa Beverley
73	1913	Simon Fitch	York & Liza Fitch
		Rosa Bowling	S. & L. Bowling
100	1913	Walter Jenkins	Felix & B. Jenkins
		Willie Anne	W. & C. Jordan
		Jordan Perror	
25	1914	Daniel L. Bibby	B. & M. Bibby
		Mittie Christian	E. & N. Christian

37	1914	John McCoy Jesie Beverly	Robert & Mary McCoy Ben & Rosa Beverly
77	1915	Daniel W. Jordan Sarah J.Christian Hayden	Squire & Sarah Jordan James & Emma Christian
103	1915	Ollie W. Wright Frances A.Jenkins	Clara Wright Felix & Betty Jenkins
37	1917	Wm. H. Beverley Candis A. Jordan	Ben & Rosa Beverley Elmore & Lottie Jordan
116	1917	John Turner Adeline Spencer	George & Eliza Turner Wash & Lucinda Childress
108	1918	Larnie Cousins Bettie G. McCoy	___ & Easter Cousin James & Susan Green

The Buffalo Ridge Band had a close tribal association as documented by the many families that intermarried within the Band from generation to generation. The researcher only needs to stand back and take a longitudinal look over two centuries--200 plus years--to see the amazing holding power of these people. A people that were broken from the Great Nation but, by instinct and/or by tribal expectations, continued to marry across many generations. Some of the marriages are as follows:

PAGE DATE	HUSBAND	WIFE	PARENTS	PARENTS
		RECORD BOOK # 2		
5 3/15/1855	F.C. Beverly	Sigis Sparrow	Rita Beverly	Bartlett Sparrow
43 12/21/1860	John Beverly	Levina Pinn	Wm. Beverly	Turner Pinn
89 12/26/1865	David Pence	Josephine Beverley	Judith Beverly Peter Pence Ellen Pence	Joisy Pinn Fred Beveray
97 9/13/1866	Jeremiah Cooper	Eliza A. Beverly	Sally Beverley D.& E. Cooper	
127 12/7/1867	Wm. Rose	Mary A. Jordan	Willie Rose	D.& C. Beverly
143 5/26/1867	Geo. Parrish	Ann Murphy	Lucinda Rose Jacob Parrish	William Hill
151 11/18/1868	John Blair	Lucie Coleman	Sarah Parish Rob. Blair	S. Hill SR. Coleman
153 11/30/1868	John A. Ware	Victoria Christian	Susan Blair N. Ware	C. Coleman John Christian
155 11/21/1868	James Christian	Emma Green	M. Ware Jesse Christian	S. Christian J. Green
161 3/13/1869	Peter Carter	Margaret Parrish	Lucy Christian Peter Carter	L. Green Preston Parrish
169 10/17/1869	Given Rose	Mary Rose	M. Carter S. & C. Rose	J. Parish Charles Rose
179 3/2/1870	Henry Christian	Mary Hughes	Lawson Christian	H. Hughes
185 9/7/1870	Hill Blair	Martha Ross	Lorine Christian Charles Blair Ann Blair	M. Hughes R. Ross S. Ross
		RECORD BOOK # 3		
17 3/1/1892	Wesley Moore	Margaret Sparrow	Allen Moore	___ Sparrow
26 5/29/1873	Daniel Spencer	Roxanna Ferguson	Carolyn Moore Wm. Spencer	Luvenia Sparrow Wm. Ferguson
54 1/6/1876	Geo.W. Beverly	Alice Knuckles	Emily Spencer Fredrick Beverly	Sally Beverly Obadiah Knuckles
236 1/11/1893	Charles Hutcheson	Nora Beverly	Sarah Beverly Jordan Beverly	Susan Knuckles Lena Beverley
269 3/29/1898	Logan Anderson	Pauline Ferguson	Mary Hutcheson Judith Irvin	
54 12/29/1875	Willis West	Martha J. Pinn	Willis West	John T. Pinn
26 5/3/1873	Wm. Beverly	R.S. Knuckles	Betsy Beverly G.J. Beverly	Joicy Pinn Obadiah Knuckles

No. / Date			
54 12/27/1875	R. Anthony Beverly	Mary A. Pinn	S.A. Beverly Lucy Beverly	S. Knuckles John T. Pinn
101 11/27/1880	Ben. Beverley	Roquene Knuckles	James Beverley Eliz. Beverley	Martha Beverly Pinn Obadiah Knuckles Susan Knuckles
145 12/24/1884	Chas. Beverly	Judith Beverly	Lucy Beverly	Aldridge Beverley
173 11/17/1887	Peter Beverly	Luzanna Beverly	Edward Beverly	Rebecca Beverly Frank Beverly
175 12/26/1887	Wm. Beverly	Anna Franklin	Sally Beverly Ned Beverly	Segus Beverly John Franklin
207 1/8/1891	Peter Beverly	Martha A. Pinn	Sally Beverly Anderson Beverly	Lucy Franklin Martha A.Pinn
41 11/25/1874	Charles Ferguson	Maria Pinn	Amelia Beverly Stephen Ferguson	Wm. Beverly
177 2/20/1888	Wm. L. McCoy	Belle Banks	S. Ferguson --Wanta McCoy	Judea Beverly Frank Banks
256 12/26/1894	Drew McCoy	Mary J. Banks	Amanda McCoy	Louise Banks Frank Banks
264 12/6/1895	Willie McCoy	Sarah Banks	Amanda McCoy	Louise Banks Frank Banks
108 7/2/1881	Calvin Knuckles	Luthena Tyree	Obadiah Knuckles Susan Knuckles	Louise Banks Reuben Tyree Luthena Tyree
193 12/16/1889	James Pinn	Laura Carter	Wm. Pinn Jane Pinn	Fred Carter Chauny A.Carter
136 2/6/1884	York Chambers	Pauline Murphy	Russel Chambers Harriet Flood	Andrew Murphy Ann Parish
143 12/15/1884	Richard Chambers	Eliza Jackson	Reubin Chambers Juda Chambers	Adderson Jackson Juda Jackson
33 1/14/1873	Washington Jordan	Candis A. Pinn	Tom Jordan Vincy Chambers Lucy Beverly	Samuel Pinn Maria Pinn
45 12/24/1884	Charles H. Beverly	Judith A. Beverly		Aldridge Beverly Rebecca Beverly
193 12/5/1889	Robert Clark	Mary Rose Penn	Nelson Clark Sophie Clark	
33 1/12/1874	Washington Jordan	Candis A/ Pinn	Tom Jordan Viney Christian	_& Ann Pinn Samuel Pinn Maria Pinn
282 4/13/1897	Elmore Jordan	Lottie Ferguson	Washington Jordan Candis Pinn Jordan	
38 7/27/1874	Felix Jenkins	Betty Pinn	Stephen Jenkins Frances Jenkins	J.J. Pinn Martha Pinn
197 4/21/1890	Andrew Johnson	Anne Banks	Lizzie Johnson	Frank Banks Louise Banks

RECORD BOOK # 4

No. / Date			
15 2/3/1902	Woodson Beverley	Nanie Jenkins	Ben. Beverley Rosa Beverley	Phelix Jenkins Betty Jenkins
20 9/15/1902	Price Beverley	Mary A. Beverly	Geo.W. Beverly Alice Beverly	Richard Beverly Aurora Beverly
55 12/2/1905	Taylor Beverly	Lilia Jenkins	Ben. Beverley Rosa Beverley	Felix Jenkins Betty Jenkins
69 4/9/1907	Charles Beverly	Cora Lee Jackson	Lucy Beverly	Andrew Jackson Lucindia Jackson
141 4/7/1913	Oscar Beverly	Mamie Beverly	Emely Beverly	A.I. Beverly Willie Beverly
159 5/10/1917	Willie H. Beverley	Candis A. Jordan	Ben Beverley Rosa Beverley	Elmore Jordan Lottie Jordan
15 1/9/1902	James Warrick	Bessie Scott	Alfred Warrick Lucena Warrick	Preston Scott Katie Scott
120 2/15/1913	Charles Carter	Rosa Nell Beverley	Geo. Carter Susan Carter	Ben. Beverley Rosa Beverley
98 7/18/1910	Issac Ferguson	Pearl Ferguson	Thomas Fergsuon America Ferguson	Charles Ferguson Martha Ferguson
125 10/21/1913	Preston Ferguson	Bessie W. Ferguson	Charles Ferguson Jenny Ferguson	R.A. Worley Ellen Worley
33 12/14/1903	James A. Ferguson	Nanny E. West Peter Ferguson	Bell Ferguson / Willis West	Martha Jane West _& Marcella Beverly
55 12/15/1905	Tom Hughes	Lucretia Penn	Barkley Hughes Jennie Hughes	
124 8/7/1913	Charles McCoy	Berta McCoy	Albert McCoy Polly McCoy	Stephen Ferguson Susan Ferguson
173 11/16/1918	Larnie Cousin	Bettie McCoy	_& Easter Cousin	James Green Susan Green
58 1/25/1906	Jesse Hutcherson	Fannie M. Ferguson	J.J. Hutcherson Matilda Hutcherson	Paulina Anderson

RECORD BOOK # 5

No. / Date			
11 11/16/1921	Pal. Beverly	Lotha Roberts	Pal. Beverly Coddie Beverly	Nick Roberts Mary Roberts
65 1/8/1929	Rucker Beverly	Martha E. Reed	Peter Beverly Mary Lou Beverly	John Reed Carrie Reed
29 7/23/1923	Charles Jordan	S. Jenkins Beverly	Elmo Jordan Lottie Jordan	Phelix Jenkins Betty Jenkins
78 8/22/1928	Houston W. Beverly	Emma V. Harris	Dany Beverly Martha Palmore	Luther Harris Elnora Harris
151 9/9/1936	Harry Beverly	Margaret Franklin	Peter Beverly Mary Lou Scott	Dillard Franklin Lena Turner
170 5/21/1938	John R. Beverly	Lillian W. Davis	Jack Beverly Maggie Smith	Raleigh Davis V. Higgin Gotham

147 6/2/1936	Robert Carter	Idah Beverly	James Carter	Wm. Beverly
31 12/1/1923	Edward Carter	Sarah Franklin	Cossie Eubanks	Anna Franklin
			Moses Carter	
			Jane Carter	

RECORD BOOK # 6

6 2/27/1943 Harris	Alfonza Beverly	Flossie Mae Harris		Jake Beverly	John
26 9/22/1943	Henry Beverly	Mamie Banks	Etta Green	Martha McCoy
			Peter Beverly	Hattie Banks
39 2/18/1944	St. Clair Beverly	Elnora R. Patillo	Mary L. Scott	Jesse Patillo
			Jake Beverly	
77 6/17/1946	Walker Beverly	Annie L. Harris	Etta Green	Jessie A. Thomas
			Wm. Beverly	Bernard Harris
70 4/17/1946	Samuel H. Jenkins	Ruby M. Anthony	Preston Jenkins	Flossie Massie
			Emma Snead	Wm. Anthony
118 3/8/1948	Dock Jenkins	Pauline Wilson	Ivanhoe Jenkins	Mary Morgan
			Cora Beverly	John Wilson
217 10/17/1953	Wilbert Banks	Mildred V. Mason	John Banks	Mary West
			Julia Childress	Sylvester Mason
				Sadie Horsley

Note: DATE refers to date of license and/or date of marriage.

Some of the other marriages of descendants of Buffalo Ridge ancestors are as follows:

DATE	BOOK	HUSBAND	WIFE
3/1/1892	3	Wesley Moore	Margaret Sparrow
5/29/1873	3	Dandridge Spencer	Roxanna Ferguson
1/6/1876	3	George Beverly	Alice Knuckles
6/6/1932`	5	Kendall Blair	Sallie B. Sparrow
6/22/1946	6	Elvin "Red" Bowling	Mildred Cousins
1/6/1876	3	George Beverly	Alice Knuckles
5/23/1942	6	Earl Beverly	Helen Banks
1/6/1900	3	Morris Beverly	Annie Roberts
5/10/1917	4	Oscar Beverly	Mamie Beverly
7/9/1892	3	Armistead Carter	Ada Blair
12/27/1910	4	Thomas Carpenter	Ada May Jordan
4/25/1912	4	Russell Carpenter	Maggie McCoy
10/28/1913	4	Edward Christian	Lelia Warrick
7/16/1914	4	Coleman Christian	Alvenia Merchant
12/21/1935	5	Robert C. Chambers	Ida Corrine Miller
4/10/1937	5	James Christian	Martha West
7/1/1947	6	Samuel H. Christian	Shirley M. West
12/26/1917	4	John Wesley Davis	Lucy I. Blair
6/24/1962	6	Gilliam M. Cobbs	Irene F. Chambers
12/29/1923	5	Robert Davis	Emily H. Elliot
12/20/1881	3	Nelson Elliott	Lucy A. Scott
4/8/1882	4	Jack Elliott	Signora Scott
12/23/1938	5	Wesley Ferguson	Etta Jane Bowling
7/29/1940	5	John Ferguson	Juanita E. Woody
3/12/1945	6	Maloney E. Ferguson	Alice A. West
12/19/1940	5	Langley Ferguson	Gladys L. Jordan
11/25/1959	6	Jesse Carol Ferguson	Sylvia K. Wiley
3/31/1957	6	Stanley Harris	Margaret Tweedy
12/28/1829	3	Howard Hutcherson	Marie Blair
6/19/1946	6	Elmer M. Hutcherson	Evelyn M. West

Date		Husband	Wife
4/28/1902	4	Hersy Hull	Annie Ferguson
7/2/1955	6	Willie R. Jackson	Mary Ann Sorrell
7/29/1960	6	Bland Dallas Jordan	Beatrice Bowling
2/12/1916	4	Frank Megginson	Laura Franklin
12/6/1895	3	Willie McCoy	Sarah Banks
8/7/1913	4	Charles McCoy	Betty McCoy
4/4/1936	5	Curtis McCoy	Isabell Beverly
5/9/1936	5	Lotts McCoy	Gertrude Beverly
2/28/1934	5	Havilah L. McCoy	Missie E. West
4/24/1929	5	Samuel Scott	Ruby H. Sparrow
3/24/1959	6	Anual D. Scott	Mary A. Sparrow
11/26/1900	4	David Scott	Mary Franklin
1/15/1955	6	Thurman Scott	Shirley Carpenter
9/17/1894	3	William Sparrow	Mary Evans
3/13/1905	4	Ernest Sparrow	Julia L. West
1/6/1917	4	George Sorrels	Carrie Giles
6/26/1945	5	Oscar West	Molly T. Thomas
9/3/1958	6	Odester West	Alease A. Waller
7/3/1918	4	Walker West	Adell Scott
12/27/1875	3	Willis West	Martha J. Penn
6/29/1963	6	Oliver C. Sorrells	Carol Ann Penn
11/8/1907	6	James O. Thomas	Annie A. Penn
5/18/1927	5	Roosevelt Sparrow	Myrtle Banks
4/28/1902	4	Hersey Hull	Annie Ferguson
8/29/1953	6	Conley E. Ferguson	Norma B. McCoy
9/20/1943	5	Henry Beverly	Mamie Banks

Many of the Ridge marriages included siblings in one family marrying siblings in another family. James and Herman Christian, brothers, married sisters, Shirley and Martha West; Curtis B. and Lotts McCoy, brothers, married Isabelle and Gertrude Beverly, sisters. This type of marriage was common on the Ridge as well as in Stonewall Mill, Appomattox County. The Buffalo Ridge members often sought spouses from Appomattox County. Otis West, son of Willis and Martha Pinn West of the Ridge, married Betty McCoy, daughter of Kitty Cousins, of Appomattox County (Dec. 30, 1902, Amherst County). Isaac Ferguson of Appomattox, son of Thomas and America Ferguson, married P. Ferguson, daughter of Charles and Martha Ferguson of Amherst (July 18, 1910, Amherst). Larnie Cousins, age 61, of Appomattox County, son of Easter Cousins, married Bettie Green McCoy, age 55, daughter of James and Susan Green of Appomattox (November 16,1 918, Amherst).

Some of the members married residents from the Buffalo Ridge section of Nelson County. Charles Carter, son of George and Susan Carter of Nelson County, married Rosa Nell Beverly of Amherst County, daughter of Ben and Rosa Beverley (Feb 16, 1913, Amherst). Some of the early Appomattox County marriages, close and distant relatives of Buffalo

Ridge's descendants, may be found in research by Jamerson, Nash, and Nash (1979). They listed the marriages of family members, including the Bollings, Cousins, McCoys, Elliotts, Fergusons, Harrises, Fieldses, Goings, Pankeys, Isbells, Megginsons, Chamberses, and Beasleys.

Some of the Appomattox relatives were considered white. Others could pass for white but chose to be classified as "colored." Those couples who were from affluent or well-to-do families frequently were not classified. Their race and parents' names were left blank on marriage documents. The clerks did not know what race to place on the documents, after the couples refused to place a designation on the application, or the clerks tried to protect prominent families' privacy.

Many of the surnames in Appomattox, Buckingham, Amherst, and other counties were generally considered Native American surnames, or names that Native Americans had adopted or acquired through marriage with settlers. The Scotts were considered Indian people in Richmond on the 1780 and 1810 tax rolls. The Gowens, Goens, Goings were classified as "mulatto" (Forbes, 202). The Goings (often spelled Gowan, Goin, or Gowen) descendants have been classified as free colored people in census reports as late as 1840 in Virginia and other states (202). After 1850, the were classified as 'M" (202).

Forbes noted that the census required only one recorded category. He explained that the system required "white" first, "black" second, and "Indian" third. Since a person could only indicate one race, if a person listed "white" first, or "black," and "Indian" second, the first selection would be counted and not the "Indian."(Forbes, 203). The system has contributed to the removal of large number of Native Americans from the census rolls.

The Dungees (Dungies) were Native Americans in Virginia, Tennessee, North Carolina, and other states. They were listed as "mulatto" on King and Queen and King William Counties' tax rolls (Forbes, 200, 201). Rosa Belle Dingess or Dungess was a teacher at the Buffalo Ridge School in the 1936-37 school year. Appomattox County had several families that were believed to be Cherokee, including the Eagles (Spout Springs, 1860), the Howells or Owls (Nebraska, 1860), and the Grows or Groahs and Eagles (Stonewall Mill, 1860).

The Two Pences, often changed to Tuppence or Two Pins, "were regarded as Indians in King William County" (Forbes, 208). Turner Pinn's daughter, Polly, married Richard Two Pence on Buffalo Ridge. It is not known where Polly's husband was born. He did, however, settle in the Indian community of Buffalo Ridge with the Pinns, Beverlys, Scotts, and other Native Americans. Halliburton indicated that the Keetoowahs were full-bloods who were committed to the "preservation of tribal traditions, not particularly sympathetic to slavery, pro-union, and strong supporters of Principal Chief Ross. They wore two common

A Pin Indian, or Keetoowah, with two pins shaped in the form of a cross. The Pin(n)s, Redcrosses, and Two Pins or "Two Pences" are believed to have worn two pins on their lapels to identify themselves as friendly Christians (1994).

pins in the form of a cross on their tunic lapels and were often referred to as 'Pin' Indians" (Halliburton, 118). It is believed that the Two Pence or Tuppence and Redcrosses were Keetoowahs. The Two Pences, Pin(n)s, and Redcrosses intermarried in Amherst County.

John Ross, chief of the United Keetoowah Band of Cherokee Indians of Oklahoma, a federally-recognized tribe, indicated in 1994 that the Keetoowah Band is in "complete support of the Buffalo Ridge Band of Cherokee in its efforts for state recognition." The Buffalo Ridge Band was invited by Virginia Senate Joint Resolution Number 15 (1992) to seek state recognition. The General Assembly asked the Virginia Council of Indians--composed of one representative of each of the eight state-recognized tribes and other members of the Council--under the Department of Health and Human Resources, to study the Buffalo Ridge Band's documentation, and "complete its work in time to submit its findings and recommendation to the Governor and the 1993 Session of the General Assembly." More than 1200 pages of documentation of the Band's history were presented to the Council. The Council, however, determined that its could not recommend state recognition while the Secretary of Health and Human Resources supported the Band's report that Cherokee were in Amherst County, and southwestern Virginia. The Department, following its usual procedure of taking the recommendation of subcommittees, abided by the recommendation of the Council and declined to recommend approval to the Governor and the Virginia General Assembly.

While the Band has strong documentation, it is believed that the political view of the Council is that the Buffalo Ridge Band is not a "traditional tribe," one that the early settlers stereotyped as "Indian" people or a group that was really directly connected with other federally-recognized Cherokee tribes (S. Penn, 1993). Wilma Mankiller, Chief of the Cherokee Nation of Oklahoma, had, at the time of the recognition proceedings, written letters to several state governors, including Virginia, advising them that Cherokee recognition should come from the federal government, not the states.

Jane Weeks, Executive Director of the Alabama Indian Affairs Commission (an Indian affairs office similar to the Virginia Council on Indians), responded to Chief Mankiller's letter to the Alabama Governor, with a letter to the effect that the State of Alabama recognizes that it has three Cherokee Tribes within the State and has every right to recognize its Native American people (March 12, 1993). Jane Weeks indicated that the Echota Cherokee Tribe of Alabama, the Cherokees of Northeast Alabama, and Cherokees of Southeast Alabama were state-recognized tribes. The State of Georgia also recognized its Cherokee residents during this same period of political disagreement and concern on the part of the Cherokee Nation of Oklahoma as to who should recognize Cherokee bands, the state or the federal government. June

Hegstrom, former Chairman of the Cherokee of Georgia, noted that the State of Georgia recognized two Cherokee tribes and one Creek tribe (Red Bear Smith, Minutes of the Unity Council, 2). The states who recognized their Cherokee Bands believed that they, more than the federal government, are closer to their state Native American history than the federal government. It is not known how Virginia's Council on Indians responded to Chief Mankiller's letter. Virginia remains as one of few states with rich Cherokee history but fails to take official action on this history (S. Penn; Whitehead).

Chief Ross of the Keetoowah Band of Cherokee stated that "the Cherokee social structure provided political alternatives to groups with differences of opinion from the main or governing body of Cherokee"(Chief Ross' letter). The general feeling among the leaders of independent Cherokee bands is that federally recognized tribes do not have exclusive rights to record Cherokee history or to exert authority over independent bands of Cherokee. Several states have supported this viewpoint by recognizing its Cherokee as official state-recognized tribes.

The ancestors/descendants of the Ridge Band include the McCoys, Warricks, Blairs, Bankses, Evanses, Sparrows, Murphys, Bowlings (Bollings), Carpenters, Clarkses, Coxs, Elliotts, Fergusons, Jordans, Megginsons, Roses, Sorrells, Scotts, Tweedys, Wares, Wests, Woods, to name a few (Fairmount Membership Roll; Fairmount School Rolls). The names on the church membership roll look like the names on the Final Roll of Cherokee, and in Starr's book, Old Cherokee Families. The Ridge has a rich Cherokee heritage.

The Buffalo Ridge Band's early ancestors are believed to be buried in "Penn Park Cherokee Grounds (Deed Book 590, p. 400, Plat Book N, 49)," founded circa 1750, including Raleigh Pinn, Turner Pinn, Samuel Scott, and other mid-eighteenth and early nineteenth century residents on the Ridge. There was a strong desire by the spiritual leaders on the Ridge to keep some of their Cherokee tradition but generally to hold fast to their Christian faith during the 1800s by confessing Christ and adopting a Christian lifestyle (McLoughlin, 34-44; Cherokee Phoenix, 1928, 4). The elders on the Ridge controlled the people with a firm hand. Anna Franklin, a descendant of the Ridge group, noted that "Fairmount members better not go to a party on Saturday night and expect to get off without repenting at the church on Sunday morning. Deacon Willis West and the other leaders were mean and firm. You had to come the right way." "You couldn't 'shack-up' or live together unmarried, you had to get married" (Frances Jordan).

The Buffalo Ridge Band did not fit the "savage" stereotype for Native Americans. They, like Cherokee throughout the Southeast, were assimilating into the main culture while at the same time adhering to their belief in one God, following the teachings of Christ, and continuing to practice their Cherokee medical and pharmaceutical skills (P. Hamel and M. Chiltoskey, 5). They did not need doctors and druggists, as some band members on the Ridge remembered the medical and pharmaceutical teachings of their ancestors and assisted the sick with time-honored remedies.

Robert Carol Chambers, a descendant of ancestors on the Ridge, remembered the Cherokee on Buffalo Ridge (interviewed 1992):

My grandmother, Frances Murphy Chambers and her mother, Ann Hill Murphy, were born in slavery. I remember Grandmother Frances telling me how they lived in cabins which had shuttered windows without glass. Great-grandmother Hill Murphy married Great-grandfather Parrish after her husband died. Great-grandmother Ann Parrish, Great-grandfather Preston Chambers and three of the children were listed as mulatto in the census. I asked my parents about slavery but I did not ask them much about the Indian side. All of my Grandmother's children had the Indian cheekbones. They used jimson weed to relieve headache. They tied it around their head. (The drug, stromonium, is made from the dried leaves of the plant and has a sedative or narcotic effect which serves as an anti-spasmodic, anti-asthmatic preparation). My Grandmother Frances mixed up different kinds of herbs and berries, and tree bark. They knew what to get to make the medicines. Grandma Ann Parrish was a midwife. She set Papa's broken arm. Amanda Murphy Lewis was also a midwife. Their slave-owner was a M.D. Like most of the Murphys, they had long, straight hair. Their complexion varied from medium brown to fair.

The Daynes are related to my mother. The Patillos are also related to us. Reverend Willie Dayne told me that he was related to my mother.

Reverend Willie Murphy (Frances' brother) helped set up Fairmount Baptist Church and preached there until they (Fairmount) got a pastor. He was my great-uncle, about the color of Amanda, light brown with straight, black hair. When I knew him he was greying around the sideburns.

I was born and grew up in Madison Heights near the Central Virginia Training Center. My father was one of their first employees. Reverend Willie Murphy, Frances Murphy Chambers, Paulina Murphy Chambers, Amanda Murphy Lewis, and Adelia Murphy Parrish lived and grew up in the Stapleton, Virginia, area near the first Fairmount Church. I liked to hang around with those old people in Stapleton. The Chambers and others in the book (The Buffalo Ridge Cherokee, 1991), the list at old Fairmount Church, I remember a lot of these people. I remember old man George Penn and old man (Willis) West. George Penn and my Mamma's father, Alfred Warrick, grew up together. Alfred lived in the Stapleton area. I heard he looked like an Indian. He was light. You couldn't tell he had any Negro in him. Alfred's

mother was half Indian and his father was full-blood Indian. My
mother's name was Lelia Anniebell Warrick Chambers.

My wife's mother, Berta Mitchell Miller, says her parents were never slaves.
She had some Indian. She was light-complexioned. She was related to
the Turners. Ms. Miller's cousin is Dean Turner. Dean looks like an Indian. A
group of Indians from Louisiana came through the area selling yard
chairs. They told her that she had to be an Indian because she looked just
like their grand-mother. They advised her to make a tea of water-
melon seeds to bring relief to a relative who had suffered a stroke.

My mother's uncle, Dan Davis, was a half-brother to our grandfather Alfred
Warrick. He was a minister and helped organized Rose Chapel
Baptist Church here in Madison Heights. He was a deacon and a minister.
Uncle Dan wore a regular hat when he was outside but when he came inside,
he reached into his pocket and took out another cap and put it on. My
mother said it was his "skull cap." It was a black cap like the top of a hat.
He was a very nice person. He lived in Charleston, West Virginia, and visited
here. He grew up in the Stapleton area. He moved to Charleston around
1918-1920. He was a stonemason in West Virginia. He was the pastor of a
church there. He always took off his hat, took his skull cap from his pocket,
and put it on his head when he came into the church, and he wore the skull
cap when he was in the pulpit.

Old man Charlie Gardner and his wife looked just like Indians. They lived in
Madison Heights. You couldn't tell them from Indians. They lived in
peculiar ways. People were scared to go around the house. Our sister, Lois,
went inside a few times and she said she saw clay items, Indian
things in the house. They were friendly with the Chambers but didn't bother
with most people. Charlie Gardner was a farmer. He wore long hair
and tied it in the back in a lock when he worked. He went barefoot when he
worked but would put on shoes to go to church. I was afraid of him because
he looked primitive-like, with his bare feet and long hair. He owned the
land and he farmed. George and Tim Penn bought the land after old man
Gardner died.

Those Indian people in the Stapleton area were friendly with other Indian
people. They had close relationship with each other because of
their Indian connection.

> (Narative recorded by Herb Chambers and author at
> the residence of Robert C. Chambers in Madison Heights).

Reverend Willie Murphy, Sr., himself of Cherokee descent (R.
Chambers), directed the church services at Fairmount Baptist Church
informally until Reverend Charles Hughes, Sr., came on the scene and

Herbert Chambers

Bernetta Chambers Pinn

Lelia Warrick Chambers

Leroy E. Chambers

Bennett Swain

served as pastor of the church in 1867. The Hughes of Lynchburg were recognized as Cherokee (Cherokee By Blood, Vol. 5, 299). The Hughes of Amherst and Nelson Counties and the City of Lynchburg have a Cherokee tradition. Fairmount was known as an "Indian" church with some black worshippers (C. Penn; D. Penn; A. Ferguson). The worshippers were listed on census reports as mulatto and free colored.

The term "mulatto" was used to classify the Chickahominy Indians in 1813. The use of "mulatto" occurred on tax rolls in King William, King & Queen, Caroline, and Essex, except the Indians living on the two small reservations in King William County (Pamunkey and Mattaponi) who did not generally appear on tax rolls (Forbes, 199). This pattern was followed in central Virginia on both census rolls (1790 Census, Amherst County) and tax rolls (Buckingham County). Native Americans in Roberson County, North Carolina, and all Virginia counties were classified as "colored" persons between 1800-1830. The whole Cherokee population of Carroll County, Georgia, was included as "colored" (Forbes, 199).

The first U.S. Census (1790, Amherst County) listed Raleigh Pinn with eight "mulattoes" in his household and Benjamin Evans with six "mulattoes." The 1850 and 1860 census records show Evans family members in the home of the Pinn residents. The Redcross family members were also related to the Pinns and Evanses (Whitehead, 1896; Amherst County Marriage Records). Eliza Redcross was the daughter of John Redcross, who was "a well-known Cherokee Indian" (Whitehead; Jordan, Vol 7, 258). Calvin Knuckles noted in Cherokee By Blood that his grandmother was Eliza Redcross and that she was Cherokee. As noted already, Benjamin Beverly, son of Betsy Beverly, married Roqueen Knuckles, sister of Calvin and granddaughter of Eliza Redcross. Calvin continued the Cherokee connection by marrying Luthena Tyree, of Cherokee descent, daughter of Reuben and Luthena Tyree (Record Book 3, page 108, 7/2/1881). Fanny M. Hughes of Lynchburg and Rosa M. Chambers of Richmond were admitted as members of the Cherokee Nation because they were related to Alice Ross Howard (Jordan, Vol. 1, 43), a resident of another state. This approach, the practice of admitting people who are related to documented roll members, has the effect of excluding a large number of Cherokee people who live in Virginia or West Virginia, for example, but do not have ancestors who were on the rolls in North Carolina or Oklahoma.

The Buffalo Ridge Cherokee history, which is believed to have started sometime long before the first U.S. Census (1790), has a very old and strong tribal tradition. The 1840 U.S. Census (Amherst County 222) shows Samuel Scott, William Harris, George Jewell, Anthony Beverley, Bartlett Sparrow, Polly Beverly, Turner Pinn, and others in a close tribal band and later census reports (1850, 1860, 1880, and 1900) reveal the strong tribal connection remaining with these Cherokee and other

Cherokee of Amherst and Appomattox Counties. Some of the early tribal members on the Ridge were are follows:

SAMUEL SCOTT, m. **Judith Scott**
Children:
Susanna Scott (b. 1800), m. Rolla Pinn
Delaware Scott, m. Nancy Foster,
daughter of James and Betsey Foster
Samuel B. Scott, m. Sally (Buckingham County)
William Scott, m. Mary
Children: Mariah, Nancy, Susan, & Betsey

Ben Scott, m. Annes Evans,
Thomas Evans' widow
Witness at marriage: Thomas Jewell

WILLIAM HARRIS, B. 1793, M. 1/28/1832, Lucy Harris
Child: Ann Harris

Brother: James Harris, m. Evelina Pinn Harris, daughter
of James and Nancy Redcross Pinn

GEORGE JEWELL,b. 1818, son of Viney Jewell,
George Jewell m. 9/13/1838,
Martha Jane Pinn Jewell,
daughter of Turner Pinn.
Witness at marriage: Jonathan Beverly

ANTHONY BEVERLY, b. 1807,
from Appomattox (Buckingham during that period) County

BARTLETT SPARROW (Sparrowhawk?), m. 12/28/1827
Maria Pinn Sparrow, b. 1802 (daughter of Turner Pinn)
Children:
James Sparrow, b. 1830
Simpson Sparrow, b. 1832
Turner Sparrow, b. 1835
Mary Sparrow, b. 1828
Joicy Sparrow, b. 1836
John Sparrow, b. 1844
Levenia Sparrow, b. 1849

TURNER PINN, B. 1770

m. Joicy Humbles
Children:
John Pinn, b. 1810
Levinia Pinn
Samuel Pinn
Polly Pinn Two Pins (Two Pence or Tuppence)
Betsy Pinn
Maria Pinn Sparrow, Bartlett Sparrow's wife
Martha Jane Pinn Jewell, George Jewell's wife
Segis Pinn, m. 1840, Daniel Jackson

POLLY BEVERLY, B. 1805
from Appomattox's Stonewall Mill area
Eliza Beverly, b. 1835
Aldridge Beverly, b. 1828, m. Rebecca Beverly,
(daughter of Judith Beverly and Charles Henry Beverly)
Mary Beverly, b. 1829
Lucy Beverly, b. 1825,
Martha Ann Pinn Beverly
Anthony Beverly, m. Mary Pinn,
(daughter of John T. and Martha Beverly Pinn)
Betsy Beverly, b. 1837
(mother of Benjamin Beverly and Willis West, Jr.)

JAMES PINN, m. 10/6/1812, Jane "Jincy" Cooper Pinn
Remarriage? (first wife, Nancy Redcross?)
Children:
Robert Pinn, b. 1813
Christina Pinn, b. 1815
George Washington Lafayette Pinn, b. 1820

RICHARD TWO PINS (Two Pence or Tuppence)
m. 1829, Polly Pinn Tuppence, b. 1805
Children:
John Turner Pinn, b. 1826
Nathan Tuppence, b. 1834
James Tuppence (brother?), m. Nov. 22, 1820, Betty Evans
(Betty Evans' mother was Annes Evans)
James and Betty Tuppence's daughter was
Susan Tuppence Merchant. Susan m.
Allen Merchant, son of Iris Merchant.

JAMES PINN, m. 1799, Nancy Redcross Pinn,
(daughter of John Redcross and

Susanna Thomas "Humbles" Redcross)
Child: Evalina Pinn Harris, b. 1805, m. James Harris,
brother to William Harris

WILLIAM BEVERLY, m.1800, Eady Pinn

RALEIGH PINN, m. Sarah
(8 "mulattoes," 1790 census)
Turner Pinn, b. 1770
James Pinn
Patsey Pinn
Anna Pinn
Edy Pinn

JOHN REDCROSS, b. 1775 or 1780, m. 1807
Susanna Thomas "Humbles" ("Suckey")

WILLIAM BLAIR, m. 2/9/1828 Clara Sale

JONATHAN BEVERLY, B. 1785
On 1810 Buckingham Census but Amherst Personal
Property Tax List in 1829
(witness at a number of weddings of Buffalo Ridge Band members:
Sparrow/Pinn, Dec 28, 1827)

These are just a few of the many early Buffalo Ridge Cherokee. The Cooper family, for example, and others are not listed above but are noted on the early census records as mulatto people and marriage records show the family connection to the Buffalo Ridge Cherokee.

Some of the members of the Stonewall Mill Band members are as follows (U.S. Census, 1850, Stonewall Mill, Appomattox):

Name	Age	Race
Anthony McCoy	77	Mu
Susan McCoy	67	Mu
Lephia McCoy	42	Mu
Delaware McCoy	42	Mu
Amanda McCoy	15	Mu
Mucra McCoy	6	Mu
Henry McCoy	3	Mu

The 1860 U.S. Census, Stonewall Mill, Appomattox, included:

Th J. McCoy	41	Mu
Sultana McCoy	30	Mu
Lucy McCoy	7	Mu
Jas R. McCoy	4	Mu
Issac McCoy	2	Mu
Albert McCoy	42	Mu
Mary J. McCoy	35	Mu
Martha McCoy	20	Mu
Mary McCoy	16	Mu
Charles McCoy	14	Mu
Peter McCoy	12	Mu
Benjamin McCoy	11	Mu
Sallie A. McCoy	9	Mu
Wm. D. McCoy	8	Mu
John T. McCoy	6	Mu
Elizabeth McCoy	4	Mu
Catharine McCoy	2	Mu
James H. McCoy	8/12	Mu
Judy A. McCoy	5/12	Mu
Semuel Tyler	41	Mu
Frances Tyler	32	Mu
Edward Beverly	32	Mu
Sarah Beverly	33	Mu
Joanna Ferguson	9	Mu
William Beverly	90	Mu
Judy S. Beverly	80	Mu
Nancy Beverly	45	Mu
Peter Furguson	44	Mu
Elmira Furguson	46	Mu
Stephen Furguson	17	Mu
Peter H. Furguson	14	Mu
Charles U.S. Furguson	12	Mu
Frederick U. Furguson	7	Mu
Stephen Furguson	72	Mu
Susan Furguson	67	Mu
Judy Furguson	25	Mu
Susan Furguson	22	Mu
Stephen P. Furguson	5	Mu

Joseph Furguson	3	Mu
Saml. Furguson	9	Mu
Nancy Furguson	8	Mu
Lucy Furguson	7	Mu
Peter Furguson	6	Mu
Hudson Furguson	5	Mu
Thomas Furguson	3	Mu
Louisa McCoy	45	Mu
Rosella McCoy	8	Mu
General McCoy	6	Mu
John McCoy	25	Mu
Nancy Furguson	23	Mu
Anthony Furguson	6	Mu
Jesse Furguson	50	Mu
Susan M. McCoy	43	Mu
Anderson Beverley	41	Mu
Pamilia Beverley	30	Mu
Chalman Beverley	13	Mu
Georgeanna Beverley	9	Mu
Calvin Beverley	7	Mu
Paul Beverley	2	Mu
Leanna Beverley	5	Mu
Peter Beverley	1	Mu

Stephen Furguson is listed on the 1840 U.S. Census, p. 4, with neighbors John R. Megginson and Archiball B. Megginson. He had fifteen members in his household. The Furgusons/Fergusons have strong family relationships with the Megginsons of Appomattox County, descendants of Pocahantas (Pocahontas and Her Descendants, Robertson and Brock, 39, 44, 52).

Stephen Ferguson (b. 1788) and his wife Susan (b. 1793) were born in Virginia (U.S. Census, Stonewall Mill, 1860). Their household in 1860 included twelve members. Anthony McCoys' household in 1850 (U.S. Census, Stonewall Mill) included seven members. Anthony McCoy (b. 1783) and Susan (b. 1793), his wife, were the parents of Albert McCoy. Albert's household contained seven members in 1850. Mary McCoy, daughter of Albert and Mary McCoy, had one child, Judith Ann, by John Dillard (R. Carson). Mary married LaFayette McCoy. Judith Ann married Hudson Ferguson and they became the parents of Mary Lucy Carson, Lelia Rose, Cassie Wills, Maxine Ferguson, Arlie Minnis, Otha Ferguson, Henry Ferguson, and McKinley Ferguson.

William Beverly (b. 1770) and Judy (b. 1780), were living in the home of Edward Beverly in 1860 (U.S. Census, Stonewall Mill). The Fergusons and the Beverlys were related. Edward Beverly's family members included Sarah Beverly, his wife, Joanna Furguson, William Beverly, Judy S. Beverly, and Nancy Beverly. The Fergusons and Beverlys were "cousins" (A. Ferguson). It is believed that Judy Beverly, the wife of William, was a "Ferguson" before her marriage to William.

The 1810 U.S. Census, Buckingham County (present Stonewall Mill area of Appomattox) listed William Beverly and two other Beverly families in a tribal setting with the Humbles family. The 1840 U.S . Census, Buckingham County (Stonewall Mill area), shows groups of Stonewall Mill Band's families together in a tribal setting; the families of Alfria Tyler, Anthony McCoy, A . Evans, Frank Beverley, Susan Umbles, and Saunders Pinn. The Howels or Howls of Appomattox County, listed as "mulatto," are believed to be connected to the Owl surname, an old Cherokee family name. It is a well-known fact that Appomattox County has numerous Cherokee families in its midst presently and had Cherokee residents during the early period, prior to and after 1800, when it was a part of Buckingham County.

The Fergusons, McCoys, and Beverlys have a strong Cherokee tribal heritage in Stonewall Mill and vicinity and the Buffalo Ridge area. Their ancestral lineage, like the Ridge members' lineage, goes back to the 1770s and possibly earlier, since all three families indicated on the U.S. Census that they were born in Virginia. These people were not "typical" Native Americans. They assimilated into their respective communities and became respected citizens.

The present United Cherokee Indian Tribe of Virginia, Incorporated (UCITOVA) consists of 315 members. Two members remember Cherokee chants from their parents and grandparents and can chant in their ancestors' traditional style, although they do not know fully what the words mean. Thirty-five members can speak and understand some Cherokee and about twenty members can write and read some Cherokee phonetic symbols. The tribe has monthly meetings. Approximately ninety-seven percent (308 members) of the membership are direct descendants of the original Buffalo Ridge and Stonewall Mill Bands whose ancestors go back as far as the mid-1700s (recorded history). Six members are possibly distantly related to the early Amherst County and vicinity Cherokee.

During the annual series of summer reunions in Amherst and Appomattox Counties and the City of Lynchburg, the Buffalo Ridge members come from California, New York, Florida, and other locations to join their local relatives as they reflect on the beautiful history of Buffalo Ridge/Stonewall Mill, their people, their ancestors' early school days (Fairmount School's class rolls; school speech), and Fairmount Baptist Church and other sister churches in the area.

The following hand-written speech was found on a sheet of Hill City Tobacco Company receipt paper. It was an unsigned, undated speech delivered by a student at Fairmount School during the 1940s on Buffalo Ridge at the official closing day of the school. The anonymous student expressed his or her love for and the beauty of school life on Buffalo Ridge:

"We come tonight to greet you on this our closing day of school. We can but recall the past when as children we reclined or disport on the grassy lawns and chased fairy winged butterflies among the blooms of fragrant flowers. Life seemed to be a little path edged with beautiful flowers.

We revere the past. Oh, the sweet years of early school life! The new books, pretty pictures, satchels containing the remembrance of a faithful father's toil and a tender mother's care, the fond teachers, happy faces and affectionate caress and words of encouragement which assured a trust in us, which has never fallen as a faithful servant for each one, large or small. Now this road seems rough and crowded, or shrouded in the mist of intricate problems to baffle every honest endeavor in making us what we are today."

(Anonymous writer)

Amherst County Schools' Elementary and High School Term Reports recorded the students who attended the old Fairmount School, near Fairmount Church on Buffalo Ridge. These documents cover a period of twenty years (1924-25 school year through 1944-45 school year). Some of the names of the students and the miles that they lived from the school are as follows:

Student's Name	Miles
1924-25 School Year	
St. Clair Beverely	3 1/2
Alfred Bowling	3
Elmer ("Red") Bowling	3
Phillip Bowling	1
Vernon Bigger	3 1/2
V.T. Davis	3 1/2
James Furguson	4
Ledwood Furguson	3
Eddie Furguson	3
Langhorne Furguson	3
Alonzo Furguson	3
James G. Furguson	3
Eugene Hull	2 1/2
Fred Hull	2 1/2

Frank Hull	1 1/2
Artie Jackson	4
Sylvester Mason	2 1/2
Abe Pendleton	3
Walker Pendleton	3
George Sparrow	1
Rosser Sparrow	1
Eldridge Turner	1 1/2
Gilbert Turner	1 1/2
Kearfott Turner	1 1/2
Sam Turner	1 1/2
Tom Vawter	2 1/2
Joe Trent	4
Sanders Vawter	2 1/2
James Vawter	2 1/2
Arthur West	1
Jasper West	1
Isabell Beverley	3 1/2
Sue Bowling	1
Myrtle Hull	2 1/2
Alice Jackson	4
Pearl Jackson	4
Lennie Lee	4
Margaret Moore	3 1/2
A. E. Pendleton	3
Louise	4
Hester Sparrow	1
Nannie Stratton	3 1/2
Viola Trent	4
Connie	1 1/2
Mary	1 1/4
W.G. Vawter	2 1/2
Lillie Vawter	2 1'2
Myssie West	1
Mary West	1

**1932-33 School Year
(Miles not noted)**
Isabell Beverley
Gertrude Beverley
Ella Bowling
Isabelle Furguson
Hattie Fitch
Marie Fitch
Ruby Mae Greene
Elizabeth Hull
Annie Pennix
Easter Pennix

143

Rosa Revely
Annie M. Trent
Mattie L. Trent
Martha West
Alma West
Elnore West
Earl Beverly
Alfonza Beverley
St. Clair Beverley
Cyrus Bowling
Joe E. Furguson
Clarence Furguson
Alonza Furguson
Joe Fitch
Ben Fitch
Frank Hull
John Hull
Farley Hull
John Pennix
Henry Pennix
Hope Key, Jr.
St. Louis Reveley
Ross Sparrow
Owen Sparrow
Clarence Sparrow
George Sparrow
Keatfott Turner
Ella Bowling
Isabel Beverley
Girtie (Gertrude) Beverley
Hattie Fitch
Marie Fitch
Elizabeth Hull
Anna Pennix
Easter Pennix
Rosa Reveley
Bettie Lee Reveley
Alma West
Elnora West

**1944-45 School Year
(Miles Not Noted)**

Robert Wesley Elliott
Conrad Fitch
Jesse James Scott
William Henry Scott
Odester Lee West

Mildred Virginia Mason
Lindy Ann Pennix
Roberta Pennix
Doretha Lula Sparrow
Mary Alice Sparrow
Jeanine Adell West
Richard Elliott
Atlena Fitch
James David West
Roy Clifton Elliott
James Edward Scott
Thurman Rufus Scott
Irene Annie Bowling
Dorothy Juanita Mason
Kathleen Virginia Sparrow
Evelyn Marie West
Shirley Maybelle West

The annual family reunions have been bringing the Ridge members together for decades. Each member may attend any and all reunions, because all the members are related to each other. The annual Ferguson Reunion, for example, may have the same people in attendance who participated in the Beverly, Pinn, West, or McCoy reunions.

An old Isbell-Bowman Company
Shoe Store sign

145

CHAPTER VII
Ga (li) quo gi (Seven))

THE CHEROKEE TRADITION IN
AMHERST COUNTY AND VICINITY

The Great Nation's Heritage Remains

Who are these descendants of the Great Cherokee Nation? What history and tradition do they remember from their ancestors? How widespread is this heritage in Central Virginia? The Amherst New-Era Progress spotlighted the Buffalo Ridge Cherokee on February 13, 1992, in the article, "Tribal Pride." Meg Hibbert focused on the Cherokee tribal connection of the Band. The article noted that two of the Band members are board members of the five-member Amherst County Board of Supervisors. Isabelle Megginson, Augustus Ferguson, Quintus Ferguson, Adlee Carter Wood, Samuel Penn, and other ancestors and descendants of the Buffalo Ridge Band were featured. While it is generally accepted that the Band members are Cherokee and have a tribal connection for more than one hundred years, very few citizens really know the whole story about the Band. Most of the ancestors have always lived in Amherst County, generally on the Ridge, while others Cherokee joined the Band later. The Band has been on the Ridge for more than two hundred and forty years. Penn Park Cherokee Grounds, the first known burial ground, has interred some of the first recorded ancestors, the Pinns, Scotts, Beverlys, and others.

Several descendants of ancestors who lived in or near Buffalo Ridge/Stapleton were interviewed to discover and record information about their oral history. Cherokees from other areas who did not have a ancestral connection with Buffalo Ridge and Stapleton, but were known to have Cherokee or "Indian" ancestry were also interviewed to determine the extent of their Cherokee oral tradition. Some white residents, who were not known to have Indian ancestry, were interviewed to gain information about the history of the area. A few of the Amherst County and vicinity residents who are known to have Cherokee ancestry, but were not directly related to the Buffalo Ridge Band, were contacted and their narratives of their oral histories were recorded. The interviewer asked respondents to provide information on their family, community, and Native American history, if applicable.

* *

Raleigh Newman "Pete" Carson

Lynchburg, Virginia
Born: April 23, 1920
Interviewed: January 21, 1991, and April 18, 1991.

My name is Raleigh Newman "Pete" Carson. Born April 23, 1920. I am 70 years old. I lived in Chicago for 30 years, Canada for two years, and the rest of the time in Lynchburg, Virginia.

There were six children born to Judith Ferguson. She was from Amherst. She was married to a man whose last name was Ferguson. We do not know his first name. She had one son by this man. His name was Sam. He was her first born son and child. She worked for Dr. Frederick Isbell in Appomattox County. She gave birth to five more children whose father was Dr. Frederick Isbell. The children were named Hudson, Thomas, William (Bill), Peter, and Lucy Ferguson. They took her last name.

Mary McCoy was Judith Ann Ferguson's mother and her father was John Dillard. Lafayette McCoy was May's husband. She had four brothers-- namely, Ben, John, Steven, and Tammy McCoy. Hudson Ferguson and Judith Ann Ferguson were born near Stapleton, Virginia, in the Stonewall District of Appomattox County.

Luther McCoy, Susie Ferguson, Deley Ferguson were sisters and brother. Their father and mother were Albert Horsley and Martha McCoy. Luther married Betty Banks. Deley married Sam Ferguson. Susie married William Ferguson. Lucy, Grandfather's sister, married Wes Ferguson. John McCoy and Betty Childress were Nanny O.K. Ferguson's father and mother.

Mary McCoy's father and mother were Albert and Mary McCoy. Their children were Ben, John, Stephen, and Tammy McCoy. Mary McCoy was married to Fayette McCoy. She had one child, Judith Ann McCoy. Her father was John Dillard. John Dillard was Judith's biological father. Judith was married to Hudson Ferguson. Hudson Ferguson had eight children:

Mary Lucy Carson was married to David Edward Carson of Amherst. Lelia Rose's husband was Fleming Rose of Lynchburg, Virginia. Cassie Will's husband was Jessie Wills of Bedford County. Maxine Ferguson's husband was Thomas Ferguson, her cousin, of Appomattox. Arlie Minnis' first husband was Jack Johnson. Otha Ferguson was married to Alva Ferguson of Appomattox. Henry Ferguson's wife was Sarah Giles Ferguson of Arrington, of Nelson County. McKinley was never married.

My grandparents, Hudson and Judith Ann Ferguson, my mother, Lucy Ferguson Carson, and other relatives always said we were Cherokee Indians. We have a great-grandfather whose name was Lafayette McCoy, who was a casket maker.

147

Raleigh "Pete" Carson

Joseph Ferguson

William Luther McCoy (Father of: Robert, Jesse, Willie Ann, Andrew, Artie, Clark, Ruben, Obey, Frank, Martha, and Herman)

He was a full-blooded Cherokee Indian. He could speak very little English. He made his own casket. He always wore his long, coal-black straight hair, parted in the middle, with two plats, with red ribbons on it. That was the way that he was laid to rest (buried).

We were told that Fayette never cut his hair. He wanted to remain as he was, a Cherokee Indian. This was a custom. He was my great-grandfather. My mother said he, her grandfather, was very quiet and reserved. He could not speak English correctly. His dialect was not clear. He was such a Cherokee that he didn't learn English. Back then, he didn't have anyone to teach him English.

My grandmother said her mother, May or Mary, was full-blooded Cherokee also. She spoke very little English. Some of the old Ferguson family members in Appomattox used English with a different accent.

My oldest brother, who is 13 years older than I am, once told me that Indian graves are all over the Stonewall area and other sections of Appomattox. He pointed out to me some of the areas that had, at one time, been cemeteries. These areas had stone markers to mark the place where the Indian residents had been interred. These people were full-blood Cherokee Indian relatives. The Fergusons at one time got mixed up with the Indians in Appomattox. The Indians were here when many of the settlers came to the area. We can't find many of the cemeteries now because the stone markers have been removed.

The houses have decayed. You can, however, see signs of their former existence. The apple and cherry trees are still spotted throughout the Stonewall area. The people canned the fruit during the summers.

My sister, Estelle Carson Young, was married to Frank Young, the owner and founder of Young Moving and Storage Company of Richmond, Lynchburg, and other locations. He died recently. The Lynchburg New and Daily Advance carried a story on him on Saturday, March 16, 1991. The story stated that "Frank Young, Jr., a prominent local businessman here in the City of Lynchburg, who founded the city's first and most enduring moving company, died Friday, March 16, 1991, at Virginia Baptist Hospital." The News and Daily Advance writer, Tony Attrino, indicated that Frank Young employed "more than 135" people and had more than "60 trucks and trailers."

Interview: with Raleigh Carson, August 20, 1994

Joseph Ferguson's sister was Betty Ferguson. Her husband was Pete McCoy. Susan Ferguson was the mother of Joseph and Betty. Joseph had a daughter named Nancy Scott. Harry Ferguson, son of William and Susan Ferguson, married Nancy Scott .She had several children: Christine, Carolyn, and Virginia.

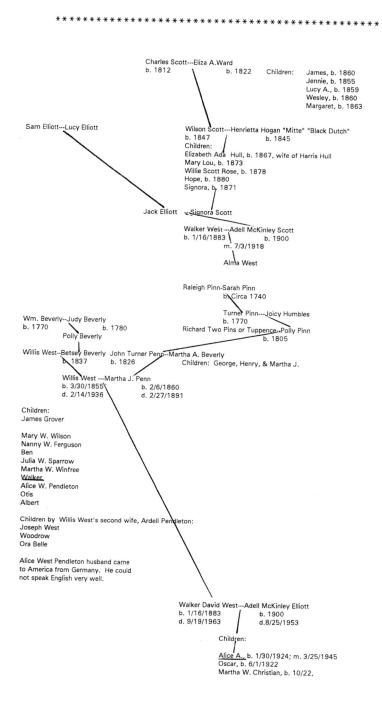

****

Charles Scott---Eliza A.Ward
b. 1812   b. 1822   Children: James, b. 1860
                                                       Jennie, b. 1855
                                                       Lucy A., b. 1859
                                                       Wesley, b. 1860
                                                       Margaret, b. 1863

Sam Elliott---Lucy Elliott

Wilson Scott---Henrietta Hogan "Mitte" "Black Dutch"
b. 1847   b. 1845
Children:
Elizabeth Ada Hull, b. 1867, wife of Harris Hull
Mary Lou, b. 1873
Willie Scott Rose, b. 1878
Hope, b. 1880
Signora, b. 1871

Jack Elliott --- Signora Scott

Walker West---Adell McKinley Scott
b. 1/16/1883   b. 1900
          m. 7/3/1918

Alma West

Raleigh Pinn-Sarah Pinn
      b. Circa 1740

Turner Pinn---Joicy Humbles
      b. 1770
Wm. Beverly--Judy Beverly   Richard Two Pins or Tuppence--Polly Pinn
b. 1770   b. 1780   b. 1805
        Polly Beverly

Willis West--Betsey Beverly John Turner Penn--Martha A. Beverly
      b. 1837   b. 1826   Children: George, Henry, & Martha J.

    Willis West ---Martha J. Penn
    b. 3/30/1855   b. 2/6/1860
    d. 2/14/1936   d. 2/27/1891

Children:
James Grover

Mary W. Wilson
Nanny W. Ferguson
Ben
Julia W. Sparrow
Martha W. Winfree
Walker
Alice W. Pendleton
Otis
Albert

Children by Willis West's second wife, Ardell Pendleton:
Joseph West
Woodrow
Ora Belle

Alice West Pendleton husband came
to America from Germany. He could
not speak English very well.

Walker David West---Adell McKinley Elliott
b. 1/16/1883   b. 1900
d. 9/19/1963   d.8/25/1953

Children:

Alice A., b. 1/30/1924; m. 3/25/1945
Oscar, b. 6/1/1922
Martha W. Christian, b. 10/22,

149

Eleanore Tinsley Jordan, b. 12/1926
James
Shirley W. Christian
Evelyn Hutcherson
Odester
Geneva Moore
Lawrence
Husazell (died infant)

Stephen Ferguson, b. 1788--Susan Ferguson b. 1793

Dr. Frederick Isbell--Judith Ferguson

Ann Megginson

Joseph Peter Ferguson--Isabell Megginson
b. 6/22/1855   b. 10/2/1856
              M. 11/13/1877

Augustus Ferguson--Nanny West
b. 1/9/1880; d. 1/10/1969   b. 8/30/1880; d. 1946

Children:

Levelt, b. 9/12/1904; d. 12/31/1963
Raymond, b. 1906; d. 1973
Ledwell Jack, b. 11/21/1909; d. 11/6/1968
James, b. 7/17/1917; d. 2/8/1992
Langley, b. 9/15/ 1914; d. 9/19/1985
Clarence, b. 1/9/1919   ; d. 4/17/1989
Isabelle, b. 3/27/1921
Edward, b. 4/10/1912; d. 6/22/1958

M.O. Ferguson---Alice Alma West Ferguson
b. 11/22/1915   b. 1/20/1924
d. 12/24/1987

Alice Alma West Ferguson
Born: January 30, 1924
Stapleton, Virginia
Interviewed: January 27, 1991

My name is Alma West Ferguson. I am 68 years old. I was born in Stapleton,
Virginia, in Amherst County. Aunt Classie Pollard, a midwife delivered me.
She lived near Jake Beverly's home house.

Susie McCoy Ferguson delivered my husband, Maloney Obrian Ferguson. She was
his grandfather's brother's wife. She was Uncle Bill (William) Ferguson's wife.
Bill Ferguson and Grandpa Pete, my husband's grandfather, were brothers.
She delivered a lot of my mother's babies also.

I lived over behind Beulah Church, about a mile and a half to two miles. We
moved up on the river, between Galts Mill and Stapleton. At that time, I was
nine years old because I remember I was nine when my grandmother died.

I started school when I was six years old. I went to school until the seventh
grade. We didn't have a high school in the area after the seventh grade.
Therefore, I didn't go to high school.

Oscar West, Eleanor West, Alphonza Beverly, Onie Sparrow, Christine (my
cousins) were in my class at Fairmount. There was a gang of them in the
school. Jack, Eddie, Buck, Folly Hull, John, Elizabeth, Myrtle Hull, Gene Hull,

Vernon Beagle, Willie Ann Trent, A.D. Jackson (Moses Jackson's cousin), George and Rossie Sparrow, Beatrice Bolling, Irene and Ella Bolling, Gene and Susie Bolling.

Our first teacher was Mr. John Wilson. He taught me for three years until he retired. Then Miss Miller from Richmond taught me for one year. Then we had Miss Dingy for one year. Then we had Mr. Bibby. Then Susie Bell Anderson taught us for two years. We were about fourteen or fifteen then. Miss Isabell Ferguson taught school for one year. I was out of school then. She taught school after I was married, around 1947 or 1948. She moved to Washington, D.C. I remember when she went over to the Irvins' house to get Rev. Irvin's sister to show her how to prepare her records to close out the school year. She knew how to complete the report.

The people in this area were very friendly. The people were very close. All colors got along well together. People were friendly and willing to help in any way that they could as neighbors. They would divide their food, butter and eggs. Even during the rough times (Depression), I heard about their generosity. Mama would go to visit them and the people would load her down with all kinds of food. Maude Pettyjohn, who lived up the road (owned Pettyjohn Island), was very helpful. Other people who were cooperative during those hard years were Mandy Morcom, Beulah Morcom, Margaret Morcom, Ellen Moore, Etta Green Beverly, Catherine Bolling, Minnie Bolling, Lizzie Stratton, Ada Vaughter, and Alice Blair. Mrs. Blair lived down the hill there. These people were just a family of folks that believed in sharing with others. Maybe one would have cows with milk and we didn't have one at the time, or they would give us butter, milk, eggs, chicken, ham, preserves, biscuits. Whatever, they would share it.

I remember Fairmount Church since I was two years old. I would go with grandpa Willis West. I would ask him if I could go to church with him on that Saturday. He would come by that next morning, Sunday. He lived about a mile from where we lived. He would come by and pick me up and I would walk behind him. People would ride to church on horses. I remember Luther McCoy, Bob McCoy's father. He was a preacher, he would come over to visit our church. People visited our church from Union Hill Church, First Baptist, Scott Zion, Mt. Zion in Appomattox, Mt. Airy, and Galilee Baptist Churches.

My father, Walker West, always said that we were related to the Cherokee Indians. When my sister and I were teenagers, they-- he and my uncle-- would always call us the Cherokee Indian girls. I had always heard the "Cherokee" term but I didn't pay any attention to it until I was a teenager. He would always say that we were related to the Cherokee Indians. I passed the tradition on to my children, that we were Cherokee Indians, just like daddy passed it down to me. (Oscar West, Alma's brother, remembers Jack Elliott having Indian hair,"long enough to sit on it" (1991)).

The Penns, on my father's side, were Indians. Betsey Beverly was an ancestor on both sides of my family. She was Cherokee Indian. Lloyd Elliott always said that he was an Indian. He insisted that he be considered an Indian.

The Fergusons, across the James River, were also mixed Indians. The Ferguson boys' father was an Isbell. The Isbells gave each of the four boys a piece of land.

Gus Ferguson, Pete Ferguson's son, came over from Appomattox to Stapleton once a month to see Nanny West. He was a farmer. They married on December 16, 1913, in Amherst County. They had to put colored on it because they could not say that they were Indian. They had to say "White" or "Colored" on the certificate.

They raised tobacco, corn, hay, cattle, mules, horses, hogs, and chickens. We lived with Gus and Nanny when we first got married on March 25, 1945. We moved into the home house with them. My husband worked on C&O Railroad for about 45 years. He went to work when he was fifteen and took retirement when he was sixty-two. He had retired for ten years when he died.

My father told me that his grandmother, Betsey Beverly, was an Indian woman. She knew about Indian methods. My father said that, when he was about five or six years old, she took his clothes off and put him on a plank over the creek early in the morning before the sun came up. He had a very bad case of asthma. But when the sun came up, he was not bothered with the asthma any more. He didn't have asthma any more. She had a way with Indian remedies. My father said that his mother has always been free Indian. When she came to this area (from Appomattox), she was a free woman. In her later years, she stayed with Willis West, her son, for a while. Later in her old age, she stayed with Ernest Sparrow (grandson-in-law), George Sparrow's father.

My mother's grandmother, Mitte Hogan Scott, was called the "Black Dutch." She was an attractive, dark lady that was possibly mixed with Indian, Dutch, and African ancestry. Jack Elliott, my grandfather, on my mother's side, was dark but had long, Indian-type hair (Oscar West, Alma's brother, remembers Jack Elliott "with his long, straight hair.").

My mother made ashcakes, an Indian recipe. The people on Buffalo Ridge dug a hole in the ashes and placed the corn meal, balled up, in the hole. They removed the ashes and ate the cake. They were delicious.

People thought my husband was white, people who didn't know him. He just let them go on and think it. He wasn't a great talker, he was a good listener. People used to wonder what we, our family, were when we went to town.

****

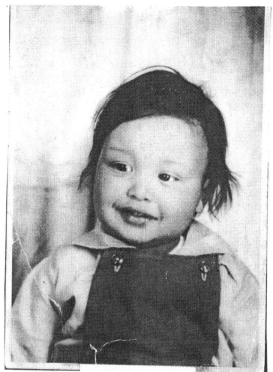

Quintus Ferguson, Sr.

M.O. Ferguson

Alma West Ferguson and
Children

Raymond Ferguson, Jr.

Dr. Frederick Isbell

Sam Ferguson, Dr. Isbell's son

Suzie McCoy Ferguson, 1865-1944

Mitt Ferguson

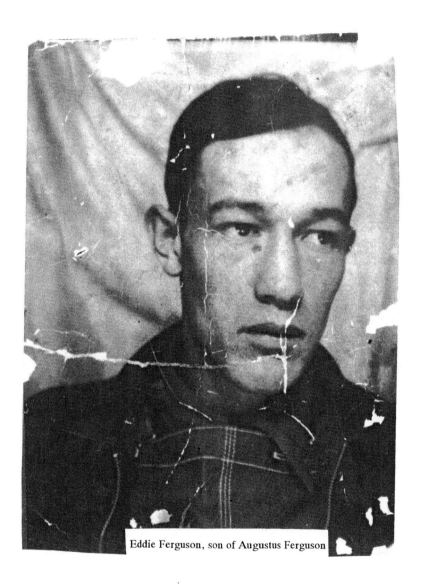
Eddie Ferguson, son of Augustus Ferguson

Ray Ferguson's Family

Back Row: Wayne, Randall, O'Neal, Clarence, Theodore, and Raymond, Jr.

Front row: Blondie, Phyllis, Ordean, Carentha, and Armentha

Sitting: Ruth Johnson Ferguson, wife of Raymond, Sr. (deceased) and mother of children

Mrs. Hopper, Lionel (son), and Marie (daughter)

M. O. and Alma West Ferguson

Leavelt Ferguson

Isabelle Ferguson Fields

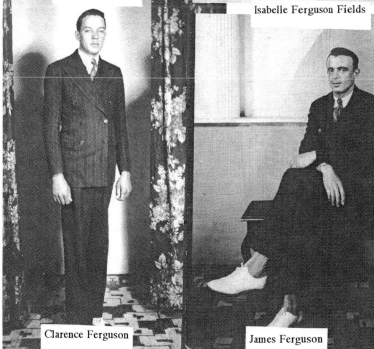

Clarence Ferguson

James Ferguson

Augustus Ferguson

Loren Ferguson, Augustus Ferguson's brother

Berta Ferguson Franklin & O.K. Ferguson, Peter and Belle Ferguson's children

Eleanor Ferguson Megginson, Augustus Ferguson's sister

Peter Ferguson

Cynthia Ferguson Jones and
friend

Hank and Hope Ferguson Melton

Rev William Luther McCoy and Betty Banks McCoy (Children in picture: Clark. Ruben. Herman. Robert. Martha. Frank. Jesse. Andrew. and Artie Standing near horse: Andrew Johnson.)

Mooney noted in Myths of the Cherokee that the Cherokee would often resort to the "universal Indian panacea for 'strong' sickness of almost any kind, viz, cold plunge baths in the running stream..." (36). Betsey Beverly was well known as a "Cherokee" woman and for her Cherokee medical practices. She resorted to the traditional Cherokee method when other methods did not work -- she lowered him into the creek to heal his asthma.

The family members are not sure about the meaning of the term, "Black Dutch." They are aware that Mitte Hogan Scott was called the "Black Dutch." They are not sure if she had some German ancestry or that her mother may have been owned at one time by a Dutch master. Mr. Bernard Humbles Penn feels that she may have been a descendant of the "Black Dutch." Dr. Charles Turner, Professor Emeritus, Washington and Lee University, Lexington, Virginia corresponded with Mr. Humbles on the subject. He noted, "'Black Dutch' refers to Dutch settlers who were dark who settled in the monasteries of Western Pennsylvania."(C. Turner, 1990). The "Black Dutch" term could refer to Mitte Hogan Scott's "Portuguese-Indian" connection (Kennedy and Kennedy, 1994, p. 20). The Irish Creek area of Rockbridge County, near Amherst County, had a Cherokee and a "Portuguese" or Melungeon tradition (Rockbridge County Historical Map, Roanoke Valley Historical Society, 1778-1865). The Irish Creek area Cherokee were called Portuguese people (Rockbridge County Historical Map). The Roanoke Historical Society, who produced the map, noted, "A few of the mysterious Melungeon people, of Portuguese and Indian Blood, lived here in the foothills of the Blue Ridge." Some Amherst and Rockbridge County residents intermarried (Dr. Plecker's letter).

M. O. Ferguson's appearance was closer to the American Indian and Eskimos. His long straight hair of the yellow-red race, leiotrichous, is evident rather than the cymotrichous variety (brown-white races) and the ulotrichous of the Negro race (Kephart, 1960, 66). His son, as a toddler, reflected more of the oriental appearance than the traditional American Indian type (see picture). M. O. Ferguson and his son, like the American Indian, are different from the Asiatic Mongoloid in that they have less nasal "facial flatness" (C.S. Coon, 1965, p. 154). Quintus, his son, reflected much more of the Oriental appearance of the American Indian ancestors, prior to their arrival in America, than his father. The fact that he and other people in this area had Indian ancestry on both sides of their families somehow magnified the "Indianness" to the degree that they, in some cases, have the oriental facial features of the earlier Indians while, in some cases, they tend to look Indian, black-Indian, white-Indian, or tri-racial.

Maloney O. Ferguson (1986), now deceased, indicated that his ancestors told him that, when General Lee's troops retreated into Appomattox, fleeing from General Grant's troops and trying to make it

Appomattox, fleeing from General Grant's troops and trying to make it to their food supply lines in Appomattox, a young Ferguson boy had a small place in Virginia history. "A hungry Confederate soldier, tired and hungry after the forced march from Richmond, begged the Ferguson child, one of Dr. Isbell's children, for a piece of his ashcake. He replied to the soldier, 'You not going to get any of this ashcake.' The soldier continued to march hastily on up the road with the other soldiers toward the town of Appomattox" (M. Ferguson, 1986; Dowdey, 368; Chilton, 1985, 17). Burke Davis, in To Appomattox--Nine April Days, 1865, 1959, indicated that soldiers were so hungry that they were "as willing to surrender to the Negro Troops as to whites; the 25th Corps north of the James (James River), with many Negroes in the ranks, took in hundreds of the surrendering Rebels" (141).

Corn (maize) products were a very important part of the Cherokee diet. Ashcakes were thought to be an Indian recipe. White settlers were not known to make ashcakes, as well as other traditionally Indian products, initially (McElwain, 1981, 45). McElwain noted the Cherokee's love for corn products and the variety of cooking methods. He indicated that the Indians had five ways of preparing corn. They included parching, parched corn soup, roasting ears, ash-boiling, and ash-baking.

Chilton noted that when the Union troops came to Appomattox County, the residents hid their valuables to protect them from the soldiers who stole food, horses, and any other valuables that they could "carry away." (Chilton, 13). Lizzie Stratton, a 97 year-old resident of Amherst County, remembered hearing stories about the Stapleton area from her ancestors. It seems that word came to the James River area of Stapleton that both armies were in Appomattox County and the Stapleton citizens hid horses and other items in the basement for protection from the troops (Stratton, 1990).

* *

Richard Harris--Pauline Harris   Andrew Johnson--Annie Banks

Stanley Harris, Sr. -- -- -- Ida Lee Johnson

Stanley Harris, Jr.

Stanley Harris, Jr.
Born: August 11, 1936
Madison Heights, Virginia
Interviewed 1/6/91

I remember one of my great-aunts (Mattie Vaughan) visiting with my grandmother, Pauline. She was living with her at the time. She had long straight hair. She spoke a different language, an Indian dialect. I heard my grandfather, Richard Harris, say he had a lot of Cherokee in him.

Willis West

Walker West

Julia West Sparrow

Nannie West Ferguson

Alice West Pendleton

Grover West

Gloria Ferguson Rice

Tara West

Rozelle Cheagle

The West Sisters

Alma W. Ferguson, Evelyn W. Hutcherson, Shirley W. Christian, Eleanora W. Jordan, Geneva W. Moore, and Martha W. Christian

Rosetta Redcross Patterson and Her daughters

Willie Ann McCoy Snead.
Daughter of Rev. Luther and Betty Banks McCoy

My wife's paternal grandmother, Mitte Jane Tweedy, was Cherokee. She had an Indian father. My wife has always heard that Grandmother Mitte Tweedy was from the Cherokee Tribe. At one time, she lived with her on Dixie Airport Road in Madison Heights.

When my father went to the VA Hospital in North Carolina in the 1940s, they put him in a ward with the Indians. They did not ask him what race he was. They just put him in the Indian ward. His skin color was copper and he had straight, black hair.

Stanley Harris is a fourth-term member of the Amherst County Board of Supervisors, He represents District One in Amherst County.

* *

Stephen Ferguson, b. 1788--Susan Ferguson, b. 1793

Susan Ferguson, b. 1838

Joseph Ferguson, b. 1857--Serena Ferguson
Children:
Joe Agee: Virginia Megginson, Jene Ware, Arlene Cooper, Irona Beard, Maxine Thompson, Obediah, Cornelius, Sears, and John C.
Walter Bass: Children--James, Charles, Ricky, Serena Higginbotham, Flossie Davis, Gwen Allen, Roberta   Womack, and Lucy Haskins.
Flossie Ferguson McCoy: Mitchell, Edward, Lawrence, Aaron, Adelia M. Knight, Betty M. Grooms, Louise M. Lewis, Hilda M. Day, and Beverly McCoy
Joseph Ferguson's other children--by first wife Susie Giles Ferguson--were **Pet** Ferguson, Estelle Ferguson Scott, Mary Ferguson, Winston Ferguson, Martha Ferguson Withers, and Hattie "Little Hattie"Ferguson.

Pet Ferguson--Henrietta Lewis
Children: "Dee," Louis, James Thomas, and Pet

Samuel "Dee" Ferguson--Virginia Tibb
b. 3/15/1915

Samuel D. ("Dee") Ferguson
Appomattox, Virginia
Born: March 15, 1915
Interviewed: August 29, 1994

My father died when my baby brother was six months old. I didn't know a lot about my daddy. He lived in Mt. Zion area. My Grandaddy Joseph lived a long time beyond his son, my dad.

My granddaddy married two times. The flu killed a lot of my grandad's children. The flu killed five or more of granddad's children. They buried two in one coffin.

Mary Ferguson Isbell, Granddad Joe's daughter, married an Isbell. I don't remember his name.

I have red skin. People tell me my skin is red. Susan, Granddad's mother, had a boyfriend. He was white. He jumped ship or refused to leave her. I heard he jumped ship so he could see her, my great-grandmother Susan.

Most of the Lewises, my mother's people, are out of state. Some are in Baltimore. Some live in the Springfield Church area. I grew up in the Springfield Baptist Church area. Uncles Bass and Joe Agee and Aunt Estelle grew up in the Mt. Zion Church area, but they lived about four miles from Mount Airy Church.

* *

Stephen Ferguson--Susan Ferguson
/
Susan Ferguson
|
Joseph Ferguson--Susie Giles

Early Scott------------------Julia Estelle Ferguson
(Cherokee)

Timothy Penn---Canolia Johnson

Jesse Scott--Ruby Mae Penn

Jesse Scott
Concord (Appomattox County), Virginia
Interviewed: August 29, 1994

My father was Early Scott. The Cherokee were the lighter skinned Indians (the Fergusons and McCoys). Granddad Joseph Ferguson had twenty-one children. All are dead now. He had two wives. The Beverlys, St. Claire and Alfonza Beverly, are related to my mother Julia Estelle Ferguson Scott. I heard we are connected to Pocahontas also.

William Mitchell here is my brother (standing near Jesse Scott). He married Elizabeth Patterson. They have three children, Ruby Mae, Joyce, and William.

I raised Sam, the Chief of the Buffalo Ridge Cherokee Band, from a baby. His mother was Adelia Ferguson Penn. Adelia's daddy was Kelly Ferguson.

The whole family is one big family circle, the Fergusons, McCoys, Penns, Beverlys, and others.

* *

The 1860 U.S. Census, Appomattox, Stonewall Mill

Stephen Furguson, age 72

156

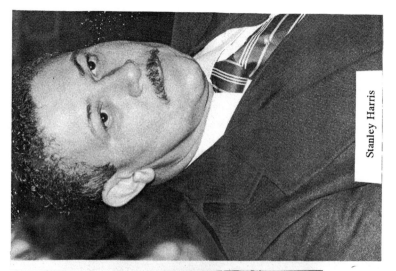

Stanley Harris

Adlee Carter Wood

Vera Pannell White

Julia Estelle Ferguson Scott

Susan Furguson, 67
Judy (Judith), 25
Susan Furguson, 22
Stephen Furguson, 5
Joseph Furguson, 3
Sam Furguson, 7
Nancy Furguson, 5
Lucy Furguson, 7
Peter Furguson, 6
Hudson Furguson, 5
Thomas Furguson, 3

(William Furguson, born 1860,
was not born at time of this census report)

Stephen Furguson---Susan Furguson
b. 1788   b. 1793

Dr. Frederick Isbell----Judy (Judith) Ferguson

Lucy Ferguson
Peter Ferguson
Hudson Ferguson
Thomas Ferguson
William Ferguson

(Sam Ferguson was Judith's son, but Dr. Isbell was not his father)

Wesley Ferguson---Lucy Ferguson, m. 10/20/1877, Appomattox County

Woodson Ferguson---Annie Willis

Children:

Alex Ferguson
Peter Hudson Ferguson
Howard Ferguson
Maud Ferguson McCoy, m. Doswell McCoy
Nannie Ferguson McCoy, m. Stephen McCoy
Laura Ferguson Pinn, m. William James Pinn
Louize Ferguson (died young, result of flu)

Harvey Johnson---Molly Ferguson Swain

Earl Ferguson----------Etta Johnson
b. Sept. 12, 1918   b. 1928

Earl Ferguson
Lynchburg, Virginia
Born: September 12, 1918
Interviewed: September 3, 1994

My parents died when I was young.. My mother died when I was three years
old and my father died when I was fourteen years old. My Aunt Laura
Ferguson Pinn raised me. I lived in Eagle Rock with Aunt Laura first and then
we moved to Huntington, West Virginia. Before Aunt Laura died, she brought
me down here for a visit. I was about nine years old, around 1927. I came to

visit Uncle Pete (Peter Hudson Ferguson) in Lynchburg, and stayed here. I had two uncles with the name "Pete." One was my great-uncle (Peter Ferguson, Appomattox, the father of Augustus and O.K. Ferguson) and my uncle (Pete), daddy's brother, in Lynchburg.

****

Onie Sparrow Born Feb. 19, 1920
Madison Heights, Virginia
Interviewed-12/15/90

I was born on Jenkins Hill, near Gus Ferguson's home house. We walked to old Fairmount Church, near Penn Park Graveyard, to worship on Sundays.

At seven or eight, I remember playing with the Turners, Trents, Wests--Oscar and Alma, the Bollings--Elvin "Red" Bolling and Irene, and the Beverlys--St Clair, Gertrude, and Alphonza.

Some of the people who lived in the Old Fairmount or Stapleton area were:

Sam Turner's family
Deacon Otis West's family
Phillip Bolling's family
Jack Franklin's family
Deacon Willis West's family
Lindy Pennix
Jack Elliott
Harris C. Hull
Gus Ferguson
David Scott (Sam Scott's father)
Wesley Moore
Will Franklin
Deacon George Penn
Deacon Charles Jackson
Deacon Henry Blair
Deacon Bernard Jackson
Deacon Elijah Revely

My daddy's mother was full Indian, coal black hair and high cheek bones.

****

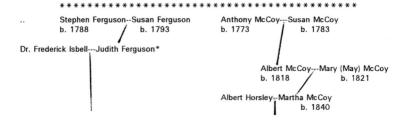

Andrew McCoy, Jr.
(Died in an airplane crash)

Captain * West Point Academy Graduate * Pilot

The Ferguson Brothers
(Picture from The Iron Worker, Courtesy of the Photo Collection
Jones Memorial Library, Lynchburg, VA)

John Ferguson with his daughter, Patricia Jordan, and
granddaughter

Children:
Luther McCoy, m. Betty Banks,
    sister of Annie Banks (m.
    Andrew Johnson)
Deley McCoy, m. Samuel Ferguson
Susie McCoy, m.William Ferguson

William "Bill"Ferguson, b. 1860 Susie McCoy
Married 12/21/1881 (Jamerson, Nash, & Nash, 1979, p.28)

John Ferguson

Children:
Conley, Cornelia, Pedether, and Patricia.

William Ferguson
Children:

Robert: b. 3/25/1906;d. 9/26/1983
Stanford: b. 9/6/1902;d. 12/11/1986
Harry:b. 2/2/1900;d. 1966
Dodridge: b. 5/25/1891; b.6/20/1944
Mott: b. 5/24/1896; d. 5/26/1964
Kathleen Ferguson White:b.3/15/1898;
                d. 2/14/1966
Martha Ferguson Boling: b.8/12/1895;
                d. 2/11/1957
Daisy Ferguson Megginson Scott:
                b. 4/1/1911;
                d. 8/2/1975
Vera Ferguson Booker: b. 4/5/1903;
                d. 12/5/1962
Vergie Ferguson Ferguson: b.10/6/1890;
                d. 4/2/1978
Molly Ferguson Swain: b. 12/25/1901;
                d. 3/6/1962
Mitt Ferguson Ferguson: d. 1928
Lucinda Ferguson Jones: b. 5/9/1889;
                d. 11/8/1942

John Ferguson
Born: January 12, 1909
Died: February 8, 1991
Interviewed January 3, 1991
Lynchburg, Virginia

I will be 82 on January 12. I was born in 1909. I still drive the car and go where I want to go.

My mother's name was Susie J. Ferguson and my father was William J.

159

Ferguson or "W.J." I think his father was an Isbell. When we went to Appomattox, I would go with him. We visited white people --kin folks. My mother was an Indian. Her hair was so long she could sit on it. She could swim across the James River. We lived on top of a mountain, about 3/4 of a mile from the James River (on the Appomattox side). Where I lived, my father had a boat, ferry, to carry a wagon across the James River. We owned an island down on the James River, just over from Stapleton, near Galts Mill. My brother, Robert, is deceased, and his wife, Ida, owns the property now. Uncle Hut's son, O.K. Ferguson's children own the other part of the land now. I am the youngest son and the last one of the children living in my family.

My father was a farmer and my mother was a midwife. She delivered babies all around Stapleton. She delivered black and white babies. I would take mother and wait for her to deliver babies. Sometimes, they gave her a chicken, a calf, or pig, because they didn't have money. Therefore, they paid her off in farm animals. (Oral tradition in many Indian communities refers "to midwifery" (McElwain, 51)).

She would catch the ferry across the James River. The ferry owner was Mr. Isbell. One of the Isbells ran the post office in Stapleton and one also had the post office in Stonewall.

My father had 197 acres. Uncle Hudson (Hut) had his ground and Uncle Pete had his. Uncle Sam and Uncle Tom lived down in Beckham, so I didn't see them that much. They lived near Mt. Zion Church. We attended Mt. Zion Church.

Uncle Hut had about four boys. My dad had work at home for his boys. Uncle Hut had his family and let them work for the white folks. Uncle Pete did the same thing. They worked for the Isbells. They lived down on the creek.

My daddy didn't allow us to go but so far. My mother would send us to get butter and milk. We had to go and come straight back. My mother had Indian appearance with long, straight hair. My father looked like a white man.

We didn't know any difference on race. One time when we were thrashing wheat, the white workers on our farm, mother let them come first to eat the meal. We couldn't understand it, the race thing. We didn't know a lot about our relatives except during church revival time at Mount Zion, that week of revival. We had work to do and we didn't have a way to get around. We had a wagon and a ferry to get across the river. We carried the wagon and plow and horse across to the island. He (his father) farmed on the island and the high land. He owned the whole mountain on the hill above the island. The ground was given to some of the brothers (by the Isbells) and they didn't like the ground. So, my daddy bought it. This is why my father had as much as he did. He bought the three brothers' land.

The light skinned students (who went for black) were able to go to school with the white kids. We went to school with the white kids.

I have one daughter who has her masters degree and is working on her doctorate at the University of Virginia.

* *

Patricia Jordan, John Ferguson's daughter, noted, "When my daddy, John Ferguson, traveled on the train, my daddy would get in the white section of the car but when we go to church, he went with the black people at the church, Mt. Zion." Pedether Wheaton, another daughter who was present during the interview, indicated, "William 'Bill' Ferguson was my daddy's father and Dr. Isbell was daddy's grandfather."

John Ferguson and his four brothers, all employed at the Lynchburg Foundry in Lynchburg, Virginia, were featured in the W.D. Lawrence's article, "The Fergusons--Five Brothers of the Lynchburg Plant" (The Iron Worker, October, 1934). The article noted:

"There are a number of instances where two brothers are found on the company's payroll. There are several families represented by three sons. In the preceding issue, four sons of one family were presented. Now, we will tell of five brothers who are working here at the same time. This rare distinction falls to the sons of Susie and William J. Ferguson of Appomattox County. When William Ferguson was married, he took his wife to his father's farm, which he inherited, and settled down to the life of a farmer. This, through hard work, thrift and good management, he improved and enlarged until he had about one hundred and eighty acres, twenty of which is an island in the James River. But he had a real need of a large place to give room to his growing family, for in response to the Divine Command to multiply and replenish the earth, seventeen children were born to him there. Of this number, twelve are living and married, with children of their own, so that now William can claim some sixty odd grandchildren..." (31 & 32).

The article stated that Dodridge Ferguson, born 1893, married Susie Davidson; Mott Ferguson, born 1897, married Erma Hamilton; Harry Ferguson, born 1900, married Nancy Scott; Stanford Ferguson, born 1902, married Ethel George; and John, the youngest, born 1909, married Bernice Wynn. Most of William's children, if not all, married spouses with known Native American ancestry. Lawrence, in his article, quoted Genesis 1:28, "And God blessed them, and God said unto them, Be fruitful, and multiply, and replenish the earth.." The Ferguson family members, and Buffalo Ridge Band members in general, have honored and obeyed the charge from Genesis 1:28 by producing large families.

161

The article noted that Mott Ferguson, "remembering that his grandfather (Dr. Isbell) was a doctor, he thought he would like to be one too..." He started college. He remained, however, at the Foundry at the end of the summer and did not return to college (31).

* *

Mary Elizabeth Pettigrew West
Born: November 12, 1905
Madison Heights, Virginia
Interviewed 2/27/91

I know that the Wests were Indians. My husband's mother, Martha Jane Penn West, was an Indian. I knew his father, Willis West. Both Martha and Willis were Indians. Willis looked like an Indian. His mother, Betsey Beverly, was Indian. Francis Jenkins Jordan's mother was also an Indian.

I think the Pettigrews had Indian in them also. We used to eat ashcakes. My father, William Henry Pettigrew, made ashcakes. We ate a lot of squash when I was growing up. We had a large farm.

I always reminded my children and relatives to put down "Indian" on their documents for race. They were Indian. It wasn't anything to be ashamed of. They had Indian in them!

I have three granddaughters and one grandson. All of them finished college. Vernetta Chambers Pinn is a teacher in the Amherst County School Division and her husband is a bank loan officer. Karen is an artist for the City of Charlotte, North Carolina. Wanda is a physical therapist at Virginia Baptist Hospital. Harry "Butch" is a teacher at E.C. Glass High School.

* *

Mrs. Vera Mary Pannil White
Born: March 29, 1924
Lynchburg, Virginia
Interviewed: February 26, 1991

William Southard —— Lucy Southard
(Cherokee)   (Cherokee)
Charles Tyree-–Harriet Southard
(Cherokee)
Dudley Reed ⌐Betsey Tyree

162

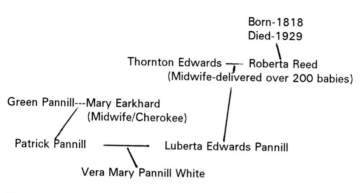

Born-1818
Died-1929

Thornton Edwards ——— Roberta Reed
(Midwife-delivered over 200 babies)

Green Pannill---Mary Earkhard
(Midwife/Cherokee)

Patrick Pannill ——————— Luberta Edwards Pannill

Vera Mary Pannill White

Vera Mary Pannill White

My grandmother always told me that her father was taken away when she was a little girl because he was a Cherokee and her mother, Betsey, was an Irish girl. They were separated. Our people were listed as mulatto. They were indentured servants.

I remember my grandmother Roberta. She used to make ashcakes for us (Indian custom). She grew up in the Pedlar Mill area, Amherst County.
* *

Vera White received the prestigious "Albert Gallatin" Civilian Award when she retired from the Bureau of Engraving and Printing, Washington, D.C..

* *

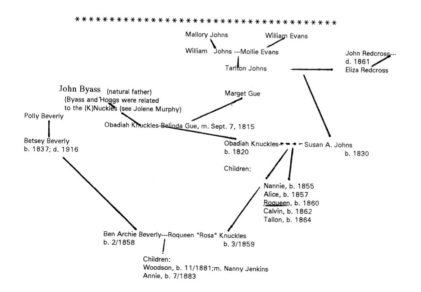

Mallory Johns   William Evans

William Johns ---Mollie Evans   John Redcross---
d. 1861
Tarlton Johns   Eliza Redcross

John Byass (natural father)   Marget Gue
(Byass and Hoggs were related
to the (K)Nuckles (see Jolene Murphy)
Polly Beverly

Betsey Beverly   Obadiah Knuckles-Belinda Gue, m. Sept. 7, 1815
b. 1837; d. 1916

Obadiah Knuckles-► ► ◄ ► Susan A. Johns
b. 1820   b. 1830

Children:

Nannie, b. 1855
Alice, b. 1857
Roqueen, b. 1860
Calvin, b. 1862
Tallon, b. 1864

Ben Archie Beverly---Roqueen "Rosa" Knuckles
b. 2/1858   b. 3/1859

Children:
Woodson, b. 11/1881;m. Nanny Jenkins
Annie, b. 7/1883

163

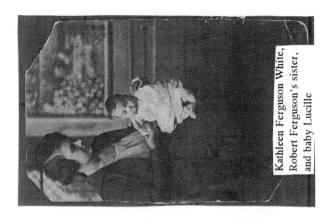

Kathleen Ferguson White, Robert Ferguson's sister, and baby Lucille

Savan Ferguson, Kelly Ferguson's brother and Samuel Penn's great-uncle

Henry Ferguson, Hudson's son

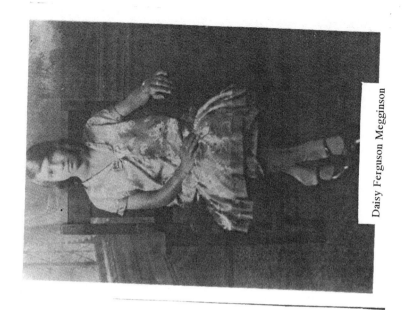

Daisy Ferguson Megginson

Mabel Ferguson Freeman

Flossie Ferguson McCoy

Joe Agee Ferguson

Ezra Ferguson's Family
Back Row: Mary (wife), Ezra, Winston (Mary Ferguson's
brother), Annie Ferguson McCoy (daughter), and
other children (second row): Thurman, Percy, Josephine
Ferguson Jackson, Mabel Ferguson Freeman,
Front Row: Susie Ferguson (died 10 yrs. old) and
George (died 2 yrs. old). Children not pictured:
Coleman, Boyd, Albert, and Fannie Ferguson Banks.

Charlie and Frances Jenkins Jordan

Grover West, Elizabeth Pettigrew West,
and Lelia Warwick Chambers

Othelle West Chambers

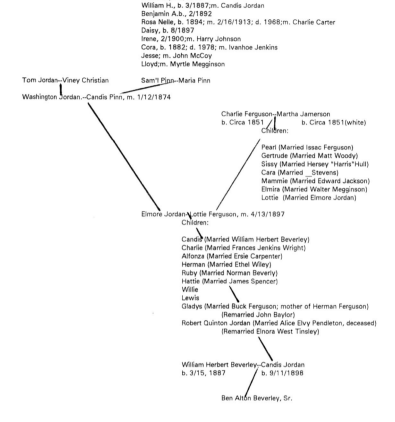

Taylor, b. 2/1885; Lelia Jenkins
Hattie C.,b. 2/1888
William H., b. 3/1887;m. Candis Jordan
Benjamin A.b., 2/1892
Rosa Nelle, b. 1894; m. 2/16/1913; d. 1968;m. Charlie Carter
Daisy, b. 8/1897
Irene, 2/1900;m. Harry Johnson
Cora, b. 1882; d. 1978; m. Ivanhoe Jenkins
Jesse; m. John McCoy
Lloyd;m. Myrtle Megginson

Tom Jordan--Viney Christian   Sam'l Pinn--Maria Pinn

Washington Jordan.--Candis Pinn, m. 1/12/1874

Charlie Ferguson--Martha Jamerson
b. Circa 1851   b. Circa 1851(white)
Children:

Pearl (Married Issac Ferguson)
Gertrude (Married Matt Woody)
Sissy (Married Hersey "Harris"Hull)
Cara (Married _ Stevens)
Mammie (Married Edward Jackson)
Elmira (Married Walter Megginson)
Lottie (Married Elmore Jordan)

Elmore Jordan--Lottie Ferguson, m. 4/13/1897
Children:

Candis (Married William Herbert Beverley)
Charlie (Married Frances Jenkins Wright)
Alfonza (Married Ersie Carpenter)
Herman (Married Ethel Wiley)
Ruby (Married Norman Beverly)
Hattie (Married James Spencer)
Willie
Lewis
Gladys (Married Buck Ferguson; mother of Herman Ferguson)
(Remarried John Baylor)
Robert Quinton Jordan (Married Alice Elvy Pendleton, deceased)
(Remarried Elnora West Tinsley)

William Herbert Beverley--Candis Jordan
b. 3/15, 1887   b. 9/11/1898

Ben Alton Beverley, Sr.

Ben Beverly, Sr.
Born:
Interviewed 2/28/91
Madison Heights, Virginia

I was born in Madison Heights near Rose Chapel Church. Pa would go to the
High Peak and Bear Mountain area to visit our relatives. His cousin and friend,
Muriel Branham, and he would visit each other all the time. This was during a
time period when I was between 15 and 30 years old. Pa died when I was 30
years old. Sometime Pa and I would eat at Muriel's house.

Pa used to sing and chant an Indian song, like a rain dance chant. (His wife,
Delores, a retired teacher and a Cherokee descendant from North Carolina,
noted that her husband also "sings and chants Indian songs, even though,
unlike his father, he does not know the meaning of what he is saying. He
makes these chants while he is working alone around the house or in the

yard"). My father's hair was straight, black. He was short in stature but tall in character and personality. He went to the mountains and cut Muriel Branham's hair. They took turns cutting each others hair. They were not satisfied with the barbers cutting their Indian hair. They wore it long. (Although M.O. Ferguson wore his hair medium long, he did not go to the black barbers. He went to a white barber in Lynchburg. They assumed that he was white. He could not find an Indian barber to cut his hair (A. Ferguson, 1991)).

My father used to take corn and make hominy. They put the corn in a tub of water with ashes and some kind of lye, I believe, and made the hominy. (His wife says that Ben loves raw vegetables. He makes sassafras tea from the root of the sassafras tree. She remembers eating several Indian goodies as a child. She noted that she ate peas and corn fritters. She said her grandfather, John Birdsong, had straight, black hair and a heavy mustache).

My father always talked about the fact that they were Cherokee Indians. He talked about it all the time. He said he was Indian and we were Indian. He said, "Don't let anyone tell you differently." People would say we are white. I said, "No. We are Indian." I have always said we were Indian.

There were eight children in the family. Even my baby sister, Jean Beverley Cardwell, remembers my father relating to us his Indian ancestry. He would always tell us to stay in school. All of the family have followed his wishes. Jean has five children. All of them have finished college. One is a teacher. One is a computer technician. Three are lawyers. All three lawyers passed the law bar examination on the first testing.

****

Raleigh Pete Carson and Ben Beverley remember the ancestors who spoke with Cherokee accents. The average Buffalo Ridge and Stonewall Mill resident, descendant of the Buffalo Ridge or Stonewall Mill ancestors, speaks some Cherokee today, unconsciously, without really intending to use the language. Simple, everyday words like yes (**v v**) and no (**tla**), written as **ᎥᎥ / Ꮟ** , are mixed with the English words, "yes" and "no," and pronounced "uh uh" for "yes" and "pnal" or "nawl" for "no." This usage of mixed English and Cherokee is common in areas that have a Cherokee heritage or a large population of Cherokee descendants. There are many other English words that are mixed up with Cherokee words and therefore give unique colloquial sounds that have similar sounds in all areas throughout the southeastern United States where Cherokee Native Americans have resided. Visitors from the north and east, whose ancestors were not Cherokee, often remark to southeastern residents, "Why do you say those words like that?"

Prentice Robinson has compiled a booklet of beginning Cherokee

Willie ((sister), Quinton Jordan, Hattie (sister), and Phillip (son)

Ben Beverley

Mattie Christian Jackson

David Gibson Beverly and son James

Willie Herbert Beverley

Beatrice Bolling Jordan, Catherine Bolling's Daughter

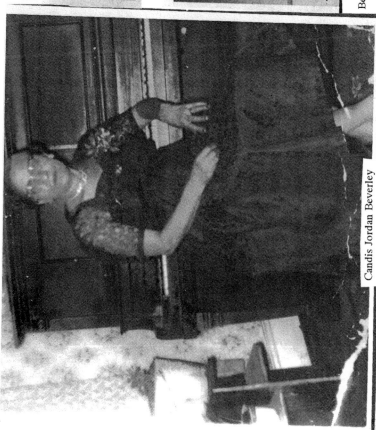

Candis Jordan Beverley

Rosa Nell Beverley, daughter of Ben & Rosa Beverley

Charles Carter, son of George & Susan Carter

Evelyn S. Wright (Redcross)

Victoria Persinger DiProsperis

language, I & II, which may be used with or without an instructor. Some of the words that are now mixed up with English words and have taken on common usage may be identified by becoming familiar with basic Cherokee language (Robinson, 1988).

****

Descendants of ancestors of the Buffalo Ridge Band are concentrated in central and southwestern Virginia and West Virginia. Eagle Rock (Virginia), for example, was a haven at one time for a large number of the Buffalo Ridge clan members. Roanoke also has a large number of the Band members. Victoria Persinger DiProsperis "Last Walker" ("She Who Walked Last"), a descendant of Buffalo Ridge and Eagle Rock ancestors, lives in Roanoke, Virginia. She has conducted extensive research on her family's genealogy and her work illustrates the strong Native American connection of the Buffalo Ridge Band of Cherokee over a two-hundred year period (DiProsperis, 1994):

****

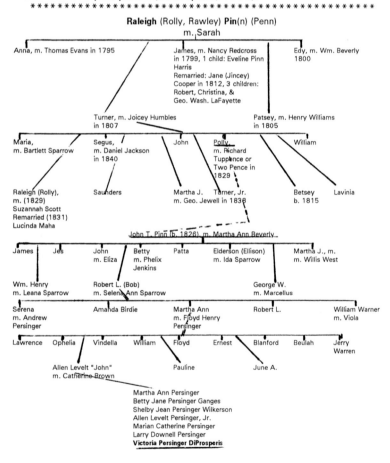

Raleigh (Rolly, Rawley) **Pin**(n) (Penn)
m. Sarah

Anna, m. Thomas Evans in 1795

James, m. Nancy Redcross in 1799, 1 child: Eveline Pinn Harris
Remarried: Jane (Jincey) Cooper in 1812, 3 children: Robert, Christina, & Geo. Wash. LaFayette

Edy, m. Wm. Beverly 1800

Turner, m. Joicey Humbles in 1807

Patsey, m. Henry Williams in 1805

Maria, m. Bartlett Sparrow

Segus, m. Daniel Jackson in 1840

John

Polly, m. Richard Tuppence or Two Pence in 1829

William

Raleigh (Rolly), m. (1829) Suzannah Scott Remarried (1831) Lucinda Maha

Saunders

Martha J. m. Geo. Jewell in 1836

Turner, Jr.

Betsey b. 1815

Lavinia

John T. Pinn (b. 1826), m. Martha Ann Beverly

James   Jes

John m. Eliza

Betty m. Phelix Jenkins

Patta

Elderson (Ellison) m. Ida Sparrow

Martha J., m. m. Willis West

Wm. Henry m. Leana Sparrow

Robert L. (Bob) m. Selena Ann Sparrow

George W. m. Marcellus

Serena m. Andrew Persinger

Amanda Birdie

Martha Ann m. Floyd Henry Persinger

Robert L.

William Warner m. Viola

Lawrence   Ophelia   Vindella   William   Floyd   Ernest   Blanford   Beulah   Jerry Warren

Allen Levelt "John" m. Catherine Brown

Pauline

June A.

Martha Ann Persinger
Betty Jane Persinger Ganges
Shelby Jean Persinger Wilkerson
Allen Levelt Persinger, Jr.
Marian Catherine Persinger
Larry Downell Persinger
Victoria Persinger DiProsperis

```
* * * * * * * * * * * * * * * * * * * * * * * * * * * * * * * * * * * * * * * * * * * *
```

Willis West--Betsey Beverly   John Turner Penn--Martha Ann Beverly

Willis West ———— Martha Jane Penn

Otis West--Betty Cousins

Havilah Hayes McCoy--Missie Estelle West

Children

Margaret McCoy Carey
Havilah Leon McCoy
Edward Stanley McCoy
Howard Eugene McCoy
Geraldine Mavis McCoy
Maitland McCoy Cooper

Missie Estelle West McCoy
Clifton Forge, Virginia
Born Sept. 13, 1913
Interviewed on January 19, 1991

My husband's people were from Appomattox County. My family lived in
Amherst County. My family always told me that my mother was on the
Cherokee side. I heard that they came from some other place and settled in
Amherst County. I'm not sure what area out of the state that these Indians
came from. My husband's people were connected to a copper-tone colored or
Indian people. He was a McCoy.

George and Isabelle
Ferguson Fields

Onie Sparrow

Missie West McCoy and her daughter, Margaret McCoy Carey

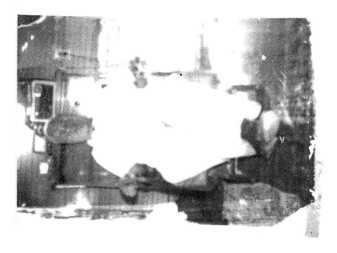

William Alonza Penn

Walter Empy

Langley "Buck" Fer-
guson

Raymond Ferguson

Annie Banks Johnson and Andrew Johnson

Allen Wright, Mrs. Jor-
dan's son (deceased)

James Ferguson

Dennis and Arelia West Harris

Alma West Ferguson, Flossie
Harris Beverly, and Brian

Samuel and Hester Sparrow Scott

Thomas Tillerson

```
*********************************************
      Raleigh Pin (Pinn)--Sarah Pinn
              /
      Turner Pinn--Joicy Humbles
                        
  Richard Two Pence/Tuppence (Two Pins)--Polly Pinn
                  /
      John Turner Penn--Martha A. Beverly
                  /
          Ellison Penn--Ida Sparrow
                  (Gladstone, Va.)
                              \
    George Empy ————————— Inez Penn
  (Lived near Eagle Rock)  /   (Born in Fairmount Area)
                          /
              Walter Empy
```

Walter Empy
Covington, Virginia
Interviewed on January 19, 1991
Born: August 2, 1908

My great-grandfather, John Turner Penn, was an old Indian. He lived in the
Galilee area (near Stapleton) of Amherst County. He moved his family to Eagle
Rock to work. We all know we have Indian in us.

There were a lot of Indians in the Buffalo Ridge/Stapleton area: George Penn,
Timothy Penn, Grover West, Otis West, Willis West. They were full blood Indians.
They lived to themselves. They were on Buffalo Ridge. They had some
connections with the Bear Mountain people.

Bernard Wade Humbles is mixed with Indian. He is a descendant of John
Turner Penn. My first cousin is Lawrence E. Penn. He lives here in Covington.
My mother, Inez Penn Empy, and his father, Alonzo Penn, were sister and
brother. Ellison Penn was the father of my mother and his father.

My father was a white man. My mother was an Indian. My mother was a full
blood Indian.

****

Lawrence Penn
Covington, Virginia
Date of birth-2/6/18
Age 73
Interviewed on 3/27/91

168

John Turner Penn (Great-grandfather)
Ellison Penn (Grand-father)
Alonzo Penn (Father)

I have lived in Covington since I was four years old. My grandfather told me about my Indian background. They lived in Amherst County.

People ask me what I am. People ask me what nationality I am. I tell them I go for black. My people, my ancestors, were full blood Indians.

* *

John Turner Pinn--Martha Ann Beverly Pinn

William Pinn---Leanna Sparrow

Ernest Napolian Crawford Orianna Penn Crawford
(Lived in Eagle Rock Area)(Left Amherst, Moved to Eagle Rock)

Clarence P. Crawford   Lucille Scott Crawford

Olemiel Bennett Randolph Doris Crawford Randolph

Doris Crawford Randolph
Phenix, Virginia (Charlotte County)
Interviewed on January 5, 1991

Orianna Penn Crawford, my grandmother, had a number of sisters and brothers. They were Wilton, Morton, Houston, Holcolm, Timothy, Artie, Ethel, Bessie and Viola.

Grandmother Orianna Penn Crawford lived in Eagle Rock, Virginia. My father lived there also. The people moved to Eagle Rock to work in the limestone quarries when times got bad in this area. They made bags of lime in 1930-47. They worked on the railroad up there also, on the extra force.

Hernandez Penn (deceased) was the last Penn in Eagle Rock. He was Viola Penn's son. She had another son, Warren Penn. He lives in Cleveland, Ohio. Viola Penn had two daughters: Rebecca Penn Rose, of Roanoke, Virginia, and Dorothy Penn Scott of Hunnington, West Virginia. I have a lot of relatives in Hunnington, West Virginia, and Cleveland, Ohio.

We were told when we grew up that we had Indian in us. I was born in Charlotte County. My parents left Eagle Rock and went back to Charlotte County in 1929 because the times were hard. When the quarries opened back up, they went back to Eagle Rock.

* *

John Turner Pinn---Martha Ann Beverly   Silas Bowling---Mary A.

Ellison Pinn----Victoria Bowling

William Henry "Buck" Wade---Estelle Humbles

Bernard Humbles

Bernard Wade Humbles Penn
Chief, United Cherokee Tribe of West Virginia, Inc.
Interviewed in Lynchburg, Virginia, on November 26, 1990

My grandfather was Ellison Penn, on my father's side. My father is William Henry Wade Penn. He is "Buck Wade" in the Alleghany County Census in 1900. My mother was Nellie Estelle Humbles. Victoria Bolling was my grandmother and married Winston Wade. She had me by William Henry Wade. The Penns were never slaves. They were listed as mulattoes, as Indians, or free colored, on the census. They would not recognize the people as Indians and therefore they would not have to pay them reparations. In 1705, the Indians were put in a nonwhite category and referred to as mulattoes. It was against the law to put the word "Indian" down as a racial identification because the colonists did not want to ever pay for lands that they took from the Indians, knowing that one day they may have to pay. So when they can, they will destroy the race of people by making them colored people, instead of Indian. They committed paper genocide; they destroyed on paper what they could not destroy physically. The Indians are all over the place. They couldn't destroy them physically, so they did it on paper. They were referred to as "free people" or "issues."

There were Cherokee people going to and from Washington, D. C. and Williamsburg, Virginia through Amherst and Rockbridge Counties from North Carolina, South Carolina, Georgia. They went through here on their way to Washington collectively to witness the signing of treaties and to collect their allotments of monies that the government had appropriated for them through the formal treaties that took place prior to and during the late 1700s and early 1800s. There were Indians coming through here and camping. Along with that, the Indians brought their slaves with them, slaves that they had intermingled with and also looked more Indian, in some cases, than the Indians did themselves. Because the Indian had then attempted to emulate the white man and they too, some of the Indians, tried to get themselves a white woman or vice verse, the racial integrity laws were instituted. Many whites that were not accepted by their own people, or did not want to marry their own people, married slaves. Consequently that created a problem. So they had to invoke what they referred to back then as a "racial integrity law." But the Indian had come into Amherst County and spent time here. Whole families traveled through Georgia and North Carolina on their way to visit the Great White Father in Washington and Williamsburg, Virginia.

It was a known policy during the first removal that several trails were used to take Indians out of the northern portions of the country. Slavers used to grab Indians, some were dark complected, and cut off their hair, and sell

170

Bernard Humbles Penn

Samuel H. Pinn (3rd from left) and his Indian friend in 1898

them for slaves. The advantage that the Indians had over the blacks was the fact that the Indians were home, in their own country. You turn him loose, and he is gone, back to his people, whereas the black was two oceans from home. But it has always been a known fact the Cherokee inhabited and traveled through Amherst County and Virginia. The oral tradition has been passed down in many families about their Cherokee connection. During the removal period, the families couldn't talk about their connection; they didn't want to be sent to Oklahoma. They told their children, and children's children, however, that they were Cherokee and told them not to say much about it to people other than the family. They did not want to be taken off their land and carried to Oklahoma with the other Cherokees. You just ask some people about their background, those people who look like Indians, black or white people, and they will probably let you know that they are connected with the Cherokee. They don't mind telling you today what they are; in 1835–38, they would only whisper to family members information about their Cherokee heritage. You don't hear any other stories, by family members, about any other tribes in this area. The Monacans have been documented in a recent book by Dr. Houck. The Monacans did not leave any oral history with many people in this area. Most thought that they were Cherokee.

There seemed to have been a campaign to make sure that there were "no more Indians." And the reinforcement of that, in the early twenties, Dr. Plecker, the Director of the State Department of Vital Statistics in Virginia, systematically went about the state of Virginia to make them all colored people instead of Indians. There were none, not one, as far as Dr. Plecker was concerned. They were primarily colored people because he made sure that they were registered on documents as colored people, not Indian; they were called black, "b," on the 1900 Census in this area. It depended on their physical appearance, and how the registrar or enumerator, how the census taker perceived the person. As a rule, a mulatto was considered either to be an Indian or a black person white enough not to have pronounced black features. In other words, he would walk in and out of buildings and the white man would not be able to tell him from another white man. If a black man in a white area looked white, if he were assumed to be or appeared to be white, he could pass for white. Some of the mixed Indian, white, and black people in Amherst County left the area and passed for white. Some of the French Huguenots were taken for black people. There were Dutch people who were referred to as "black Dutch" (C. Turner).

The Cherokee had a connection here in the state of Virginia long before the coming of the white man. If you are able to unearth villages that are four or five hundred years old, you know that they were here and if you find artifacts that reinforce that, then they were here. No matter what a person says, you don't go around digging up Indian artifacts and say that they were from a different tribe other than the tribe that was known to make these particular type of arrowheads or use these different type of corn grinding stones, or whatever. The Cherokee traveled all over Virginia and traded items with other tribes. You can find arrowheads in the ground that are made of rocks that are not found in this area. You will realize that other tribes brought the items from other areas of the state or country.

In one of the books written (Houck, 1984), Rena Redcross mentioned that she had always heard her people referred to as "Cherokee." It has been said that we depend on surnames, surnames were not always correct. You have people in Rockbridge County by the name of Clark. The Clarks are on the Cherokee Rolls. You also have people in Amherst County whose surnames are Bolling, and Bolling is on the Cherokee Rolls in Tahlequah, Oklahoma, as well as Cherokee, North Carolina. It is also on the rolls of the Choctaw and Chickasaw in Philadelphia, Mississippi, where the Choctaw and Chickasaw reservations are and those people, for the most part, their physical appearance, is that of a black person. Because the United States Government says that from 1866 on that they were Indian, I am not going to dispute my government; though there are people who will do that now. There are many Cherokee surnames in Amherst, Covington, Clifton Forge, Rockbridge, all the way back to the northern end of the old Cherokee borders. The people are all over the place. Just look at them, they are white and Indian; black and Indian; Indian; Indian, black, and white.

We have what is known as the United Cherokee Indian Tribe of West Virginia, whose members are descendants of, primary descendants of Ellison Penn, his sons' children, who in turn came from or were born in Beckley, West Virginia. The Cherokee Tribe in West Virginia is based on people whose surname is Penn. We have accepted membership from people in Virginia, even people whose names are Adkins, who are Chickahominy. They wanted to become members and members they are. There are people named Horne, these are surnames of people, Cherokee people. There are people named Penn. There are names I can't mention because of confidentiality. My name is Penn, so I can talk about me. My people were from Virginia and moved over to West Virginia. The Penns that are there do not deny that they are descendants of Ellison Penn and are descendants of John Turner Penn and Martha Ann Beverly, full blood Indians. You must remember that the Beverlys are members of that family group.

We have people in Kentucky, duly incorporated. They are the Evanses. They claim descent from the Evanses.

When Indians were captured, at night, many of them took off and when they reached Amherst County, they sought shelter in the areas known as Buffalo Ridge. Indians were there. There was an amalgamation of blacks, whites, and Indians. A lot of the Cherokees stayed and did not go with the Indians to Oklahoma. Even when the threat of removal was past, the Indians remained in the area because they liked the place. I read a documentation in the

Rockbridge County Militia's notes that the Rockbridge County Militia killed a number of Cherokee people on their way to Washington. They killed the Indians and some were taken prisoners. Some of the women were kept.

In 1866, the Cherokee had to by decree of the United States Government, three years after the Emancipation Proclamation, had to release from bondage people that they held as slaves. They agreed to take these people that they had held in bondage and free them. Make them full members of the tribe, and give them land (Cherokee Treaty). In Philadelphia, Mississippi, you will find people who are very diverse in color, but have physical characteristics as African-Americans.

Indian is not exclusively white as many people think. You will notice that there are marriage books in Amherst Court House where Indians tried to keep their identity by putting down in the marriage books such names as Delaware Jones or Pocahontas Smith. Delaware being an identification of a group of people who used the Cherokee dialect. These people tried to document in their own way in the marriage ledgers in the 1700s, 1800s, and 1900s their Indian connection. Some wrote Indian as their race and the clerk tried to deny their existence by writing "mixed."

Nobody goes around calling themselves Delaware, unless they were trying to let people know who they really were. Many people, white and black in Virginia, especially in southwest, central, and the Alleghenies, have Indian in their blood, with the primary tribe being Cherokee. Look at their names--straight from the Cherokee tribal rolls, then look at their appearance.
* * * * * * * * * * * *
Chief Bernard Humbles Wade Penn has been a active worker in West Virginia to obtain official state recognition of American Indians in West Virginia. He "obtained a proclamation from Gov. Gaston Caperton naming June 13, 1989, as Native American Day" ("Native American Center opening," The Dominion Post, Friday, June 23, 1989). "In addition to working to obtain funding for Indians in West Virginia (something he cannot take money for, Humbles said), he also is working to help families discover their Indian ancestry. His ancestry, also West Virginia, is both black and Indian, and 'many blacks are not aware they may have Indian blood,' he said" (The Dominion Post, Friday, June 23, 1989).

The Delilah Whitecloud United Cherokee Indian Tribe of Kentucky, Inc., is "the official American Cherokee Indian Tribe of the Commonwealth of Kentucky" (Wallace Wilkinson, Governor, 1991).

Mr. Humbles provided information about the acquisition of Cherokee land by white settlers(July 25, 1994). His narrative is as follows:

The Treaty of Lochaber had several problems. The treaty was held in Lochaber

(Abbeville), South Carolina. Why convene a meeting so far away from the land on which you are negotiating? According to Dr. Larry Ware, Professor Emeritus, Erskine College, Due West, South Carolina, Lochaber or the meeting place was a cabin on a creek in Abbyville County, South Carolina. Dr. Ware is a resident and teacher at Erskine College, Due West, South Carolina. He indicated that those people who were present at the meeting were the British King's representative, John Stewart, and twelve chiefs of the southern Cherokee tribes.

These people met to participate in the charade or game called land acquisition. The treaty occurred so far away from the actual area involved because the chiefs who were trading ownership of these lands probably did not know they existed as part of their domain and cared less about the land and vicinity where the middle Cherokee towns were, the areas of Virginia, West Virginia, Ohio, and Kentucky. At this time in history, Virginia and West Virginia were one state. The Cherokee Nation was divided into three sections. Upper Cherokee included sections of Illinois. Middle Cherokee included sections of Virginia, Ohio, and Kentucky. Lower Cherokee covered areas in Tennessee, the Carolinas, and west to Texas and beyond.

Calling these lands "hunting grounds" would make one believe that residents were not living in a setting in the areas of southwestern Virginia and vicinity, and West Virginia. This was a skillful stretch of the imagination. It was a falsehood. What will it take for researchers to acknowledge that Cherokee were in southwestern Virginia and vicinity, including part of central Virginia? What will it take for Virginians and West Virginians to catch up with their Cherokee history? What will it take for Virginian researchers--historians, archaeologists, anthropologists--to acknowledge that more should have been written on the subject and now is as good a time in history as any to concentrate on the research? There were residents in this part of the Cherokee territory. Unless more research is conducted and written on the Cherokee, archaeological sites may be inaccurately classified. The view that this was just "hunting ground," that the Cherokee didn't really live in the area, may cause problems in documenting history. The view that "Cherokee were not in the area, so this site or those Pisgah ceramics must be related to some other tribe" will force the decline of the Cherokee heritage in Virginia and West Virginia. How did the Cherokee protect and keep their land from other Native American tribes, the Six Nations, or settlers if they, some of the numerous bands, were not living in Virginia? Even a child would question those who hold the belief that the "Cherokee claimed the land but just hunted on it, they didn't live there." Why are so many central and southwestern Virginia and southern West Virginia residents claiming to have Cherokee ancestry? If they just hunted in the area and left after each hunting trip, then they would have had problems with others moving in when they left and staking claims for the land. The British settlers and colonists accepted the fact that this was Cherokee land, so they treated for the land. The Cherokee would have had to wage war each time they returned to the area to hunt, if they did not have bands in the area and if they didn't have a way of knowing who were moving in on their property. They would dispatch several bands to protect the land when the permanent Cherokee settlers notified the main bodies that they needed more "military assistance, that intruders were moving into the area.." Most of the recorded history of the Cherokee in Virginia, and West Virginia, was transferred to England after the Revolutionary War. There also are records in France, Germany, and Spain.

****

Thomas V. Parker, in 1907, provided a concise history of some of the treaties with the Cherokee in his book, The Cherokee Indians:

YEAR   EVENT

1721   Governor Nicholson of South Carolina, prompted by jealousy of French encroachments, entered into an agreement with the Cherokees. This agreement defined the boundaries and undertook to begin some systematic superintendence of Indian affairs in the Colony.

1730   North Carolina concluded a treaty with the Cherokees in which the sovereignty of the King of England was acknowledged and the Indians agreed to trade only with the English.

1755   There was a treaty and purchase negotiated by South Carolina.

1756   A treaty of alliance with North Carolina followed (in 1756).

1760   A subsequent alliance with the French brought defeat at the hands of the English and a   consequent treaty of peace in 1760 followed by a more decisive one the next year. The Indians were not principally to blame for the hostilities of this period, as they were treacherously dealt with by Governor Lyttleton.

1768   In 1768 there was another purchase-treaty with South Carolina.

1770   In 1770 there was a treaty with South Carolina settling the boundary.

1772   In 1772 there was a treaty of purchase with Virginia.

1773   A similar one was concluded with a British official.

1777   In 1777, after hostilities, a treaty of purchase   was concluded with South Carolina. Some time   after   this Cherokee territory   was practically confiscated by North Carolina.

1783   In 1783 the dispute in regard to this was adjusted by a treaty which was, however, so favorable to the whites that the Indians were far from satisfied.

1785   In the War of Independence the Cherokees were allied with the British. Peace was not concluded between the tribes and the United States Government until 1785, when the Treaty of Hopewell ended the war. Prisoners were exchanged, peace and friendship were pledged. Article nine of the treaty allowed Congress to pass laws regulating trade with them and to manage all their affairs for the protection and comfort of the Indians. They were to be allowed to send a deputy to Congress. No whites were to be permitted to settle on their lands.

1788   Congress issued a proclamation forbidding unwarranted intrusion upon the Indians' territory, but scant respect was paid to it by the offenders whose actions called it forth.

1789   The Secretary of War Knox characterized these encroachments as a "disgraceful violation" of the Treaty of Hopewell by the whites. Angered by the failure of the whites as individuals to respect Cherokee rights, and by the failure of the Government to protect them in their rights, the Indians kept the neighboring settlements in a state of uncertainty and terror by sudden, hostile incursions.

1791   In 1791 a second attempt was made to secure a permanent peace and the result was the Treaty of Holston. The Treaty of Holston was in many respects, however, similar to its predecessor--that of Hopewell. It provided for an exchange of prisoners and for permanent boundary lines. The United States was to pay an annuity of $1000 for the extinguishing of a claim to territory lying beyond a certain described line.

1794   In 1794 there was a treaty dealing with the stealing of horses, but which also reaffirmed the Treaty of Holston.

Jones, in License for Empire (112), summarized the Cherokee land cessions between 1720-1775. She stated that the Cherokee gave up 11,258 square miles of their land between 1721-1755, 850 square miles in 1768, and 48,217 square miles between 1770-1775 (1982; Royce, 1887, 378).
     ****

Dr. Larry Ware, Professor Emeritus, Erskine College, Due West, South Carolina, made the following observation and narrative about the Treaty of Lochaber (January 10, 1995):

In June, 1770, the governor of Virginia notified the superintendent of Indian Affairs that Virginia would cooperate in an effort to alter and to extend the Hard Labour Line of 1768 which marked the Indian boundary line in western

Virginia. The colony was willing to offer L 2,900 to cover the costs of gifts required for the Indians at a congress which would be convened with the Cherokees. The congress was scheduled for October at Lochaber, the South Carolina frontier plantation of Mr. Stuart's deputy, Alexander Cameron, who had named his plantation for the place of his birth in Scotland. John Stuart lived in Charleston, but his deputy, who was married to a Cherokee woman, lived up near the Cherokee lands. Lochaber was on Penney Creek, a small tributary of Little River within four or five miles of the Indian boundary line. Today, it lies on S.C. Highway 71 about ten miles west of the town of Abbeville. The site is marked by a historical marker which is a part of the "Bartram Trail." Six years after the Treaty of lochaber, the famed naturalist William Bartram recorded in his Travels how he spent the night with Cameron at Lochaber. A short time after this, Cameron took the side of the Loyalists and fled into the Cherokee nation for refuge, and at the time the Whigs or "Patriots" burned his home.

The Cherokee chief, Oconostota, had advised that the tribe expected a sizable compensation for the surrender of additional land. He said, "We shall give no part of our land away unless we are paid for it and indeed we want to keep the Virginians at as great a distance as possible, as they are generally bad men and love to steal horses and hunt for deer...but what are a few goods in comparison onto good land. The land will last forever and will yearly produce corn and raise cattle."

Nonetheless, Oconostota led over one thousand Cherokees southward in the fall of 1770 to meet with John Donelson, the representative from Virginia, and his party of Virginians as well as John Stuart and Cameron. The congress at Lochaber convened on October 18, 1770. The chief controversy was over the Cherokees' reluctance to give up the Long Island of the Holston (which lies in present day Kingsport, Tennessee). The line which was finally agreed to was called the Lochaber Line and was surveyed in the spring of 1771 by John Donelson and Alexander Cameron and the Cherokee leader, Chief Attakullakulla.

++

William Pinn---Leanna Sparrow   Thomas White--Milly Scott White

    Children:
    Holcombe
    William J.
    Orianna
    Samuel
    Wilton

        Samuel Houston Pinn---Rosa White Pinn

        Dr. James Taylor---Melvina Pinn Taylor

Melvina Pinn Taylor
Born: July 13, 1920
Lynchburg, Virginia
Interviewed: June 16, 1991

Vivian Pinn-Wiggins, M.D.

My daddy, Samuel Houston Pinn, hopped a freight train from Eagle Rock, Virginia, to Hampton, Virginia. He had one penny when he arrived in Hampton. He went to apply for admission to Hampton College. They tried him out by giving him a job of dusting and cleaning to see what kind of worker he was. They said he did a fairly good job, so they took him in.

The college officials lodged him in the Indian Wigwam section of the campus. He lived in an Indian wigwam until he finished college. He was an Indian and college officials knew that he was Indian. He graduated with the highest honors at Hampton College in 1898. We have a picture with him and his classmates. Some of dad's college classmates were Joe Hooker, Henry Tapaosa (Indian), Bassit Pride, John Brown, and Edward Ukipata (Indian). I have always known that I have Indian ancestry.

My father came to Lynchburg after his graduation from college. He took the postal examination and made a high score. He was the first man of color to make a 100 on the test. He worked in the post office a while. Then he went into the transfer business in 1920, the year I was born. He went into business with Dr. Francis Whitehouse and John Morton. Dr. Whitehouse and John T. Morton had the financial backing and dad had the transfer business knowledge. He got his trucks and went into business with them. The business grew to Morton Manufacturing Company. He had four trucks. He worked there until he died in 1947 or 1948.

* *

Dr. Vivian Pinn-Wiggins, the daughter of the late Carl F. Pinn and the late Francina Evans Pinn (of Halifax, Virginia), and the step-daughter of Annie Chambers Pinn, is the first full-time Director of the Office of Research on Women's Health (ORWH) at the National Institutes of Health (NIH). She was appointed to this position in November, 1991. Prior to her appointment to her present position, she was Professor and Chairperson of the Pathology Department at Howard University, College of Medicine. She earned a B.A. From Wellesley College in Massachusetts and her M.D. from the University of Virginia School of Medicine. She returned to Massachusetts to complete her postgraduate training in pathology at the Massachusetts General Hospital, during which time she also served as a teaching fellow at the Harvard Medical School. Her research interests have been in the field of renal pathology. She served as Director of the Central Pathology Laboratory of the Collaborative Study of Adult Glomerular Disease, a national joint study to determine prospective indices of kidney diseases, from 1972-1984. She has authored and co-authored more than 35 publications and nine abstracts, most of which are related to diseases of the kidney or minority medical education.

Dr. Pinn-Wiggins belongs to and has held offices in numerous professional organizations. In addition to her election to the position as

President of the National Medical Association, she had previously served as Speaker of the National Medical Association House of Delegates and a member of the Board of Trustees. Dr. Pinn-Wiggins served as a member of the Scientific Advisory Board of the Armed Forces Institute of Pathology from 1984 to 1988. She has medical licenses in Virginia, California, Massachusetts, and the District of Columbia. Dr. Pinn-Wiggins was featured in the April, 1990, Ebony Magazine. The article, "NMA President leads national crusade for equal health care," focused on Dr. Pinn-Wiggins" concern for and work with the "growing plight of the poor and minority populations" (58 & 60).

Since assuming the position of Director of ORWH, Dr. Pinn has presented the initiatives of the ORWH to numerous national and international scientific, professional, political and legislative, community, and advocacy groups. She represented the U.S. Government in the technical discussions on Women, Health, and Development in Geneva, Switzerland in May, 1992. In April, 1993, she received a plaque in recognition of her outstanding leadership and dedicated service to the promotion of women's health issues by Women in Medicine, Howard University.

Mrs. Taylor, Dr. Pinn-Wiggins' aunt, is a retired teacher with the Lynchburg City Public Schools. Her husband, Dr. James H. Taylor, Jr., earned his doctorate from Duke University. Dr. Taylor is a former member of the James Madison University's Board of Visitors. He retired from the Lynchburg Public School System as an assistant superintendent.

Mrs. Taylor's sister, Geradine Pinn Oldham, retired from Tuskegee University as an assistant professor in the Department of Education. Mrs. Oldham's daughter, Karen Rutherford, is an assistant to the President at Benedict College in Columbia, South Carolina. Mrs. Taylor's twin, Melvin T. Pinn, Sr., is the father of Melvin T. Pinn, Jr., M.D., of Charlotte, North Carolina.

Samuel Houston Pinn was a 1901 graduate of Hampton Institute. His file listed him as a resident of Eagle Rock, Virginia. His school records revealed that he later became a grade school principal in Glen Wilton, Virginia. A letter from Nannie Barnette Black, a Hampton Institute graduate, to Hampton Institute on January 7, 1908, indicated that Houston Pinn was the principal of a grade school in Glen Wilton, Virginia, and that he had been there four years. She wrote that he "has done a great work carrying out the Hampton thought in word and deed" and that this was her second year working with him as a teacher. She indicated that he was married to Rosa White and that they had a little boy (Courtesy of Hampton University Archives Department). His file includes a picture of Samuel Houston Pinn with one of his Indian classmates.

Virginia, includes a Cherokee student from Amherst, Virginia. Clarence Stein Branham, listed on a "Cherokee of Virginia" card, attended Hampton Norman and Agricultural Institute in 1914 and 1915 (Courtesy of Hampton University Archives Department). Whitehead noted in 1896 that the Cherokee residents may be able to go to the "Indian school at Hampton to accomplish great good amongst the 258 descendants of these original Indian settlers. There are a number of bright youths amongst them, who would gladly welcome the chance to get an education at the Hampton school, and return home to lift their people to a higher plane of moral and religious life" (Richmond Times). Clarence became one of these young men who, eighteen years later, attended Hampton, and fulfilled the expectation of his people and of Edgar Whitehead that a young man from the settlement would attend Hampton. Clarence Branham, like many of the Amherst County residents, remembered and kept the Cherokee connection alive in 1914 and 1915, a time that was just 76 years after the Cherokee "Removal" period. In this short period of time, Clarence Branham could not have forgotten his tribal connection. Hampton's Cherokee rolls included students with Wolf, Owl, Bird, and other Cherokee surnames (Courtesy of Hampton University Archives Department). Dawnena Walkingstick, in The Journal of Cherokee Studies, 1976, indicated that Hampton Institute "maintained a Government-supported department for Indians" (87). Walkingstick noted, "Mr. (Frell) Owell, one of six children from his family who attended Hampton, was Valedictorian of his graduating class"(88). Hampton University Archives Department files indicated that the Owls attended Hampton (Courtesy of Hampton Achives Department , 1991).

****

George Hicks---Maggie Hicks   Alex Johns---Lila Duff Johns

Frank Hicks---Mary Elizabeth Johns Hicks

Tessie Lee Hicks

Angus L. (Hicks) Thomas **(RC)**
("Thomas" is his adopted name,
his step-father's surname)
Born: December 29, 1946
Madison Heights, Virginia
Interviewed: June 19, 1991

Our people were Indian and many of them wouldn't say what they were. My mother, Tessie Lee Hicks, took us to Maryland when we were young. We came back home when I got out of the Army. I remember my grandparents, my grandmother, going out into the woods and bringing back tree bark. She made herbal teas to help you get over some medical problems. We were treated at home. I remember, I went with her as a child to get the herbs. When we were sick, we didn't go to the doctor, we were treated at home. My

Angus Thomas and his daughters, Mary and Tracey

When we were sick, we didn't go to the doctor, we were treated at home. My grandmother chewed tobacco and my great-grandmother smoked a pipe. Nanny Hicks, Mary Elizabeth Johns Hicks, chewed Red Man tobacco.

We were related to the Rainwaters and Whiteclouds. I remember when they had the Pow Wow here locally, off Route 29, the Indians would visit my grandparents' home on a regular basis. There was an Indian from Oklahoma that came into the area and visited my grandparents. After a rain, he followed the streams with a tobacco pouch and would not return for several days. When he did return, he would have little gold nuggets in his pouch. He went to the mountains to look for the nuggets. I remember the last time it happened, when he came for a visit, it was 1958.

I have always told people that I am Cherokee. Some of my relatives are the Branhams, Terrys, Beverlys, Hickses, Johnses, and Redcrosses. My sister's hair is not the color of my hair. Her hair is jet black.

My grandparents were featured in the newspaper as Cherokee. I remember reading about my grandparents' connection with the Cherokee.

* *

William J. O'Neill's Washington Post article, "The Amherst Cherokee-- Virginia's Lost Tribe," noted that Angus Thomas' grandparents, Frank and Liz Hicks, "are among the descendants of the Cherokee Indians who settled in Amherst, Virginia (June 15, 1969). The article quoted Captain Edgar Whitehead. Captain Whitehead, "an old and honored citizen of Amherst," indicated that William Evans, a Cherokee Indian, lived on Buffalo River, in Amherst County and that his daughter, Mollie Evans, was the wife of William Johns, son of Mallory Johns. Whitehead noted that a tradition existed among the Indians as late as 1896 that "Mallory Johns, William Evans, and John Redcross, all came from the South, and it may be that they belonged to the Cherokees of North Carolina, who found their way here in the visits of the Indians, then made on foot along the air line from North Carolina, to Washington to see the Great Father...and that either in going or returning they stopped by the way and took up their abode here" (O'Neill, 1969; Whitehead, Richmond Times, 1896). Whitehead indicated that "William Evans, a Cherokee Indian first resided, about the time of the Revolutionary War, on Buffalo River, in Amherst County. His daughter, Mollie Evans married one, William Johns, son of Mallory Johns, an Indian, sometimes called a Portuguese..." Angus Thomas indicated that he remembers visits to his house by Indians from other areas of the country. Whitehead indicated that John Redcross was a "well-known Cherokee Indian."

* *

William Morse--Frances Mitchell Morse   John Martin--Jenny Carter Morse

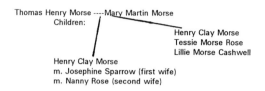

Thomas Henry Morse ----Mary Martin Morse
Children:

Henry Clay Morse
Tessie Morse Rose
Lillie Morse Cashwell

Henry Clay Morse
m. Josephine Sparrow (first wife)
m. Nanny Rose (second wife)

Rev. Henry Clay Morse
Born: April 11, 1911
Lovingston, Virginia (Nelson County)
Interviewed: April 24, 1991

I was born in Lovingston (Nelson County). Tom Henry Morse was my daddy. My mother was Mary Martin Morse. Both were raised in Nelson County. My father had Indian background. I believe my mother did also. She had long, black hair. There were eleven children in our family. It is said that my mother gave birth to 19 children. Ten are living now. I recently lost one sister, Leola Cashwell. My mother and father married young.

My dad was a real good farmer. He left Nelson County as a young man and worked in the coal mines in West Virginia. He came back home to help his sisters and brothers on the farm. His mother had died. Many people think I am Indian, Chickasaw Indian. I am not sure exactly what type of Indian I am. I have heard a lot of talk about the Cherokee. But I know that I am mixed up with one or several tribes.

I am a very good hunter. I have lived alone. I used to do construction work in Washington during the summer and work in the hotels in the winter. I used to own about 27 horses, mules, and ponies. I lived in Arrington, Virginia, then. I have lived alone most of my life.

I work with roots. People used to be afraid of my power because they didn't understand me. I help people. I can make herbal medicines. I make sassafras tea. It thins your blood following the spring and fall. I make a tea out of wild cherry bark. It will get rid of pneumonia. It will build up your appetite. If you have the problem. You will get so hungry that you will feel like eating bark off of a tree.

People used to come to me when they had swollen joints and bad limbs. They drank some of my herbal teas and they were cured. I have helped people's sick dogs. At times, when I am working with the sick people, the dog owners will look me up to help their dogs. People paid me more than I charged them. I don't have much education but I have the Holy Spirit and the power to heal. I believe that I lost some of my power when I had my long beard cut.

The herbal and medical knowledge are from the Indian's ancestors. I worked

Rev. Henry Clay Morse

Rev. Morse

Jesse and Ruby Penn Scott

Barbara Page

Evelyn Lewis Donigan and
Janay

with a doctor. There was a time when the doctor gave up on the patient--he went as far as he could go--I could help them. After I prayed, I went to the mountains to get the herbs to make the tonic.

* *

Reverend Morse is a descendant of the Morses who have a long tradition of being Native American, with most of their descendants in Nelson and Amherst Counties claiming Cherokee ancestry. The Gileses and Morses of Nelson County have a Native American heritage. The Fergusons of Appomattox County and Bowlings of Amherst have married into the Giles and Morse families.

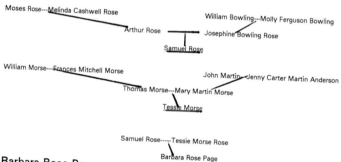

Moses Rose---Melinda Cashwell Rose

William Bowling---Molly Ferguson Bowling

Arthur Rose ——— Josephine Bowling Rose

Samuel Rose

William Morse---Frances Mitchell Morse

John Martin--Jenny Carter Martin Anderson

Thomas Morse---Mary Martin Morse

Tessie Morse

Samuel Rose-----Tessie Morse Rose

Barbara Rose Page

Barbara Rose Page
Age: 50
Piney River, Virginia (Nelson County)
Interviewed: April 24, 1991

As a child and an adult, people have asked me about my Indian ancestry. They indicated that I looked like an Indian. My father told me that we were mixed with Indian and Irish ancestry also. My people are the Carters, Morses, Robinsons, Andersons, Cashwells, and Murphys.

* *

Barbara Page's ancestors were the Roses, Bowlings (Bollings, Boldens), and Fergusons. The Roses, Bowlings, and Fergusons have a strong Cherokee heritage in Amherst and Nelson Counties. Barbara Page is an elementary teacher in Nelson County.

* *

Mary Catherine Bolling
Madison Heights, Virginia
Interviewed on 12/13/90

I am not sure how old I am (believed to be between 95 and 100 years old).

The people at Old Fairmount did all right as farmers. Betsey Beverly lived with her son, Willis West. When he married, his mother left and moved in with Julia West Sparrow. She stayed with Julia, her granddaughter, Hester Scott's mother, until she died. Ben Beverly, her youngest son, moved from Fairmount area to Madison Heights. Rose Nellie was Ben's daughter and the mother of Adlee Carter Wood, the wife of Rev. Roy Wood.

Willis West's father looked white. Ben carried his mother's name, we don't know who his father was.

Betsey worked on the farm and raised her children. Willis West married Missy (Martha) Penn. Betsey lived with them. Betsey Beverly had a family at old Fairmount but they all moved away. Lucy was Betsey's sister. Lucy married a Penn. She married Marcellus Penn.

I remember Bartlett Sparrow. He belonged to Old Fairmount. He was colored. He got killed by his nephew. He was married to Mary Jane Moore. This was Margarette Elliott's sister. Mary Jane Sparrow was the sister to Margarette.

Some of the people near Old Fairmount moved to Covington. Lots of the people moved back to Covington.

The people worked up there at Old Fairmount on the farm. Some worked on the white farm. Henry Clay Blair owned a little farm. He was a deacon at Fairmount. Willis owned his own farm. It was a pretty good farm. Walker West moved out when he got married. Walker moved up to Wright Shop Road area when he got married. When I joined Fairmount, 32 people joined with me. I'm the only one living. I was fifteen years old then.

Jake Beverly's sister, Lizzy Beverly Ross, married and moved to Covington. A lot of our people left to go to Covington.

Peter Ferguson lived in Appomattox. He used to visit Fairmount anytime. He married Belle Megginson. Betty Penn married old man Felix Jenkins. She was Mrs. Francis Jordan's mother. I remember the Isbells. They lived in across the James River from Stapleton. They were white people.

All of the Wests were Fairmount Baptist Church members. Walker West was Willis West's son. Julia West was Onie's (Sparrow) mother. Some of the people lived close to the church. They had church on the first and third Sundays of the month. Rev. Merchant was the pastor for forty some years. I remember Rev. Merchant. I confessed Christ and joined the church under Rev. Merchant. The Jordans lived in the Galilee area. The people were related to Fairmount members.

184

I heard my grandmother talking about slavery. She told us children how the people were mean to our people during slavery. My grandmother was Mary Catherine Beverly and my mother was Mary Lou.

I remember Wilson Scott. When we were children, we used to go up to his house to play every Sunday. Charles Rose ran an old mill, Mundy Mill, back out there at the Ridge near Old Fairmount, near the creek. I heard that they called her the Black Dutch. Wilson was a light-skinned yellow man. His wife, Mitt Scott, was dark.

It was said that we were Indians way back. My grandmother was related to the Indians. My grandmother was Catherine Beverly. I have her name too. Betsey Beverly was related to Catherine Beverly way back.

* *

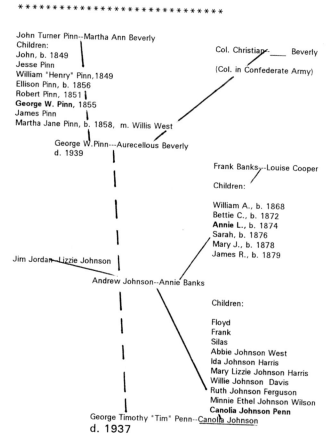

John Turner Pinn--Martha Ann Beverly
Children:
John, b. 1849
Jesse Pinn
William "Henry" Pinn, 1849
Ellison Pinn, b. 1856
Robert Pinn, 1851
George W. Pinn, 1855
James Pinn
Martha Jane Pinn, b. 1858, m. Willis West

Col. Christian ____ Beverly

(Col. in Confederate Army)

George W. Pinn---Aurecellous Beverly
d. 1939

Frank Banks--Louise Cooper

Children:

William A., b. 1868
Bettie C., b. 1872
Annie L., b. 1874
Sarah, b. 1876
Mary J., b. 1878
James R., b. 1879

Jim Jordan--Lizzie Johnson

Andrew Johnson--Annie Banks

Children:

Floyd
Frank
Silas
Abbie Johnson West
Ida Johnson Harris
Mary Lizzie Johnson Harris
Willie Johnson Davis
Ruth Johnson Ferguson
Minnie Ethel Johnson Wilson
Canolia Johnson Penn

George Timothy "Tim" Penn--Canolia Johnson
d. 1937

Canolia Virginia Johnson Penn

185

Sitting: Canolia Johnson Penn, Ruth Johnson Fergsuon,
and Lucille Johnson Davis.
Standing: Ruby Penn Scott, Alline Penn Thomas,
Ida Johnson Harris, and Eager Penn,
Canolia's son.

Sitting: Irene and Lawton Wright.
Standing: (Children) Florence McDaniel, Ida Mae Minifee,
Lawton, Elaine Perkins, Eunice Eldridge, Francina Ferguson,
and Bernice Wright

Rev. Armenthia Ferguson Moore.
Daughter of Raymond and Ruth Johnson Ferguson and Granddaughter of
Augustus and Nanny West Ferguson and Frank and Annie Banks Johnson.

Born: April 28, 1901
Madison Heights, Virginia
Interviewed: December 14, 1990
Joint interview with Canolia Johnson Penn and Ida Johnson Harris, her sister.

Ida Johnson Harris, mother of Stanley Harris, Jr.
Born: May 17, 1904

Mrs. Penn:

I was born between Riverville and Amherst. My parents were Andrew Johnson and Annie Johnson. I grew up in Lynchburg with my aunt. I lived in my young years in the Galilee (Church) area. My childhood friends were Martha McCoy, daughter of Luther McCoy. I wasn't allowed to go around with any and everybody. Mr. McCoy was my mother's sister's husband.

My father was Andrew Johnson Jordan. His daddy was a Jordan. Mr. Jim Jordan was a white man. Mrs. Francis Jordan and my husband were first cousins. Charlie Jordan was my cousin. They come in on my father-in-law's side. They were mixed in with the Indian. Some were bright and some children were a pretty brown with long hair.

Some went to Eagle Rock to work, up near Buchanan, near Covington area. They went to work in the mines. They had Indian and white blood in them. They went for black, however.

My husband was George Timothy Penn. My sister, Ida Lee Johnson Harris, was born May 17, 1904.

All the Fergusons stayed in Appomattox except the ones that married in Amherst; Annie Ferguson married Robert Carpenter and Gus married Nannie West.

Flossie Ferguson married my cousin, Robert McCoy. Her dad was called Joe Ferguson. Robert was Luther McCoy's son.

We were mixed in with white and Indian. The whole family looked like Indians. We were called Negroes or black. Our people chose to go for black. We could have chosen the white side but we went for black. The brother of my father-in-law went white. Last we heard from him, he went to Richmond.

My people chose to go for black even though we had Indian in us. They are out of the Eagle Rock and Covington area. They originated near Amherst County. I heard my father-in-law, George W. Penn, say he was mixed with Indian.

186

My mother-in-law's mother was Martha Beverly.

Mrs. Harris:

Signora Scott, Alma West Ferguson's grandmother, used to fix a good table at Fairmount during revival time. We had to go to her table to eat on Revival Sunday. She thought a lot of us. She was around 35 or 40 at that time. Signora was dark, with straight black hair like her daughter Adell's hair.

Francis Jordan is my husband's first cousin. My husband is 11 years older than I am. They were one year apart children, Francis and my husband. So, she is about 98 or 100. She is about 11 years older than I am. I told her this when I saw her last.

The Jenkinses are my father-in-law's nieces. My grandmother said she was Indian.

Mrs. Penn:

"My daddy's mother was part Indian. His father was part Irish. He was white. His name was Jim Jordan. Daddy's mother raised his four or five brothers by this Irish man, he was born over here I guess. My mother was part Indian, Annie. My mother's mother was named Louise Cooper. She said her mother was part Indian. Father was named Frank Banks.

My daddy's mother was a Johnson, Lizzie. My daddy was supposed to be a Jordan but went by Johnson. He was part Irish and part Indian. My father's father, Mr. Jordan, was an Irishman. He brought apples and other things to my daddy. Mr. Jordan married a white woman. When he died, his children by the white woman told my father, their half-brother, that they were sorry that they didn't ask their half-brother to the funeral of their dad. They gave my daddy a horse and apologized. My mother was Indian, I don't know what else.

Louise Cooper was part Indian. Mother's mother was Louise Cooper and my mother's father was Frank Banks, he was part white but went for colored. I am related to Ben Beverly.

The people in this area were more Indian than black. When I was a kid, I was 10 or 12, a peddler came through and told my grandmother that we were part Indian and that we ought to put up a church to ourselves (away from Fairmount). The whole group down there were Indian. I was waiting in line once for oil assistance, and a white lady asked me if I would get insulted if she asked me a question. I said, "No." My sister, Ida, was with me. She asked, "You white or colored?" I said I am part Irish and part colored Indian, but I am on the black list for oil assistance.

187

Eunice Ferguson Henderson,
O.K. Ferguson's daughter

Nannie McCoy Ferguson

O.K. Ferguson (sitting), son of Peter and Belle, and
father of Warren, Manley and Mack (standing)

Raymond, Jr. and Katherine
Cousin Ferguson (1952)

Christina Humbles Penn, granddaughter of Chief Humbles Penn

Leavelt Ferguson

Hazel and Leonard Ferguson

Jo Ann Wooding

George and Sadie
Ferguson Wooding
(O.K. Ferguson's
daughter)

Jo Ann Wooding

Mrs. Harris:

I was blond when I was young but changed.

Mrs. Penn:

My hair was black when I was young. My dad's hair was jet black. My son Clarence's hair was jet black also.

Mrs. Harris:

My husband's people, from Nelson County, the Morses, were Indian also. I would love to know what color our people were when they were sold years ago. My great-grandmother had some children in slavery—they were given around to different people. The Mundy's raised grandmother. Her mother was sent to Tennessee, and sold on the auction block and the baby was just beginning to start to walk. She wasn't sold but they sold her mother.

They looked like Indians. They sold grandmother's mother right in front of her children. They would not let her say goodbye to her baby. Her mother moved to Tennessee. Grandmother Banks was living during slavery but was not a slave. She was free (see U.S. Census, 1810-1860, the Bankses were "mulatto" and "free colored").

****

Dr. Frederick Isbell—Judith Ferguson   Ann Megginson

Joseph Peter Ferguson---Isabelle Megginson   John McCoy---Betty Childress

O.K. Ferguson--Nannie McCoy

Glenwood Henderson---Eunice Ferguson

Eunice Ferguson Henderson
Age 76
Lynchburg, Virginia
Interviewed: December 24, 1990

My name is Eunice Henderson. I am the daughter of O. K. Ferguson. We lived about a mile from the James River in Appomattox County. We went to Old Fairmount Church. They had a ferry boat, called the Stapleton Ferry. It hauled wagons, horses, and cattle across. I rode on it when we crossed the James to the Amherst side. My people were farmers. They worked on shares. They owned a small farm, about 30 acres, but this was not large enough to live on. So they sharecropped.

Gus Ferguson was 89 years old when he died. My daddy, his brother, was 94 when he died.

Rupert Lee

Some of Mrs. Donigan's Baskets

* *

Charlie "Rupert" Lee
Minton Ridge, Madison Heights (near Galts Mill area).
Interviewed on March 19, 1991.
Born 1909, Age 81

I have lived in Amherst County all my life. My father came from Appomattox County, near Red House. My father was a farmer. He moved on the Floyd Place to farm.

Indians have lived here. I know that there were Indians here because I have found all kinds of Indian artifacts. I have arrowheads, tomahawks, soapstone bowls, clay pottery, stone drills, clay and stone smoking pipes, and many other Indian items. I found them on the surrounding hills, in the tobacco fields, on the river bank (James River), and all over the area.

I believe that the Indians came up here near my house years ago to shoot squirrels. I know that because I have found a lot of arrowheads around my house, near these nut trees. They probably attracted the squirrels and the Indians came up here to hunt them. After a rain, you can see the arrowheads shining in the freshly plowed fields.

Some of the Indians were probably local tribes because they had these large bowls. They were too heavy for the traveling Indians to carry around. Therefore, many of the Indians lived in this area. Some of the arrowheads and other items were made from stones that are not in this area. It is likely that the local Indians traded with Indians who were traveling through this section. They may have been given to the local Indians as a gift by traveling Indians and they may have given the travelers gifts to take home with them.

Collecting Indian artifacts is a hobby with me. I have dug for arrowheads as far as Buchanan, Virginia. I leave the artifacts when I dig for them away from home. The collection that I have here at home came from this area around where I live.

* *

Mr. Lee has more than 900 Indian artifacts in his collection. Marie Gresock, in an article in The Lynchburg News and Daily Advance, December, 31, 1983, wrote that for the past 47 years he has been unearthing Indian relics in the fields near his home and that he has about 900 arrowheads, tomahawks, and pottery pieces.

* *

Evelyn Lewis Donigan

Madison Heights, Virginia
Born-September 1, 1927
Interviewed March 16, 1991

Edward Ashbey Donigan, Jr. ---- Evelyn Lewis Donigan
B-July 9, 1926 D-Aug 6, 1962

I have heard that my father's father, Turner Morris Lewis, was on the last ship that brought slaves to America. He came as a child with his mother, Lettie, and two brothers, Tom and Charles. Tom escaped from slavery and went or was sent to Ohio. Charles died in slavery. Lettie also died in slavery. My great-grandmother Lettie worked in slavery as a rock mason. She was a skillful rock mason. Some of her work may be seen at Speed-the-Plow Peach and Apple Orchard, near Elon. She built the rock walls and the chimney work. It was called Dearing's Plantation at that time.

My father learned basket weaving as a teenager. I watched daddy as he worked and learned the craft. I can do any of the work that he did. I do chair bottom and basket weaving. I am scheduled to display my work in the Smithsonian Institution. My name is listed in the Smithsonian files as a folk artist. It is a lost art because no one is making them in this style but me. Ferrum College's Blue Ridge Institute field representative contacted me and indicated that this is a lost art. They would like to preserve it with some of my works.

I have one basket that I made 32 years ago. The basket is still strong. I cut the white oak strips from the tree and weave it into a basket. My baskets are durable and will last a long time. These baskets were originally used for measuring products on the farm, a bushel or gallon. My dad made them for measuring. This basket is a gallon basket (she held up the basket that she had made). I plan to leave a set of my work for the Smithsonian Institute. The chair bottoms that I weave also last a long time.

I have always known that grandma Maggie and grandpa Richard Lee, both sides, were Indian. If you saw them, you would know that they were Indians. We don't know what type or tribe they were. Mrs. Virginia Herndon used to say that her grandmother, her mother's mother, was sent back to the Indian reservation by the government because she was a full blood Indian. Her mother married my great- grandfather, Charles Brown. Charles Brown was the grandfather of my mother, Maggie Lee Lewis.

****

John Turner Penn DOB 1824┬Martha Penn DOB 1822

George Washington Penn DOB 1855---Aurcellous Penn DOB 1861
    Died 1939   Died 1926

George Timothy Penn (b. 1891-d. 1937)--Canolia Johnson (b. 1901)

                 Kelly Ferguson--Pearl Austin

       George Dennis Penn--Adelia Ferguson

         Samuel Houston Penn
President/Chief-United Cherokee Indian Tribe of Virginia, Inc.

My grandmother Penn, my grandfather was deceased, she always told me that we were Indians. They grew up in the Stapleton Area and attended Old Fairmount Church. My paternal grandparents and great- grandparents are buried in Penn Park, at Old Fairmount Church, on Buffalo Ridge.

My research into my family history has revealed that my ancestors were Indians. The census records and their physical appearance verified that they were in fact Indian. The oral tradition among our relatives, that lived near Old Fairmount as well as those that moved away from the area, indicated that they were members of the Cherokee Tribe.

* *

Written Statement from Chief Samuel H. Penn, Sr., September 5, 1994:

"Our ancestors began a great journey in Amherst County, over two hundred and fifty years ago. The raw history cannot be disputed. Cherokee Indians lived, worked, and died (buried at 'Penn Park Cherokee Grounds' in the mid 1700s) on Buffalo Ridge in Amherst County, Their great desire to become a part of the community and survive forced them to live as colored, black, or white. They mingled in by living with, marrying, and working and worshiping with the people of the area.

The United Cherokee Indian Tribe of Virginia, the Buffalo Ridge Band, was formed to bring the tribe together in a progressive form. In December, 1991, almost two hundred and fifty years after the group started informally, a small core group held its first formal meeting. Officers were elected, by-laws written and adopted, and our movement began. We have over three hundred members at this time. Members live in Virginia, Florida, Maryland, New York, North and South Carolina, Michigan, Georgia, New Jersey, Connecticut, Indiana, California, West Virginia, Pennsylvania, and the District of Columbia--all having roots from the Buffalo Ridge of Amherst County.

With more than 1,500 pages of collected research and information, we attempted to achieve state recognition, but were told that we didn't

Chief Samuel H. Penn

Reverend Roy and Adlee Carter Wood

Canolia Johnson Penn, age 16

Mr. and Mrs. Samuel H. Pinn
(picture taken in 1949)

Leona Ferguson Benn

Wayne Lamont Penn

Laverne Penn Haskins, Samuel Penn's sister

have enough information and documentation. We refuse to be held back and continued to build within.

There is no way that we are going to allow bureaucracy to wipe out two hundred and fifty years of rich oral and physical history with the stroke of a pen. We will attempt the state-recognition process again, in the future, but, notwithstanding acceptance, we will continue to build, educate, and spread the rich history of the Buffalo Ridge, Amherst County, Virginia, Cherokee.

We receive phone calls and written request from individuals all over the country, stating interest in our tribe. In some cases, other tribes refer them to our band. One of the primary requirements for membership, however, is that an applicant must be related to ancestors or descendants of the Buffalo Ridge Cherokee.

The time has come that no one has to hide his or her heritage! Our ancestors endured this because they had no other choice--hiding their true identity because of fear of being set aside or considered outcast. Our ancestors kept the tradition and tribe going since the 1700s, with their strong kinship and marriage structure. They must have known that at some point in history, someone would stand back, look over the two centuries of rich tribal history, and document their activities and the facts about the Buffalo Ridge Band of Cherokee. They are firmly rooted. I encourage all members, present and future, to read the material on the Buffalo Ridge Cherokee Band and gain knowledge of the rich history that has been placed on the shelf for the past 250 years. Our band members are charged with the task of carrying forth the truth and living the life that was hidden for so many years. Carry the history torch, regardless of how many people try to extinguish it.

So without remorse, pave a course down the muddy road so future generations can hold their heads high and be proud of the ancestors of Buffalo Ridge and Stonewall Mill, and the rich heritage that they left to us."
****

Herman Christian
Madison Heights, Virginia
Born: 1916
Interviewed March 19, 1991

Willie Henry Christian--Julia Christian __?__ Robinson--Carolina Robinson
    (White)   (wife/Full-blooded Indian)

    Samuel H. Christian---Roberta Candace Robinson
                        Wilson Scott--Henrietta Hogan Scott

    Willis West-Martha J. Penn   Jack Elliott-Signora Scott

```
              \        Walker West--Adell Scott West
               \                    |
        Herman Christian--Shirley West Christian
```

I remember my grandmother Robinson. My mother's hair was very long. I don't remember what tribe they were members of. My ancestors were out of Buckingham and Nelson counties. I heard the old ones and mama talk about their Indian background.

* *

The Christians were considered white and Native American on Buffalo Ridge. Many of the Christians owned land on the Ridge and intermarried with the Buffalo Ridge Band members.

* *

```
James Aldolphus Pankey--Fannie Frances Cragway
(Mixed, light skinned Indian)        (Indian--African American, black, straight hair)

               /        Stephen Buchanan Johnson Beasley--Mary Cornelia Johnson Beasley
              /         (Slave name, "Johnson,"--Free Black)        (Free black)

Eugene Pankey--Berta Susan Beasley Pankey
b. Circa 1890        b. Circa 1893
d. Circa 1955        d. 1978

               Nine Children
```

Thelma C. Pankey Henderson (deceased)
Cora F. Pankey
William P. Pankey
Arabelle Pankey McCoy
Margaretta Pankey Christian
Robert Anderson Pankey (deceased)
Ellen Pankey Haynes
Odessa Pearl Pankey
Rachael A. Pankey (deceased)

Arabelle Pankey McCoy
Born: November 21, 1921
Appomattox, Virginia
Interviewed: March 12, 1991

I have heard that I have Indian in me on both sides, Pankey and Beasley. None of my ancestors that I heard about were ever slaves. It is a common fact that the Pankeys were not slaves. They got the Pankey name from the whites, however. I heard that daddy's grandfather, "Bob" Robert Pankey, sold slaves.

My husband, Paul Woodson McCoy, was born on January 11, 1923 and died on June 10, 1988. His father and mother were Stephen and Nannie Ferguson

Herman and Shirley West Christian

Richard Lee Johnson,
Mattie's first cousin

James Christian

William Christian, Mattie
Jackson, Herman, & James' brother

Herman Christian

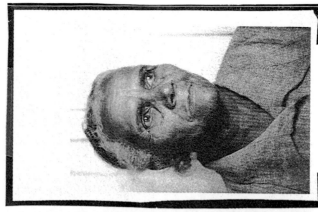

Nanny Ferguson McCoy

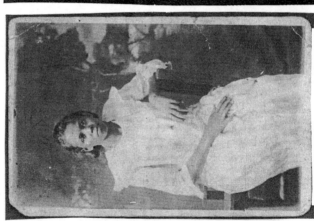

Martha McCoy, Martha Morris'
mother

Arabelle, Vanessa, and Paul McCoy

McCoy. We have five children:

Francine M. McCoy
Paul Lawrence McCoy
Wanda McCoy McKoy
Marcia McCoy Hudson
Valarie McCoy

****

Stephen & Frances Jenkins   John Turner Penn — Martha Ann Beverly
(Married July 27, 1874,
Amherst County Marriage Book
6, p. 38)

Felix Jenkins ———— Betty Penn

Children:

Frances Jenkins Wright Jordan
Felix (married Bessie Megginson Jordan)
Walter (Married Willie Jordan)
Ivanhoe (Married Cora Beverly Jenkins)
Joe
George
Betty Jenkins (Married Harry Johnson)
Nannie (Married Woody Beverly)

Frances Jenkins Wright Jordan
Amherst, Virginia
(Age--Says she is "90 something." She is believed to be 95 to 100
        years old (C. Penn, 1990).
Interviewed: November 10, 1990 and March 2, 1991

My mother, Betty Jenkins, was a half-blood Indian. They always said they
were half-Indian. Martha (Ann Beverly) Penn was my mother's mother. She
married John Turner Penn.

My daddy raised hogs, cows, chickens. We had plenty of food on the farm. My
mother put corn meal and milk together like you make bread and placed it
down near the ashes. She cleaned the area up and baked the ashcakes until
they were brown.

We had hominy corn also. They put lye in the pot so it could eat up the hulls
on the corn. When it came off, they washed it clean and nice. Then they
cooked it until it got done. It was good. I enjoyed squash, beans, and other
types of food that my people cooked.

194

My dad had straight, black hair. Like the Indians and white folks.

Betsey Beverly was the mother of Willis West and Ben Beverly. She had to make do because she didn't have any income. My parents gave them food. Papa raised hogs, four or five, each year. My sister, Betty Jenkins, and I always went with Cousin Betsey home to help carry the food that daddy gave to her. We had to walk four miles to Old Fairmount. They lived on the left side across from Old Fairmount Church, way back in the woods.

Our folks were Indians. Most of the other Penns went to Eagle Rock to work in the quarries. They went to West Virginia, on the other side of Eagle Rock.

Jack Elliott married Signora Scott. I remember when they married at Old Fairmount. Rev. Merchant performed the marriage. We all went to the wedding.

Adel West, their daughter married my first cousin, Walker West.
Nanny West was Willis West's daughter. She married Gus Ferguson.

A man and a woman could not live together like they do today. Rev. Merchant and the church would not let people live together on Buffalo Ridge.

They had a boat that carried cattle across to Appomattox, down near the depot at Stapleton. When revival came at Old Fairmount, Gus would come, all the Fergusons were courting and came over to see the girls. Nanny was my first cousin. She had Indian in her. The Fergusons were white looking people. They came over to court the pretty girls on the mountain.

* *

The Jenkins' Clan

Phelix (Felix) Jenkins--Betty Penn
Children:
George Jenkins
Frances Jenkins
Lelia Jenkins Beverly m. Taylor Beverley
Joe Jenkins
Theodore Jenkins
Nannie Jenkins m. Woody Beverley
Felix Jenkins .m. Bessie Megginson Jordan
Ivanhoe Jenkins m. Cora Beverley
Children:
William Jenkins m. Armon Johnson
Dock Jenkins m. Pauline Wilson
Clint Jenkins m. _____ Ferguson

COMMONWEALTH OF VIRGINIA

DEPARTMENT OF HEALTH - DIVISION OF VITAL RECORDS

(1) PLACE OF BIRTH

County of *Amherst*

District of *Court House*

or Inc. Town of _____

or City of _____

COMMONWEALTH OF VIRGINIA
STATE BOARD OF HEALTH
BUREAU OF VITAL STATISTICS

Registration District No. *5D*   File No. _____

Primary Registration Dist. No. _____   Registered No. _____

If birth occurs in a hospital or other institution, give name of same instead of street and number.

(No. _____ _____ St.; _____ Ward)

(2) FULL NAME OF CHILD *Dock Rerovelt Jenkins* supplemental   If child is not yet named, make supplemental report, as directed.

(3) BOY OR GIRL? *Boy*   **(4) Twin, triplet, or other?** _____   **(5) Number in order of birth** (To be answered only in event of plural births)   **(6) Legitimate?** *yes*   **(7) DATE OF BIRTH** *October 28, 1912*
(Month) (Day) (Year)

FATHER	MOTHER
(8) FULL NAME *Swanhoe Jenkins*	**(14) FULL MAIDEN NAME** *Cora Beverly*
(10) RESIDENCE OF FATHER *Walkers Ford Va* Amherst Count	**(15) RESIDENCE OF MOTHER** *Walkers Ford Amherst County*
COLOR OR RACE *Indian + White* **(11) AGE AT LAST BIRTHDAY** *29* (Years)	**(16) COLOR OR RACE** *Indian + White* **(17) AGE AT LAST BIRTHDAY** *25* (Years)
BIRTHPLACE *Amherst County*	**(18) BIRTHPLACE** *Amherst County*
OCCUPATION *Farmer*	**(19) OCCUPATION** *Housewife*

Number of children born to this mother, including present birth *3*   **(21)** Number of children of this mother now living, including present birth *3*

CERTIFICATE OF ATTENDING PHYSICIAN OR MIDWIFE*

I hereby certify that I attended the birth of this child, who was *born alive* (Born alive or Stillborn), at *9* (Hour A.M. or P.M.) *A.M.* on the date above stated.

When there was no attending physician or midwife, then the father, householder, etc., should make this return. A stillborn child is one that neither breathes nor shows evidence of life after birth.

When added from a supplemental _____ 191___

(23) (Signature) *Nannie Beverly*

(24) *Midwife* (State whether Physician or Midwife)

(25) Address of Physician or Midwife *Walkers Ford Va*

(26) Filed *Oct Report* 191 *2*   *W W Gilbert*   LOCAL REGISTRAR

REGISTRAR

This is to certify that this is a true and correct reproduction or abstract of the official record filed with the Virginia Department of Health, Richmond, Virginia.

DATE ISSUED   **APR 26 1991**   *Russell E Booker Jr*

Russell E. Booker, Jr. State Registrar

VS 15B

VIRGINIA DEPARTMENT OF HEALTH · VITAL STATISTICS

Lawrence William "Ned" McCoy (Son of Robert and Flossie Ferguson McCoy

Cliff Jenkins
Elva Jenkins m. Curtis Harris,
brother of Flossie Harris Beverly

Dock Jenkins
Born: October 28, 1912
Pauline Rosa Wilson Jenkins(wife)
Born: May 23, 1913
Amherst, Virginia (Union Hill Community)
Interviewed on April 17,1991

Mrs. Jenkins:

My family came from the Cherokee group and Dock's people came from the
Indians in Nelson County. Both groups are mixed. Dock Jenkin's grandfather
from Nelson County. Dock's father was Ivanhoe Jenkins and his mother was
Cora Beverly Jenkins. Dock is Monacan.

Mr. Jenkins:

I am a certified Indian. It is on my birth certificate. The news people called
me a Negro but they retracted it after they were informed and saw proof that
I was an Indian.

People in the community did not know that I was Indian until the newspaper
article about me came out. I didn't want people to think that I thought more
of myself because I was Indian. I didn't tell anyone that I was Indian until
they read about it in the newspaper. Ben Beverly's father, Willie Hubbard
Beverley, was the brother of my mother, Cora Beverly Jenkins. My daddy,
Ivanhoe Jenkins, and Frances Jordan were sisters and brothers.

Mrs. Jenkins:

We used to eat ashcakes all the time. There is nothing better than a glass of
buttermilk and ashcakes. We had our own cows (had plenty of buttermilk).

Our family, the Wests, is from the Cherokee side. I grew up in the Fairmount
area. Dock's grandmother is Rosa Knuckles Beverly. My mother was a
midwife. Mother became a midwife after she had her eleven children. Willis
West (Jr.) and Martha Jane Penn West were my mother's parents. She
delivered a lots of babies, black, white, and Indian babies.

My daddy was a teacher for a number of years at Fairmount School on Buffalo
Ridge.
****
Dock Jenkins' father, Ivanhoe Jenkins, and mother, Cora Beverly
Jenkins, were both listed as "Indian and white" on Dock Jenkins' birth

certificate. Cora Beverly was a member of Fairmount Baptist Church and was interred at Fairmount Cemetery. Dock's parents refused to yield to the social pressures to drop the "Indian" family connection on official documents. Many other Amherst and vicinity families were forced to place "colored" or "white" on these certificates. The Jenkins and Beverly families knew "who" they were--Indian and white-- and withstood the social harassment as they asserted their heritage. Dock and Pauline Jenkins, members of the Buffalo Ridge Band (UCITOVA), have been always admitted that they had Native American ancestry.

Dock and Pauline Jenkins have one son (Alfred Jenkins, M.D.), one daughter-in-law (Mary Collins, daughter of Horace and Louise Collins), and three grandchildren. Dr. Jenkins earned his pharmacy degree from Howard University, Washington, D.C. He was a military pharmacist at Gallup Indian Medical Center in Gallup, New Mexico. He later returned to college to study medicine. He received the Doctor of Medicine degree from the Medical College of Virginia, Richmond, Virginia. Dr. Jenkins is presently an anesthesiologist at the Good Samaritan Hospital in Dayton, Ohio.

The Jenkins in Amherst and Nelson Counties have a Cherokee tradition. The Jenkins are listed on the Cherokee census rolls.
****

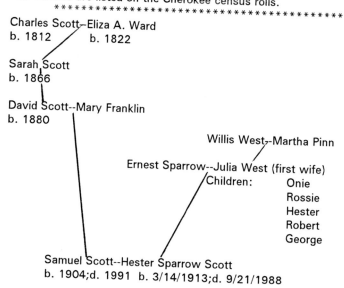

Charles Scott--Eliza A. Ward
b. 1812   b. 1822

Sarah Scott
b. 1866

David Scott--Mary Franklin
b. 1880

Willis West--Martha Pinn

Ernest Sparrow--Julia West (first wife)
Children: Onie
                 Rossie
                 Hester
                 Robert
                 George

Samuel Scott--Hester Sparrow Scott
b. 1904;d. 1991 b. 3/14/1913;d. 9/21/1988

Samuel Scott
Stapleton, Virginia
Age 86
Interviewed November 21, 1990

197

I was born on June 26, 1904 near this house. Signora Scott and my father, David Scott, were cousins. My mother was Mary Franklin Scott.

We called the old Fairmount area Buffalo Ridge and Icey Mountain. George Sparrow, Onie Sparrow, Robert Sparrow, and Ruth Sparrow were kin to the Indians. I married Hester Sparrow. Hester's mother and father were Indians. Hess (Hester) and Bee (M.O. Ferguson) were first cousins. Hess' mother and Bee's mother were sisters. Hess' mother was Julia West and her father was Ernest Sparrow.

****

Tom Jordan--Viney Christian   Sam'l Pinn--Maria Pinn
b. circa 1825   b. circa 1830   b. circa 1832   b. circa 1837

Washington Jordan, Sr.--Candis A. Pinn, m. 1/5/1873
        b. 1850   b. 1856

                Charlie Ferguson--Martha Jamerson (white)
                (Jamerson, Nash, & Nash, 1979 ,p. 27)
                Married 2/8/1885

Elmore Jordan--Lottie Ferguson Jordan, m. 1897

        Lottie's Sisters:

                Pearl (Married Isaac Ferguson)
                Gertrude (Married Matt Woody)
                Sissy Annie (Married Hersey Hull)
                Cora (Married __?__ Stevens)
                Mamie (Married Edward Jackson)
                Elmira (Married Walter Megginson)

Elmore and Lottie Jordan's Children:

Candis (Ben Beverly's Mother)
Charlie (Married Frances Jenkins Wright)
Alphonza (Married Ersie Carpenter)
Herman (Married Ethel Wiley)
Ruby (Married Norman Beverly)
Hattie (Married James Spencer)
Willie
Lewis
Gladys (Married Buck Ferguson) Mother of Herman Ferguson
        (Remarried John Baylor)
Robert Quinton

        Willis West, Sr.--Betsy Beverly   John Turner Pinn--Martha A. Beverly

                Willis West---Martha Jane Penn

198

Abe Pendleton--Alice West

Robert Quinton Jordan--Alice Elvy Pendleton
(Deceased)

Robert Lewis Jordan
James L.
Charles Washington
Phillip D.
Elmore
Norman A.
Stewart D.
Danny A.
Joseph D.

Robert Quinton Jordan
Madison Heights, Virginia
Interviewed March 9, 1991

Washington and Daniel Jordan were twin brothers. A brother named Joseph moved to Chicago. Washington "Wash" had three children:

Washington Jordan, Jr.
Lelia Jordan
Willie

All three children lived in the Amherst Area.

Abe Pendleton came to the United States from Germany with Duncan Campbell. I'm not sure about the year. Nobody knew much about him. He stayed to himself.

He married Willis West's daughter, Alice West. He lived in Stapleton and Madison Heights. He was a German. He talked very good English but it had a German accent.

He had three children--Abe, Walker Hamilton, and Alice Elvy (Jordan). He died in the early forties.

My people never did talk a lot about our Indian heritage and background. Back then, if you had any black in you, they made you black. They didn't mind going for black, even though they were made to feel like they were black. People would ask me about my color. I said, "You can see as well as I can."

My grandad Charles Ferguson lived in the Galts Mill area of Amherst County,

199

between Stapleton and Madison Heights. I went down to Galts Mill to help him on the farm on the road near Bernard Jackson's place, turn off the road to the left beside his (the Jacksons) house. When I rode the train to granddad's place, the conductor would not let me ride in the colored section. He made me get up and go to the white section.

* *

Eleanora West Jordan, his second wife, indicated that she remembers her relatives telling her that she and her sisters "were Cherokee creek girls" (referring to their Indian appearance and the Cherokee oral tradition, and the fact that they lived over near the creek).

* *

Joe Moore--- "Annie"Ann Megginson

Children:

Bell, m. 1883 Peter Ferguson, son of Judith Ferguson
and Dr. Frederick Isbell

Albert, m. Berta Ferguson

Norvell,Sr., m. Maggie Moore, daughter of Rev. Spencer
Moore
Norvell, m. Emma Bell Ferguson'
James
William Clifford
Ollie
Norvell, Jr.
Nathaniel

Norman, m. Elisa Davidson, daug. of Scott Davidson
b. 1866   b. 1866
Children:
Norman
Debrew
Louise
Elva

Rosa

Clinton, m. Lizzie Davidson--
Children:
Harry
Reva, m. Harry Smith (Native American)
Ida, m. Robert Ferguson. son of William
Ferguson
Hezekiah,m. Beatrice Goff
Curtis, m. Ann Bolling
Spurgon
Wyman, m. Spouse from W. Virginia
Hersey
Eldridge
Ann Laura, died, 14 years old
Ida m. Robert Ferguson
Gentry, m. Eveleen Bolling, Ann's sister
Rosa, m. Arthur Davis
Claudia

Clifford, m. Jennie Davidson
Irona, m. Henry____, "Indian" in NY

Joe Moore--Annie Ann Megginson   Rev. Spencer Moore--Fannie Moore
(former slave)

Norvell, Sr.---Maggie Moore

Charlie Johnson---Betty Patterson

William "Clifford" Megginson--Helena Johnson

Truemellon Ferguson Carpenter, Alma Ferguson Wheaton, Robert and Ida Megginson Ferguson, Margaret Ferguson Watson, and Eloise Ferguson Colmore

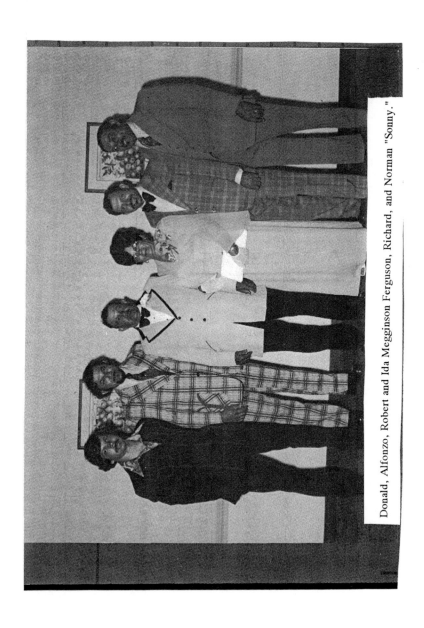

Donald, Alfonzo, Robert and Ida Megginson Ferguson, Richard, and Norman "Sonny."

Lizzie Davidson Megginson

William "Clifford" Megginson
Born: 1909
Lynchburg, Virginia
Interviewed: January 8, 1994

(Annie Ann) Ann Megginson was a very good farmer. She had one hundred hands (workers) on her farm. The second father of Ann's children was a Moore (Joseph Moore). He left a large farm to her near the James River.

A horse threw Ann and she died. The people beat her children out of her land after she died. Ann was a half Indian.

* *

Clinton and Lizzie Davidson Megginson had a large family. Large families were typical for the Megginsons, McCoys, Fergusons, and Bollings. A view of the genealogical structure of two of their children will show the close tribal connection between these families:

Dr. Frederick Isbell—Judith Ferguson   Joe Moore--Ann Megginson

William Ferguson--Susie McCoy Ferguson   Clinton Megginson---Lizzie Davidson

Robert Cabell Ferguson--Ida Estelle Megginson

Children:

Alma Ferguson Wheaton
Robert Ferguson, d. 12/19/1969
Kathleen Ferguson Pankey
Norman "Sonny" T. Ferguson--Sabra Scruggs
Truemellon Ferguson Carpenter--Howard Carpenter
Richard Ferguson
Alphonso Ferguson, m. Ella Morgan
Eloise Ferguson, m. Leon Colmore
Margaret Ann Ferguson, m. Walter Watson
Donald Ferguson, m. Linda Reed

* *

Joe Moore---Ann Megginson   __Isbell--Maria Bolling Wm. Ferguson--Susie McCoy

Clinton Megginson--Lizzie Davidson   Herman Bolling--Martha Ferguson

Curtis Megginson, Sr.--Ann Bolling (deceased)

Children:

Evonne Megginson (Deceased)
Curtis Megginson, Jr., m. Evelyn Ferguson

Curtis Megginson, Sr.--Elnora Scruggs (second wife)
* *

Roosevelt Key--Lillian Napier Key   Saint Branham--Lena Lollis Branham

Elenora Key Branham---Harry Howard Branham
DOB- Aug. 10, 1929

Elenora Key Branham
Born: August 10, 1929

Amherst, Virginia
Interviewed: March 2, 1991

I heard that George Key and Maude Key, my grandparents from Nelson County, were Indian. I know that Key is a Cherokee surname.

My Aunt Nannie Key Coles used to say her mother, Mrs. Maude Key, was an Indian. I believe she did say something about her mother being Cherokee. I go for black but I do have a little Indian in me. My husband, Harry Howard Branham, is an Indian.

Harry Howard Branham noted, "I have heard that I am Indian. I know that my parents were Indian".

* *

The family of Willis West is typical of some of the large Indian families in Amherst County and vicinity. A view of this family, for example, shows how extensive the Native American connection runs in the area.

Legend indicates that Willis West came to this area, circa 1855-56, while working on the packet boat on the canal to and from Richmond, or working in the Stapleton vicinity. It is believed that he was a white-Indian visitor that met and liked Betsey Beverly. Betsey, who was born around 1837, had a son, Willis, by the Senior Willis when she was approximately 19 years of age.

The Cherokee Census (Chapman Roll, 1852, Blankenship, 63) shows a Will without a surname, a Will a gus kih, four Willises, and six Wests. The Hester Roll, 1883, has two Will Wests listed (Blankenship, 83 & 84) and the Churchill Roll, 1908, has a Will West listed (Blankenship, 99). It is not known, however, if there is a connection between these individuals and the Willis West of Stapleton. Did he leave the Cherokee Territory area to the south and travel up the Blue Ridge Mountains to Amherst County? Could he have worked on the packet boats that traveled to Stapleton? Did he return to his home and show up on the 1883 Hester Roll and/or appear on the 1908 Churchill Roll? Was he a relative of the Cherokees in Georgia? Willis West did leave the Buffalo Ridge area and his whereabouts are not known to this date. The Cherokee tradition runs so strongly in Amherst and vicinity that an answer to one or two of these questions could be in the affirmative. It is strongly believed that Willis West, Sr., was a member of the Jacob West family, Etowah River, Floyd County, Georgia (Tyner, 1974, p. 60).

A review of some of the history of the canal revealed that the first canal was constructed near Richmond in 1795. The organization of the James River and Kanawha Canal in 1835 was due to the work of George Washington. The canal was constructed to Lynchburg in 1840 and through the Blue Ridge mountains to Buchanan by 1851 (Adkinson, 1978).

Ann Woodlief, in In River Time–The Way of the James, 1985, indicated that the canal, that was built to transport mule-pulled packet boats, had been completed to Lynchburg by 1840, and 197 miles of canal were completed by 1851(99). Irish immigrants and slaves comprised the labor for the construction of the canal.

Betsey Beverly became the Indian ancestor for a large number of grands, great-grands, great-great-grands. She obeyed the commandment, "Be fruitful, and multiply, and replenish the earth..." (Gen. 1:28):

William Beverly--Susan Beverly
b. 1770   b. 1780

Polly Beverly
b. 1805

Willis West (Senior)–Betsey Beverly
(White/Indian)(Full or three-quarter blood Indian)
(Betsey Beverly's second son was Ben Beverley)

John Turner Pinn--Martha Ann Beverly

Willis West---Martha Jane Penn West

Children   **Grandchildren**

Mary West Wilson
    Pauline Jenkins
    Josephine Jones
    Mary Lizzie Pannell
    Vital
    Bennie
    Preston
    Maggie Wilson
    Sadie Payne
    Martha Kyle
    Effie Douglas
    Hortense Wilson

Martha West Winfree
    Charlie Winfree
    Mary Hendricks
    Ed

Ester Hendricks
Ella Virginia Vaughn

Julie West Sparrow
George
Robert
Onie
Rossie
Hester Sparrow Scott
Ruth Sparrow Albert

Nannie West Ferguson
Maloney Ferguson
Raymond
Jack
James (Jim)
Langley
Clarence
Edward
Isabell Ferguson Fields

Otis West
Bertha West Johnson
Landrum
Catherine West Johnson
Arthur
Missie West McCoy
Jasper
Mary West Jackson
Arelia West Harris
Andrew

Alice West Pendleton
Abe
Elvy Jordan
Walker

Walker West
Alma West Ferguson
Oscar
Martha West Christian
Shirley West Christian
Evelyn West Hutcherson
Odessa
Geneva West Moore
Lawrence

Albert West   (No children)

Grover West

    Othell West Chambers

    Willis West   Ardell Pendleton West
                (Second Wife)

    Joseph West
    Woodrow West
    Ora Belle West

* *

Beulah Morcom Hudnall
Stapleton, Virginia
Interview on 3/16/91

My father-in-law, Thomas E. Morcom, came from Cornwall, England. He lived in Stapleton, Virginia. I married his son, Wood Lee Morcom, Sr., on October 2, 1924.

I own the land near Partridge Creek on the left side. Mr. E. Carson, Jr., owns the land on the right side.

After the flood of November, 1985, my son, Wood, Jr., and I walked over there to see the land. He saw the remains of what had been an Indian camp site: charcoals, pieces of broken pottery, burnt rocks. I saw the skeletons. I saw part of the skeleton in a fetal position. It was partly buried. I saw a side of its face.

My son saw its arms before we really knew what it really was. The people from Sweet Briar College came over and examined it.

My father-in-law, Thomas Morcom, owned the hotel. It was on Partridge Creek. The passengers on the canal boats spent the nights as they traveled on the canal. They kept the packet boat mules in a barn near the hotel. My mother-in-law's brother and his wife, the Colemans, kept the place. They cooked for the guests and ran the boarding house.

There was a village called Hartsville. It had a store and at least seven houses up there, going toward Buffalo Ridge. The road, 624, went from Stapleton to Sweet Briar Station. The place really started from mining sand that was used for glass manufacturing, iron ore, copper. This whole area is full of mine shafts. The area called Sugar Ridge is cut up with roads where they had been mining.

Willis West was living up the creek, beyond Carter's Hole, about a mile, near

Carter's place. He lived near the swimming hole. You go a little farther, you will find the old Willis West place. Walker West lived there with his dad until he was married.

One day Willis was building a barn for us. He scraped his hand. He came up here to get it bandaged. He said, "Look at my hand, it is as white as yours." I said, "It is whiter." He said, "I am not a colored man, I am an Indian."

My son, Wood, and Ed Hesson, our neighbor, were the first to see the rows of post holes or beams. They were from the posts that were used for the Indian buildings. They contacted Sweet Briar College's archaeologist.
****

Wood Morcom, Jr.
Retired, Air Force NCO
Retired, Captain, Amherst County Sheriff's Department
Stapleton, Virginia
Interviewed March 16, 1991

I find Indian artifacts in my yard all the time. I have arrowheads, a tomahawk that is almost perfect. I found a perfectly round stone ball. I have found arrowheads all over the place; at my new place, at my other house, and down around the low ground area. I know that the Indians were in this area. Rupert Lee has a large collection of artifacts. He finds the things on his farm.

Jake Beverly told me that he was Indian. He worked for the C&O Railroad. He had a small car that ran on the railroad tracks, seven days a week. He had to check out the tracks for the railroad, a three-mile section. We would talk on Sunday mornings as I watched our cows near the area where he worked. We had a long talk. He said he was Indian. He had the high cheek bones and straight hair. He looked like an Indian.

****
Alfonza, one of Jake Beverly's sons, was married to Flossie Harris Beverly. Flossie Beverly wrote a poem about Alfonza for her children. She dedicated it to her husband(1985):

Dear Dad

You worked out in the blowing snow
and under the scorching sun,
In wind chills that reach 40 below
and the heat of a hundred and one.

But now you've driven your last spike
and laid your last mile of rail,

Ruth Sparrow, Onie Sparrow's sister *Vernell Rose Sparrow, Onie Sparrow's wife*

Jake Beverly (Deceased)
Trustee, Church Sexton,
Fairmount Baptist Church

You've built your last crossing, thrown the last switch
and told them to forward your mail.

The steel-toe boots, and that damn hard hat,
now sit upon the shelf.
Now you'll sit back, on the old front porch
and reflect upon yourself.

In all the years of struggle
and the hardships that you've heard,
You'll wonder if you've done some good
or if anybody cared.

You kept the tracks that carried the coal,
that lit the homes and stores,
The tracks that carried troops and steel,
that helped to win the wars.

The trains that hauled the corn and grain
to make our daily bread,
And the automobiles shipped from Detroit,
all traveled on your gravel bed.

You helped to keep the country strong,
so pat yourself on the back.
The things that made people's lives better,
depended on your track.

For 43 years you did your part
and earned mom's respect, and mine,
So thank you, Dad, for a job well done.
Now RELAX...Its the end of the line.

Written by Flossie Harris Beverly,
wife of Alfonza Beverly
(Alfonza Beverly retired from the C&O
Railroad after 43 years on the job.)

Anderson Beverly--Pamilia Beverly
b. 1821   b. 1830
Appomattox County

Children:

Chalman, b. 1847
Georgeanna, b. 1851
Calvin, b. 1853
Paul, b. 1858
Leanna, b. 1855
Peter, b. 1859

Robert "Pete" Beverly--Mary Lou Scott Beverly
b.1859   b. 1873
d.1938   d. 1951

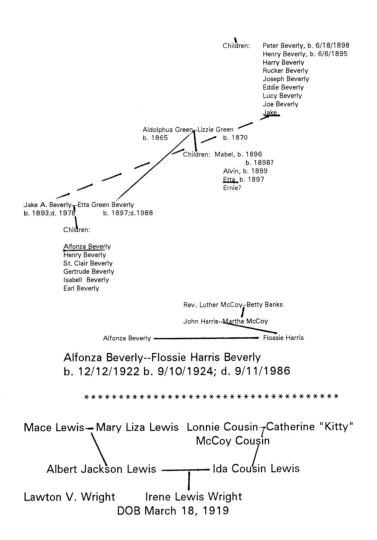

Children: Peter Beverly, b. 6/18/1898
Henry Beverly, b. 6/6/1895
Harry Beverly
Rucker Beverly
Joseph Beverly
Eddie Beverly
Lucy Beverly
Joe Beverly
Jake

Aldolphus Green--Lizzie Green
b. 1865   b. 1870

Children: Mabel, b. 1896
b. 1898?
Alvin, b. 1899
Etta, b. 1897
Ernie?

Jake A. Beverly--Etta Green Beverly
b. 1893;d. 1978   b. 1897;d.1988

Children:

Alfonza Beverly
Henry Beverly
St. Clair Beverly
Gertrude Beverly
Isabell Beverly
Earl Beverly

Rev. Luther McCoy--Betty Banks

John Harris--Martha McCoy

Alfonza Beverly ——————————— Flossie Harris

Alfonza Beverly--Flossie Harris Beverly
b. 12/12/1922 b. 9/10/1924; d. 9/11/1986

* *

Mace Lewis--Mary Liza Lewis   Lonnie Cousin--Catherine "Kitty"
McCoy Cousin

Albert Jackson Lewis ——————— Ida Cousin Lewis

Lawton V. Wright   Irene Lewis Wright
DOB March 18, 1919

Irene Lewis Wright
Gladstone, Virginia
Interviewed February 12, 1991

I was born in the Tower Hill area of Appomattox County. My paternal grandparents lived in Tower Hill, the Lewises. My mother's parents lived in Appomattox County near Bent Creek on Route 26 (Cousins). I have heard that we had Indian background.

We lived in the Riverville area of Amherst County before I got married in 1936. I have seven children and fifteen grandchildren.

208

My mother, Ida Cousin, had long, coal black hair. She was light-skinned. She died in 1936. I am related to the Cousins, McCoys, Fergusons, and Wests. My aunt was a West, Betty Cousin. She married Otis West.

The majority of the Lewises are in the State of Maryland.

I am an active member of Springfield Baptist Church in Appomattox County.

****

Thomas M. Tillerson
Farmville, Virginia
Interviewed 3/24/91

My parents seldom discussed their Indian heritage. They were not ashamed but did not like to talk about it to other people in the area. They didn't want people to think that they didn't want to be Negroes or that they think that they are more because of their skin color and hair. My great-grandmother smoked a pipe and could make her own pipes. She was very artistic and very frugal. She made a good living. My mother is still living. She looks very much like an Indian. My mother's people made a good living off the farm. They were skillful farmers.

My father had few relatives. His mother was Sallie Tillerson. She was born of a Caucasian and Cherokee Indian. Her father was Finger Tillerson. Her mother died at a very early age.

My mother is Thelma Burgess Tillerson. She lives in the Spartanburg County, South Carolina, area. Her father was Elbert Burgess. His father was Felix Burgess, an African American. His mother was Margaret Moore Burgess, a Caucasian. Elbert's parents were born slaves. Felix, his father, was born a slave on the Cox Plantation in Columbus, North Carolina (Polk County). My mother's mother was Candance Wilkins Burgess. Her father was _____ McMillian, a Caucasian. Grandmother Candance Burgess's mother was Fannie Wilkins, a full blood Cherokee.

I have never mentioned my Indian background. People are always asking me, "What are you?" or "Are you one of us?" I say I am African American. I don't explain the other part because some people would not understand it or appreciate it. I am proud of my background, however.

****

Mr. Tillerson is a college librarian at Barber Scotia College. The Wilkins have been classified in Spartanburg County as white, mulatto, and black. Some of the Wilkins families had members with "Finger," a Cherokee surname, as first names or surnames. The whole area, including Cherokee County, Cherokee Springs, Fingerville, Chesnee,

Boiling Springs,Travelers Rest, Spartanburg, Wilkinsville, and Pacolet were near the scenic Cherokee Foothills Scenic route. The North Carolina cities of Rutherfordton, Caroleen, Brevard, and others were on the northern side of the Cherokee Foothills Scenic route. Many residents in Upstate South Carolina and neighboring Western North Carolina acknowledge that they have Cherokee ancestors. Numerous streets, creeks, and town/cities have Cherokee names. These sections of North and South Carolina were once a part of the Cherokee Nation and the surnames and descendants remain as a testimony to the greatness of the Cherokee Nation.

****

Alice Robinson Brown
Gordonsville, Orange County, Virginia
Age 59, Date of Birth: May 25, 1931
Interviewed on April 1, 1991

Great-grandfather-Great-grandmother   Great-grandfather?
(Cherokee)   Cherokee   (Cherokee)

Ernest Robinson -Lulabelle Taylor   Thomas Snead
(full-blood)   (Cherokee)

John Robinson ——— Cora Snead Robinson
(Died-Age 65)   (Died-Age 62)

Alice Robinson Brown

My father's mother, Lulabelle, was a Taylor. They had some white ancestry. They were born and raised in Madison County, Virginia. The Robinsons are from Orange County, Virginia. My father had coal-black, curly hair. My father's father, Ernest Robinson, had Cherokee on both sides. In my youth, the kids used to call us half-breeds. I wondered why they called us half-breeds. Finally, my people told us. They said we are full of Cherokee Indian. My husband, Reginald, has Indian also in his family, on his mother's side. His mother has some Indian in her; you can see it.

****

Alice Brown's daughter, Robin Brown Haithco, a graduate of Mary Washington College and the Virginia Union School of Theology, has completed her internship at the University of Virginia Hospital's Chaplain Internship Program. Mrs. Haithco has physical features that are similar to the people of Japan. As is the case with Quintus Ferguson, both of her parents have Cherokee/Indian ancestry and therefore her facial features have the appearance of Asiatic Indian.

****

210

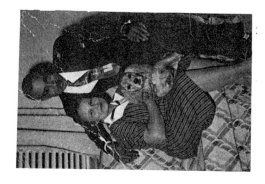

Louise Riddick Redcross and her husband, Arthur.

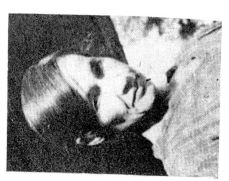

Katie Faison

Louise Langhorne Spraggs
Age: 68
Cumberland, Virginia
Interviewed: May 14,1991

My daddy, Temple Clyde Langhorne, met my mother, Katie Faison, in Faison, North Carolina, in 1917. My mother was born in 1899. They married shortly after they met. She had Indian ancestry. Her hair was so long that she could sit on it. She wore it in two braids. My sister often wears Indian attire.

****

Cherokee lived throughout Virginia, North Carolina, and other states, and have descendants remaining in these areas. A large number of residents, now classified as "black" and "white," in Spartanburg, Cherokee, and other counties in South Carolina, have Cherokee ancestry.

****

Bessie Hopkins Hopkins
Columbus, Ohio
Born: March 15, 1905
Interviewed: May 6, 1991

Rachael Hopkins--Hopkins was the slave name--she had three sons by the slave master, and one daughter. She had two daughters, twins, but one died at birth. My grandmother, Rachael, and my daddy's baby brother, Virgil Hopkins, raised me. When Elizabeth Triplett Hopkins, my mother died in 1910, my grandmother, Uncle Virgil, and his wife, Aunt Carrie, raised me.

My great-grandmother was part Indian. They didn't feel that young people should know much back then, so we didn't get all the answers about our family background. We lived in Blairs, South Carolina, back then. My grandmother looked like a real Indian. She was a big woman and had red skin. Her hair was worn in braids. We have hair like her today.

I had a brother that died last July. He was 90 years old. My brother and I are darkskinned and have straight, Indian coal-black hair. My sister, John Coleman's mother, wore her hair in two braids. The Indian appearance is throughout our side of the family.

My grandmother Rachael told me that she lived in a shack with a dirt floor with a fireplace. She taught me as a little girl of eight years old, she taught me how to make ashcakes. You take your broom and brush the ashes back from the fireplace After it cooked and got done, she took a towel and wiped off the ashes. It was very good and delicious.

My grandmother Rachael smoked a clay pipe. She always asked me to light the pipe for her. I took some small coals from the fireplace and put them in

Hilda, Margaret, Johnny, Kathy, and John Coleman

her pipe. She used chewing tobacco in her pipe. I sometime used a lighted stick to light her pipe. I was five and a half when my mother died. Grandmother raised me. She was a sweet woman.

****

John Coleman
Cleveland, Ohio
Interview date-January 18, 1991

I have some Indian background. My daughter, Kathy, has been researching the family history. We grew up in Blairs, South Carolina. I left South Carolina in the 1950s, when my wife, Margaret and I married, and moved to Cleveland, Ohio. My Indian background was from my mother.

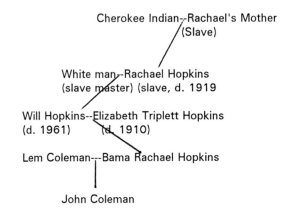

Cherokee Indian--Rachael's Mother
(Slave)

White man--Rachael Hopkins
(slave master) (slave, d. 1919

Will Hopkins--Elizabeth Triplett Hopkins
(d. 1961)   (d. 1910)

Lem Coleman---Bama Rachael Hopkins

John Coleman

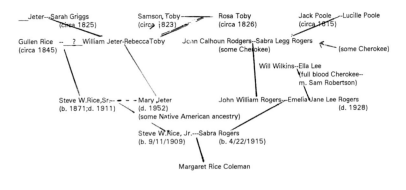

Jeter--Sarah Griggs
(circa 1825)

Samson Toby----- Rosa Toby
(circa 1823)   (circa 1826)

Jack Poole---Lucille Poole
(circa 1815)

Gullen Rice -- ? William Jeter--RebeccaToby
(circa 1845)

Jean Calhoun Rodgers--Sabra Legg Rogers
(some Cherokee)

(some Cherokee)

Will Wilkins--Ella Lee
(full blood Cherokee--
m. Sam Robertson)

Steve W.Rice,Sr.-- - - -Mary Jeter
(b. 1871;d. 1911)   (d. 1952)
(some Native American ancestry)

John William Rogers--Emelia Jane Lee Rogers
(d. 1928)

Steve W.Rice, Jr.---Sabra Rogers
(b. 9/11/1909)   (b. 4/22/1915)

Margaret Rice Coleman

****

John Coleman's wife, Margaret, also has Cherokee ancestry. She was born and grew up in Pacolet, South Carolina (Spartanburg County), near Gaffney (Cherokee County). Her mother's maternal grandmother was

Sabra Legg Rogers
Lived 106 years

John William Rogers

full-blood Cherokee and it is believed that her mother's paternal grandmother also had some Cherokee ancestry.

George Rogers, brother of Sabra Rice and Margaret's uncle, made the following statement (1992):

Grandmother Ella Lee was full-blood Cherokee. She was unmarried (until later when she married Sam Robertson). She was born in Cherokee County but lived on old Pacolet Mill Road, near Green Bethel Baptist Church. Will Wilkins (biological father) lived in Henrietta, North Carolina. He was tall and light-skinned. He looked like a white man. He went for colored (believed to be mixed with Caucasian and Native American ancestry). Grandfather Will stayed in Henrietta. He was a bricklayer. He built smokestacks for factories in Henrietta, Caroleen, Cliffside, Rutherfordton, and other places. William Leonard, my brother, left Cherokee County, South Carolina, and went to work with Granddaddy Will Wilkins. He went everywhere to build the stacks. Buddy (William Leonard) said he was so far up in the air (on the smoke stacks) that he got tired of pulling the bricks up in a bucket that far up in the air. He had to pull the bricks up in a bucket first. Later, as they got higher and higher up in the air, he had to pull one brick at a time on a string.

Will Wilkins met Ella Lee in Cherokee County. He came to see Grandma Ella. Ella's hair came almost down to her knees. She wrapped it up every night with brown paper strings. She talked with an accent. She was full blood. She said she was full blood. She was dark and had straight, long Indian hair. She died around 70 years old. Deacon William Thompson at Green Bethel Church remembers her. Ella had a brother named Phil Lee. He lived in Cherokee County. Amelia (or Emelia) Jane was her daughter.

****

George, who died in 1994, allowed his hair to grow very long. He was placed in his coffin, looking like an Indian, with his straight hair almost touching his lower neck. He always kept his hair cut closely around the sides and medium length at the top. He was not interested in cutting his hair, however, just before he died, as if he wanted to let his family see his long, straight hair at his funeral.

Sabra Rice indicated that her Grandmother Ella "was known as a root and herb worker. She was full-blood Cherokee. Grandmother Ella believed that people could do things with those roots. Mother Emelia Jane was a very good person. She kept us in church and brought us up right. She worked hard all of her life. Grandmother Ella later married Sam Robertson. He made mother and grandmother work hard on the farm. Mother married John William Rogers, my daddy. I was about twelve years old when Mama Emelia died, in 1927 or 1928. She died very young."(1990).

Note the Cherokee names in both families: Hopkins, Coleman, Rogers, Lee, Legg, and Wilkins.   Sabra means "native born" (Uris and Harissladis, 1960, 228).

* *

The Cherokees have descendants in Amherst County, Virginia, and other areas of the United States, with the strongest concentration of residents living within the limits of the former and present Cherokee territories.   The oral histories that have been kept by the descendants have preserved the Cherokee connection.   The Cherokee names, physical features, and oral traditions have been retained.

Molly Ferguson Swain with children, Bennett and Raymond.
Daisy, Molly's sister, is standing.

CHAPTER VIII
Tsa ne la (Eight)

THE 1900s

A Remnant Faces Political Opposition

The turn of the century, the early 1900s, presented some challenges to the "social security" of these Indian people. The degree of social unrest and upheaval on the part of the residents was depended upon, to a large extent and in a direct relationship to their level of **consciousness** or **awareness** of their Cherokee or Indian heritage. During the period of racial discrimination in Virginia against Negroes and Indians, many Indians, who were **aware** that they were Indian, left Virginia because they could not claim "Indian" on marriage, birth, and death certificates (Houck). Many Indian people left the state to avoid the discrimination that resulted when they desired to marry individuals of another race or other Indians. Some just wanted to escape the discrimination that came with the "black" or "Negro" designation.

With the Stapleton group, it seemed that the more informed family members, those who **knew** that they were "Indian" or mixed with Indian, refused to keep quiet their knowledge. This **awareness** of their Indian ancestry resulted in resistance of the "status quo." They resisted the racial pressures by insisting that their children remember that they were Cherokee (A. Ferguson; E. West). These people, generally, accepted the "black" term placed on them for purposes of control and subjection (Humbles, 1990). The most rebellious of the group, however, made sure that they kept the Cherokee oral tradition alive in the hearts of their descendants.

The 1705 state law that required "Indians" to be classified as "mulatto" and the change in the census record classification in 1900 ("Mu" became "B"), plus the development of the "racial integrity" files, created untold tension for the people. They kept the pressure within, untold, and did not reveal it to the public. These Cherokees were very good at adjusting to their environment (Humbles Penn, 1990). Cherokees learned to survive by adjusting to, not resisting, their environmental conditions. These people quietly accepted their lot. Actually, most of the people enjoyed the security of being labeled "black." They were not caught between two forces, as was the case with many of the Indians. Some were refused schooling by whites but they accepted the offer by blacks to attend their schools. Most of these people attended "black" schools. Some, however, attended school with whites, although they

215

went for "black" (J. Ferguson, 1991).

Dr. W. A. Plecker, State Registrar of Vital Statistics, in a December, 1943, letter (in the Racial Integrity Files), chastised the registrars and clerks of courts in Virginia. He, by taking advantage of the facts that Indians had been denied the opportunity of using their "Indian" classification on legal documents and that they were, by that time, listed on the census as "black," wrote a letter to clerks in the state reprimanding them for allowing individuals to place "Indian" on official records.

Earlier, in January, 1943 (Plecker, January, 1943), he sent a letter to local registrars and clerks of courts with a list of mixed surnames of families that he wanted to be prevented from claiming to be "white" or "Indian." In December, 1943, he wrote (*Plecker, December, 1943,):

"In our January 1943 annual letter to local registrars and
clerks of courts, with lists of surnames, we called attention
to the greatly increased effort and arrogant demands now being
made for classification as white, or at least for recognition
as Indian..."

(*Dr. Plecker's letters are included in the Racial Integrity Files at the Bureau of Vital Statistics, Richmond, Virginia.)

These people knew that they were Indian or part Indian! With poor results in his efforts to keep these people from recognizing their Indian heritage, he wrote his December, 1943, letter of reprimand. He stated:

"This loose practice (to state it mildly) of a few clerks is
now the greatest obstacle in the way of proper registration
of race as required of the State Registrar of Vital Statistics
in that section. Local registrars, who are supposed to know
the people in their registration areas, of course, have no excuse
for not catching false registration of births and deaths."

Many Indians were passive to these actions and played along with the "Plecker game," while others vehemently objected to these rules. The difficulty of proving their Indian connection after the "B" for race was placed on the 1900 census reports, however, caused most of the Indians to stay in the local area and accept their lot. Realizing that it was easier to "play the game" rather than to go to jail for attempting to violate the law, they accepted the "B" classification. Plecker informed the clerks that these people were being put in prison for resisting his efforts. He said (Plecker, January, 1943), "Three of these negroes from Caroline County were sentenced to prison on January 12 in the United States Court at Richmond for refusing to obey the draft law unless permitted to classify themselves as 'Indian.'"

Many of the Indians attempted to tell people that they were Indian by noting the "Indian" on legal documents. Plecker (January, 1943) sent a list of family surnames to clerks of courts and registrars. A few of the counties and surnames are as follows:

County	Surnames
AMHERST	(Migrants to Alleghany and Campbell County) Adcock (Adcox), Beverly (Dr. Plecker noted: "This family is now trying to evade the situation by adopting the name Burch or Birch, which was the name of the white mother of the present adult generation."), Branham, Duff, Floyd, Hamilton, Hartless, Hicks, Johns, Lawless, Nuckles (Knuckles), Painter, Ramsey, Redcross, Roberts, Southard (Suthards, Southerds, Southers), Sorrells, Terry, Tyree, Willis, Clark, Cash, Wood.
BEDFORD	McVey, Maxey, Branham, Burley (See Amherst County)
ROANOKE	Beverly (see Washington)
ROCKBRIDGE	(Migrants to Augusta) Cash, Clark, Coleman, Duff, Floyd, Hartless, Hicks, Mason, Mayse (Mays), Painter, Pultz, Ramsey, Southards (Southers, Southards, Suthards), Sorrells, Terry, Tyree, Wood, Johns.
WASHINGTON	Beverly, Barlow, Thomas, Hughes, Lethcoe, Worley.

It should be noted that these counties were known to have Cherokee Indians as residents. The respective county histories relate the Cherokee heritage. The Cherokee did not disappear during the Removal Period. Actually, the politics of the "Removal Era" forced many of the Cherokee in the Cherokee Nation, in its reduced territorial limits, to move away from the political hot spot. Like the movement of water after a rock has been dropped into the river, the Cherokee, who were able to escape, moved in every direction except in the direction of the trail to Oklahoma. They moved into southwest and central Virginia and joined their relatives (Santini; Humbles Penn). Washington County had a large number of Cherokees in its midst as recorded in their early history (Summers, 1971). The Beverlys and others, in southwest Virginia, claim Cherokee ancestry. These people are considered descendants of European settlers but acknowledge that they have some Cherokee ancestry. Rockbridge County was known to have a very large group of Cherokee Indian within its borders (Tompkins and Davis, 1939, 82):

"In a certain portion of Rockbridge County, away back in the mountains, lives a tribe or clan or aggregation of people who are distinct in color and other characteristics from either the purely white or the black race. They claim to have descended from the Indians... The facts which he said he unearthed were as follows: About a hundred years ago a large party of Indians from a far Southern state were on the way to Washington to visit the 'Great White Father.' They encamped for the night in the edge of what is now Rockbridge County. Next morning several of the party were found to be sick, and they delayed departure on this account. Presently it was discovered that they were sick with small-pox... The community was aroused. They compelled the Indians to remove to the most remote region to be found in the county, back in the mountains. There they were left, and told to live or die as circumstances might determine, but not to come out from there.

Those who survived remained there, finding the situation to their liking, and so their descendants are to be found there today..." (He noted that one of the Indians came to the clerk's office and gave his Indian 'much name' or long name-- 'Alexander Farander Fundigundi Way-out-yonder Nathan Tyree Tolley Pott Tommy Jones Tomorrow Watson.')

The Clarks and Tyrees in Rockbridge County, the Irish Creek area, are Irish and Cherokee. They lived "in little groups." The Irish Creek people are the Clarks (Elmore Tyree, May 21, 1991). Jean Tyree Tomlin, an Amherst County resident, noted that her ancestors were the Clarks and Tyrees of Rockbridge County and that they have some Cherokee ancestry. There are many other owners of surnames other than the Clarks and Tyrees who have Cherokee ancestry (Huffer). Huffer, in Fare Thee Well, Old Joe Clark--History of the Clark Family of Rockbridge County, listed a large number of Clarks, Coopers, Peters, Sorrells, Southers, and other family surnames of Rockbridge County people. Some of these families admit that they have Cherokee and Irish ancestry while others prefer to be known as "white" citizens.

Amherst, as well as many other counties on Plecker's list, has Indians within its borders and knows the truth of this fact. The Native residents suffered greatly because of the "racial integrity" files and the efforts of state and county officials to deny them a chance to document and retain on legal documents their rightful heritage, acts which in time would contribute to the destruction of the Native American population in the area."

Vogel indicated that if Native Americans were classified like the Negro-- that is, that if they had one drop of "non-white" blood, they would be "non-white" or "black"--the number of Native Americans in the United States would number in the "millions" (Vogel, 1972, 30). The "one drop" myth or racial control procedure has recently been discontinued or outlawed in all states in the United States that previoused used it except one.

The mixture of English Americans and Native Americans has resulted in a "high degree of racial mixture" (Vogel, 30). The mixture of African Americans with whites and Native Americans has brought forth the term "tri-racial isolates" (30). The 1990 Census has "uncovered a fascinating phenomenon: an explosion in the American-Indian population, which has increased by 38 percent since 1980" (Richmond Times-Dispatch, March 18, 1991). The answer to this large increase has been attributed to a "resurgence in ethnic pride, a reaffirmation of roots." This seems to be the case with the Amherst County Indians. They do not mind admitting that they are Cherokee. At one time, Cherokee was a hush word, as many of the Indian descendants noted (see interview section).

Today, they do not mind stating, proudly, that they are white and Indian, black and Indian, or white, black, and Indian. Buffalo Ridge and other areas in Amherst County have a large number of Indian citizens with racial intermixture. Some of the people are Caucasian and Indian; some are Negro and Indian; and others are Caucasian, Negro, and Indian. The Buffalo Ridge group's physical appearances and skin color appear to be more Indian/Caucasian while some of the citizens appear to be tri-racial. The common racial characteristic in the Buffalo Ridge people is that all are Cherokee Native Americans. Throughout the period of paper genocide by officials on legal documents and census records, the Band members passed on to their descendants the Cherokee legacy. They did not want the 240 year plus legacy about the Cherokee remnant to die.

CHAPTER IX
So ne la (Nine)

SUMMARY
A Cherokee Remnant

The "rocks have cried out"--arrowheads all over the farm grounds in Stapleton (Hesson, 1990; R. Lee, 1991; and W. Morcom, 1991); the James River's swollen flood waters have excavated historic Indian artifacts (Amherst New-Era Progress; Lynchburg News and Daily Advance); the people's physical features provide and have given non-verbal evidence that Native Americans were and are "here;" and the oral Cherokee tradition has been widely proclaimed in the county and vicinity. With these and other factors challenging the public to be cognizant of the existence of Cherokee Native Americans, why have citizens been so resistant, consciously and/or unconsciously, to educate themselves to the facts?

It has been said that the Cherokee have been very skillful in adopting successful practices within the environments in which they find themselves. Many of the Amherst and vicinity Native Americans have been successful, educationally, professionally, and socially. Their members are farmers, brick masons, architects, nurses, lawyers, teachers, politicians (two card-carrying Buffalo Ridge Band members are board members of the five-member Amherst County Board of Supervisors), steel mill supervisors and workers, lawyers, physicians (five known M.D.s), pharmacists, and lab technicians, to name a few.

They present themselves in all colors. Some have black eyes while others have blue eyes. Some have blond and black hair while others are redheads. Some are darkskinned while others are lightskinned; however, they are all family. Some are closely related while others' genealogical relationship with other members is more distant. It has been said that if the Band members had intermarried more closely with close and distant kin, they would have "violated the law. They were members of a tribe that has been bound by a close family or kinship structure that reached as far back as the 1700s" (S. Penn, Chief, UCITOVA).

They are German-Native-African Americans. They are Irish-Native African Americans. They are Anglo (English)-Native-African Americans, Native-African Americans, German-Native Americans, Anglo-Native Americans, Irish-Native Americans. The common thread that runs through all of these groups is the Native American, the Cherokee thread. This thread, this heritage that has not broken and will not break, has been the force that has united this band of people, individuals mixed with a variety of ethnic and racial backgrounds. They come with different educational, vocational, economic, and social backgrounds that would divide most families. This group, however, has a bond that ties them together, their Cherokee heritage and the knowledge that its members are a remnant of a once great Nation. What a variety of cultures, what a melting pot of people! What a location, Amherst County and vicinity, in which to live or from which to have ancestors!

The Cherokee Band on the Ridge and at Stonewall Mill greeted white settlers as they moved into its areas in the 1700s. Cherokee Native Americans maintained a friendly, supportive relationship with their neighbors.

The Buffalo Ridge Cherokee are survivors. Their Native American ancestors assimilated into the general environment by becoming successful farmers, carpenters, and other skilled professionals. They refused to be stereotyped as "poor Indians," isolated on the Ridge, although some were poor. Some were considered white, some were considered Native American or colored. Yet, they were Indian! They defied the odds of trying to make it on their own as a tribe. Cherokee Native Americans did not wear feathers and dress like stereotypical Indians. They dressed like the rest of the general population in Amherst, Appomattox, Buckingham, Campbell, Rockbridge, and other central Virginia counties, as well as southwestern Virginia counties. They did not draw attention on themselves by looking different, and setting the stage for manipulation as helpless people by outside forces.

They were Native American Cherokee. A longitudinal, global view of the Buffalo Ridge Band of Cherokee's recorded history from the mid 1700s to the present time reveals their close knit culture, medical and pharmaceutical practices, love for God and Jesus Christ, religious fellowship, and Cherokee farming skills. They are as much or more "Indian" than many reservation Indians due to their intermarriage over the period of more than two centuries and their strong commitment to "pass on" to descendants their Cherokee heritage.

They encouraged their members to stand on their own two feet. The "nobody owes you anything" philosophy prevailed. They have not sought handouts, money, or land from others; actually they were engaged in real estate transactions of the Ridge long before many of the European settlers arrived in the late 1700s.

They were atypical Indians because they did not allow themselves to be classified as an isolated, withdrawn, socially introverted band on the Ridge and in Stonewall Mill. If these Native American people had not been respected, average citizens during the late 1700s and early 1800s, they would have been manipulated and removed from the area by land-hungry white residents. Some of their ancestors have modeled the possibilities, the vocational successes, that exist for a dedicated, united band of family members. They believed in education, vocational training, maintaining their faith in God, and the principle of hard work.

This longitudinal overview has documented the Buffalo Ridge Band's close tribal relationship and Native American customs. They were and are a remnant of a once great and powerful Nation. The Cherokee had a great fall but some of the broken pieces of the Nation have survived. The Cherokee Nation of Oklahoma, the Qualla Band in Cherokee, North Carolina, and, the United Keetoowah Band of Cherokee Indians in Oklahoma, all federally recognized Cherokee tribes, are the big pieces of the Nation. There are many other bands that are as much "Cherokee" as the federally-recognized tribes. Some of these bands may not have as much historic tribal documentation as the Buffalo Ridge Band but some are as much Cherokee as the Ridge Band. These bands are scattered along the bases and ridges of the Allegheny and Blue Ridge Mountains, and have been forced to flee to other states beyond the original Cherokee Nation boundary (Smith, Redbear, Unity Council Meeting of 39 Cherokee Bands in Jasper Tennessee, 1993). The bands are living testimonies of the Cherokee persistence, their instinctual, moral and intestinal fortitude. They are living reminders of the great Nation, whose broken pieces can survive even when their Nation has been broken, who can still live without being connected to its head or under one leader.

Thirty-nine Cherokee groups--some state-recognized Cherokee bands--held a meeting in Jasper, Tennessee in 1993 to confirm that they are broken pieces of the once unified Great Nation. The Nation has had a great fall, all the kings men and horses during the 1700s helped to make the fall great for the Nation. It has been suggested that to put the Cherokee Nation back together, as an "original whole," is just as impossible as it is to put a broken egg back together that has fallen to the ground. The Cherokee spirit, its will to survive, is greater than an egg. Look at the broken pieces all over the southeast and in other areas of the United States! Look at their residual heritage, their will to stay "Cherokee." What a miracle! Look at the broken pieces all over the U.S.; they are survivors, even when larger pieces--some of the federally-recognized Cherokee tribes-- do not recognize them as part of the once whole nation.

Whitehead, in 1896, criticized the State of Virginia officials for their failure to follow the lead of other states in documenting the State's history. He wrote an article about the Amherst County Cherokees. He used the article to illustrate how the State of Virginia had lagged behind other states in actively seeking and recording its history. He wrote:

> "It is regretted that so little is known and so little has been published by the present generation of the history of each county in our State, so full as they are of historic interest"

(Whitehead. "Amherst County Indians--Highly Interesting History of an Old Settlement of Cherokee." <u>The Times</u>, Richmond, Virginia, April 19, 1896).

The history of the Cherokee in Virginia and in some of the other states has been generally ignored and forgotten, actually very little has been written on the subject other than those Cherokee writings that are mentioned in various counties' histories in a particular state. While it is acknowledged that the Cherokee once owned a section of southwestern Virginia--and that some bands resided as far as central Virginia-- some researchers believe that the Cherokee did not actually live in the area, just hunted there. Why are so many residents of Virginia, West Virginia, and other states noted in <u>Cherokee By Blood</u>? Why are there so many people with Cherokee surnames and oral histories in southwestern and central Virginia? Why is Amherst County so heavily populated with people who claim Cherokee ancestry? Many residents of Amherst County and vicinity, as well as residents of southwestern Virginia, will challenge anyone who believes that the Cherokee did not live in Virginia (V. Santini; S. Penn; H. Chambers). Not only were their ancestors living in the area for more than 200 years, their descendants are still in the area. Their ancestors would not have left such a wide legacy across a large part of Virginia, if it were not true. Actually, they asserted their heritage even though it was to their disadvantage during the early 1900s to claim Native American ancestry. In spite of the Racial Integrity Laws, they kept the Cherokee legacy alive. Each band kept its own history. The chief, family members, and historians are frequently requested to provide information on the Buffalo Ridge history for historical societies, schools, colleges, and public libraries in Virginia and other states (<u>The Buffalo Ridge Review</u>, Spring, 1992, 1-2).

If we accept the facts regarding the strong Cherokee heritage in Virginia, why do we only look to Oklahoma and North Carolina when the word "Cherokee" is mentioned? It has been said that written history has been controlled to the point that only descendants of ancestors who were on the immigration rolls and those ancestors on the rolls of the Qualla Band have the right to claim Cherokee. While Cherokee were already living in Virginia during the 1750s-1770s (the Pinns, Beverlys, McCoys, Scotts, Fergusons, Evanses, Redcrosses, and others), many escaped before and from the March to Oklahoma and headed to the hills and back woods of Alabama, Georgia, and areas of the Blue Ridge and Allegheny Mountain, including the Virginia area. They hid out and did not seek attention. Many did not desire to leave a public record of their Cherokee ancestry. Some Cherokee were already in Virginia, long before the American Revolution and the "Removal Period."

This level of thinking--that you have to be on a roll-- is akin to believing that only descendants of Japanese Americans who were detained in detention camps during World War II are real Japanese Americans today. The belief that all Cherokee went to Oklahoma during the Removal Period, all were taken from southwestern and central Virginia, is just as unbelievable or preposterous as a belief that all Japanese were taken to and kept in detention camps--"The detention records will document all the real Japanese descendants." The belief--that the only way you can prove Cherokee ancestry is to find the respective rolls--is the result of unconscious twisting of historical facts. All the Cherokee, including those who lived in southwestern Virginia, were not removed to Oklahoma.

When Virginia was ceded, the Cherokee residents stayed on their farms. They were not put in a moving van and removed to Oklahoma. They stayed on and became white citizens or black citizens with Cherokee ancestry. They dressed like the white people, just like the Buffalo Ridge group. Why do citizens look for loin-cloth attired Native Americans when they conduct Native American research? If they didn't wear feathers and wear a loin-cloth, they must not be Indians. If nobody wrote history about the "Indian village," the Native Americans on the Ridge, they must not be Indian. Why do Cherokee people have to fit a stereotype to be what they are? Some did wear their hair long, some had trouble speaking English, many practiced medicine, most had Cherokee customs, but they managed their own affairs and dressed like the average citizen. Should that take away their Indian "village?"

Raleigh Pinn, Turner Pinn, and John Turner Pinn were successful farmers and land owners. The Buffalo Ridge people were carpenters, coopers, and other professionals. They did not wear feathers and loin-cloths. The Fergusons, Beverlys, and McCoys engaged in farming, carpentry, shoemaking, casketmaking, and other skilled professions. They dressed like the other people in the population. Why detract from your success and your ability to assimilate into the general environment by dressing like you are poor, with a loin-cloth, long hair, and bare feet? Some of the Cherokee people did dress like that and earned a reputation for being different from the other people in the community (Robert Chambers' Interview; Raleigh Carson Interview). The pictures of John Ross and "Major" Ridge (Kah-nung-da-cla-geh), great Cherokee leaders, show that they did not wear feathers and traditional Indian clothes (Halliburton, Jr., 12, 14). There are research methods, much harder work, of course, than looking for feathered, loin-cloth attired Indian people to prove that they are "Indian" (Humbles Penn). Researchers need to stand back and take a longitudinal view of tribes in states throughout the Eastern United States. Cherokee Bands were not restricted to North Carolina and Oklahoma.

Donald E. Coones, Chief of the Chickamauga Cherokee in Republic Missouri, indicated that the removal (to Oklahoma) did not get all Cherokee. Many remnant populations of Cherokee are scattered throughout many of the southeastern states and many are still located within the original territory (Coones, November 12, 1993; Jane L. Weeks, March 12, 1993, Whitehead, 1896). Look at them! They cried out to the world that they were still in the original Cherokee territory-- and had scattered in other areas. They cried out from South Carolina, Texas, Missouri, West Virginia, Virginia, and other states (Jordan, Cherokee By Blood; Guion Miller). Their cries for attention implied, "We're over here, you forgot to include us in the census, we are Cherokee too!" Some Cherokee in central and southwestern Virginia did not cry out, as if to say, "Why bother, they, the claims officials, have made up their minds that you can't be Cherokee unless you live in the current official Cherokee boundary or have a relative on the Removal rolls!" It is sad, this painting or whitewashing of Cherokee history in the respective states and counties.

This "all inclusive" approach--the belief that all Cherokee were removed, not one was left in Virginia or in other Cherokee-inhabited states that once were a part of the Cherokee Nation--has been one of the reasons for the genocide of history pertaining to Cherokee in America. Many citizens who have had to rely on current history on the subject, those who do not have Cherokee ancestry and do not know the truth, believe that all the Cherokee are **gone** from Virginia, **if they were ever here**.

Historians need to look to additional methods, other than names on immigration rolls, to document people who are descendants of Cherokee. The immigration roll method, however, is an easy, less energy-expending technique for researchers.

The technique of researching Cherokee history only in North Carolina or Oklahoma has generally been the most popular approach for documenting Virginia Cherokee history. Granted, those two states have had and still hold a wealth of historical resources regarding Native Americans, and this research is a valuable method for historians and genealogists. It is, however, much more prudent for the respective state to seek its history from its own rich archives in addition to other documentation, if applicable, from North Carolina and Oklahoma. The fault of this method, of only looking to other states for the answers, lies in the fact that it only identifies part of the divided Cherokee Nation.

It has been said that memory is not like wine or cheese, it does not improve with time or age. In the case of memory or history, not wine or cheese, the passage of time is its worst enemy. The inaction or failure of historians to document Virginia's Cherokee history during the 1700s and 1800s has helped to destroy some of the heritage of the once great Cherokee Nation, as part of the Nation's territory was southwestern Virginia. Mooney has suggested that it even extended to the Peaks of Otter in Bedford County and to the Blue Ridge Mountains in the east (Mooney, Bureau of Ethnology, 14). The "Peaks of Otter were the line of demarcation between the hunting territories of the

Susquehannah Indians to the north and the Cherokees to the south" (Roanoke Historical Society, Map of Botetourt County).

W.L. Bickley, M.D., and others helped preserve the Cherokee tradition in Virginia with their work on Cherokee archaeology sites (Bickley. History of the Settlements and Indian Wars of Tazewell County, Virginia; C. G. Holland, 1970, 58-61; Keel, 1976, 223). Dickens noted that Pisgah sites "have been found as far north as Lee County, Virginia.." (1976, 16). The Crab Orchard Museum and Pioneer Park pamphlet provides information about the archaeological site. It reads, "See local crustaceans and mastodon remains millions of years old. Artifacts from the Native Americans 10,500 years ago. A real life diorama of a Cherokee settlement once on our nationally known Crab Orchard Archeological Site." The historical settings are located on U.S. Routes 19/460 west of Tazewell, Virginia. The area, Tazewell, Pocahontas, Cedar Bluff, and Richlands, as well as other areas of southwestern and central Virginia, has a Cherokee tradition.

States that have procedures for recognizing their Native American tribes should follow the lead of Alabama, Georgia, and other states that have researched the history of and recognized their Cherokee people. It has been overdue, the recognition of Cherokee in the State of Virginia, especially when it is generally known by residents in Amherst County and vicinity, the Cherokee residents in the State, and Cherokee Bands in other states (V. Santini 1994; John Ross, 1994) that the Buffalo Ridge people are Cherokee. The "all inclusive" view, that all Cherokee have been removed elsewhere, has hindered the thinking of researchers too long.

The former great Nation has been divided, but a small piece--one of many pieces throughout the United States--has been preserved. The Buffalo Ridge Band has not forgotten its parent, that great Nation from which it was born. An oyster--in protecting its body by producing a substance to cover foreign objects and irritants that have entered its shell--makes a pearl. The Buffalo Ridge Band, an indigenous people, banded together and produced a **precious heritage** over a two hundred plus period as a survival technique against aggressive forces that would have injured or destroyed its body. The paper genocide, the omission of Cherokee history in Virginia, and other opposition efforts against the Band have forced this group over time to preserve within the membership its pearly Cherokee heritage for its historical survival!

226

REFERENCES

Ackerly, Mary D. and Lula E. Jeter Parker. Our Kin. Harrisonburg, Virginia: C.J. Corrier Company, 1976.

Acts of the Assembly. "An Act to Preserve Racial Integrity." Approved March 20, 1924.

Addington, Luther F. History of Wise County. Wise County, Virginia: Bicentennial Committee (Now published by Genealogical Publishing Co., Baltimore, Maryland), 1956.

Addington, Robert M. History of Scott County, Virginia. Privately Printed, 1932.

Adkinson, Ann S. "A Visit to the James River Kanawha Canal Locks at Big Island, Virginia." Unpublished Manuscript, 1978.

Alabama Indian Affairs Commission. "The Echota Cherokee Tribe." Montgomery, Alabama.

A Letter from the Governor to Peter Randolph and William Byrd. Williamsburg, Virginia, December 23, 1755 (Including Indian Treaties).

"American Tribalism." Richmond Times-Dispatch. Monday, March 18, 1991.

Amherst County Historical Museum. The Poindexter Papers. January, 1994.

"Amherst County Indians." Richmond Times. Richmond, Virginia, April 19, 1896.

Amherst County Marriage Records--1855-1957. Amherst County Courthouse, Amherst, Virginia.

Amherst County Marriage Records (with Cherokee Surnames and Oral Histories). Compiled by Horace Rice, 1993.

Amherst County Marriages --Some of the Family Members. Compiled from Amherst County Marriage Records, Horace Rice, 1992.

Amherst County Schools Term Report--Elementary and High Schools. Courthouse District, Fairmount School, 1925-1945, Amherst County Schools, Amherst, Virginia.

An Act to Preserve Racial Integrity. Chapter 371 [S B 219] March 20, 1924.

Andrews, Matthew Page. Virginia--the Old Dominion. Richmond, Virginia: The Dietz Press, Inc., 1949.

Anonymous Writer. Fairmount School Speech. Undated.

Area Directory Madison Heights: Dominion Directory Company, 1989.

Ashley, Leonard R. Whats In a Name? Baltimore, Maryland: Genealogical Publishing Company, Inc., 1989.

Attrino, Tony. Lynchburg News and Daily Advance. Lynchburg, Virginia, March 16, 1991.

Barrett, Theodosia Wells. Revolution and Despair. 1978.

Barrett, Theodosia Wells. Russell County. A Confederate Breadbasket. Tazewell, Virginia, 1981.

Bauer, Fred. Land of the North Carolina Cherokee. Brevard, North Carolina: George E. Buchanan, Printer, 1970.

BCEA Bicentennial Commission. Bedford County. Bedford County, Virginia.

Beale, Calvin L. "American Tri-racial Isolates: Their Status and Partinence to Genetic Research. " The Eugenics Quarterly. Vol. 4, 187-196, 1957.

Beale, Calvin L. "Census Problems of Racial Enumeration." In Race: Individual and Collective Behavior. Edgar T. Thompson and Everett C. Hughes, Eds., New York: Free Press of Glencoe, 1958.

Berry, Brewton. Almost White. New York: MacMillian, 1963.

Beverley, Ben. Interview. Madison Heights, Virginia, February 28,1 991.

Beverly, Bernard. Marriage Certificate. July 2, 1921.

Beverly/Clark Marriage Certificate. Amherst County, Virginia, Register # 5, Page 205, October 21, 1940.

Beverly, Houston. Marriage Certificate. Amherst County, Virginia, Register # 5, Page 6, 1921.

Bickley, W.L., M.D. History of the Settlements and Indian Wars of Tazewell County. Virginia.

Blankenship, Bob. Cherokee Roots. Cherokee North Carolina, 1978.

Blankenship, R.B. Facts of Interest About Amherst county, Virginia. Amherst, Virginia, April, 1907.

Blumenthal, Walter H. American Indians Dispossessed: Fraud in Land Concessions Forced Upon the Tribes. Salem, N.H.: Ayer Company, 1975.

Bolling, Mary Catherine. Interview. Madison Heights, Virginia, December 12, 1990.

Bolling, Robert. A Memoir of a Portion of the Bolling Family in England and Virginia. Richmond, Virginia. W.H. Wade & Company, 1868.

Boxley, Mary Frances. Gravestone Inscriptions in Amherst County, Virginia. Amherst, Virginia. Amherst Chapter of the Daughters of the American Revolution, 198

Bradshaw, Herbert Clarence. History of Prince Edward County, Virginia-- From Its Earliest History in 1754 to Its Bicentennial Year. Richmond, Virginia: The Dietz Press, 1955.

Branham, Clarence Stein. Hampton Institute Student Registration. September 23, 1914.

Branham, Elenora Key. Interview. Amherst, Virginia, March 2, 1991.

Brock, Robert Alonzo. History of Montgomery County. New York: H. H. Hardest & Company, 1884.

Brown, Alice Robinson. Interview. Gordonsville (Orange County), Virginia, April 1, 1991.

Bruce, Phillip Alexander. Institutional History of Virginia in the Seventeenth Century. 2 Vols, New York: 1910.

Bundy, Nellie White. Sketches of Tazewell County, Virginia--Early History. Montgomery-Floyd Regional Library, Christiansburg Branch, July, 1976.

Bureau of the Census. "American Indian Population by Tribe for the United States, Regions, Divisions, and States: 1990 (CPH-L-99), Missouri-- West North Central Region.

Carson, Cathy S. Matohe--A Labor of Love. Lynchburg, Virginia: Warwick House Publishing.

Carson, Raleigh Newman. Interview. Lynchburg, Virginia, January 21, 1991.

Chambers, Robert C. Interview. Madison Heights, Virginia, May 14, 1992.

Cheagle, James. Interview. Lynchburg, Virginia, July 15, 1992.

Centennial Bulletin--109 Years. Fairmount Baptist Church, 1967-1976, July 4, 1976.

Central and Potomac Telephone Directory. Lynchburg, Virginia: Central and Potomac Telephone Company of Virginia, 1986.

Chang, Claudia. Telephone Interview. Professor of Anthropology, Sweet Briar College, Sweet Briar, Virginia, November, 1990.

Charlottesville Contel Telephone Book. Charlottesville Contel Telephone Company, December, 1987.

"Cherokee" at Hampton Institute. Records of Cherokee at Hampton Institute, 1894-1920. Hampton University Archives and Library (Including records of students from the Owls' Family), Hampton, Virginia.

Cherokee Phoenix. New Echota, Vol.1, No. 4, Thursday, March 13, 1828.

Cherokee Phoenix, and Indians' Advocate. New Echota, Vol. 1, No. 48, Wednesday, February 11, 1829.

Chilton, Harriet A. Appomattox County, Virginia During the War Between the States. Falls Church, Virginia, 1985.

Christian, Herman. Interview. Madison Heights, Virginia, March 19, 1991.

Clarke, Mary Whatley. Chief Bowles and the Texas Cherokees. Norman, Oklahoma: University of Oklahoma Press, 1971.

Clement, Maud Carter. The History of Pittsylvania County, Virginia. Baltimore, Maryland: Regional Publishing Company (Genealogical Publishing Company), 1976.

Clifton Forge-Covington, Iron Gate, Potts Creek, Virginia, Telephone Directory. August, 1990.

Coleman, John. Interview. Cleveland, Ohio, January 18, 1991.

Colonial Archives, Pennsylvania. Vol. 7, 1787.

Commonwealth Studies Program. Indians in Virginia. Silver Burdett Company,

1983.

Coon, Carleton S. The Living Races of Man. New York: Alfred Knopf Publishers, 1965.

Coones, Donald E. Principal Chief, Chickamauga Cherokee, Republic, Missouri. Letter to Horace Rice, November 12, 1993.

Cottle, Basil. The Penguin Dictionary of Surnames. Baltimore: Penguin Books, 1967.

Crab Orchard Museum and Pioneer Park of Southwest Virginia (Pamplet). Tazewell, Virginia.

Cresap, Bernard. The Story of General E.O.C. Ord. New York: A.S. Barnes & Company, Inc., 1981.

Criteria for Membership--UCITOVA. 1994.

Davis, Bailey Fulton. Amherst County, Virginia Miniatures--Marriage Data. Amherst Courthouse, 1965.

Davis, Bailey Fulton. The Deeds of Amherst County, Virginia, 1761-1807, and Albemarle County, Virginia, 1748-1763. The Jefferson-Madison Regional Public Library, Charlottesville, Virginia.

Davis, Burk. To Appomattox-Nine April Days, 1865. New York: Rinehart & Company, Inc., 1959.

Davis, Julia. The Shenandoah. New York: Farrar and Rinehart, Inc., 1945.

Deed. Second Fairmount Baptist Church, Amherst County, Virginia, Deed Book # 61, Page 570, January 3, 1897.

Deed. Third Fairmount Baptist Church, Amherst County, Virginia, Deed Book # 162, Page 342, April 1, 1953.

Dial, Adolph and David Ellades. The Only Land I Know: A History of the Lumbee Indians. San Francisco: The Indian Historical Press, 1975.

Dickens, Roy S. Jr. Cherokee Prehistory--The Pisgah Phase in the Appalachian Summit Region. Knoxville, Tennessee: The University of Tennessee, 1976.

Dictionary of American History--Cherokee. New York: Charles Scribner and Sons.

DiProsperis, Victoria. Interview. Roanoke, Virginia. December 10, 1994.

Donigan, Evelyn Lewis. Interview. Madison Heights, Virginia, March 16, 1991.

Dowdey, Clifford. Lee's Last Campaign. New York: Bananze Books, 1960.

Egloff, Keith and Deborah Woodward. First People--The Early Indians of Virginia. Richmond, Virginia: The Virginia Department of Historical Resources, in cooperation with The Jefferson National Forest, Roanoke, Virginia, 1992.

Ehle, John. Trail of Tears--The Rise and Fall of the Cherokee Nation. New York: Archer Books, 1988.

Empy, Walter. Interview. Covington, Virginia, January 10, 1991.

Executive Journals. Council of Colonial Virginia, Vol. III-VI, Williamsburg, Virginia.

Fairmount Baptist Church. Centennial Bulletin, 1867-1976. July 4, 1976.

Fairmount Baptist Church. Membership Roll. 1969.

Farrar, Stuart M. Census--Appomattox County, Virginia--1850. Appomattox, Virginia, 1984.

Farrar, Stuart M. Census--Appomattox County, Virginia--1860. Appomattox, Virginia, 1984.

Ferguson, Alice Alma West. Interview. Stapleton, Virginia, January 27, 1991.

Earl Ferguson. Interview. Lynchburg, Virginia, September 3, 1994.

Ferguson, James A. Marriage License. 1903.

Ferguson, John. Interview. Lynchburg, Virginia, January 3, 1991.

Ferguson, M.O. Interview. Stapleton, Virginia, March 11, 1986.

Ferguson, Raymond Jr. Interview. Lynchburg, Virginia, January 7, 1992.

Ferguson, Samuel "Dee." Interview. Appomattox, Virginia, August 29, 1994.

Fields, Isabelle Ferguson. Interview. Washington, D.C., January 25, 1991.

Fleischmann, Glen. The Cherokee Removal. New York: Franklin Watts, Incorporated, 1971.

Forbes, Jack D. Black Africans and Native Americans. "Native Americans as Mulattoes." New York: Basil Blackwell, Incorporated, 1988.

Franklin, Benjamin. Indian Treaties--1736--1762. Philadelphia, Pennsylvania: The Historical Society of Pennsylvania, MCMXXXVIII.

Gallant, R. Ancient Indians--The First Americans. Hillside, New Jersey: Enslow Publishers, Inc., 1989.

General Index to Eastern Cherokee Applications. Report Submitted by Guion Miller, May 28, 1909. National Archives Microfilm Publication.

Goetz, Philip W. The New Encyclopaedia Britannica. Chicago: Encyclopaedia Britannica, 1989.

"Good Morning , Virginia." TV Interview, Tab O'Neal with Perry Tortellotte, U.S. Forest Service Archaeologist, WSET TV, January 29, 1991.

"Good Morning Virginia." TV Interview, Tab O'Neal with Dr. Peter Houck and Phyllis Hicks, WSET TV, January 28, 1991.

Haislip, Alex W., Sr. Interview. Cumberland, Virginia. February 21, 1991.

Hale, John P. Trans--Allegheny Pioneers. Raleigh, North Carolina: Derreth Printing Company, 1971.

Halliburton, R., Jr. Red Over Black. West Port, Connecticut: Greenwood Press, 1977.

Hamby, M.E. Interview. Cumberland, Virginia, February 21, 1991.

Hamel, Paul B. and Mary U. Chiltoskey. Cherokee Plants--Their Uses--A 400 Year History. 1975.

Hamm, Olliemaye Freeman. Montvale--From Indian Trails to Park Ways. Montvale, Virginia: Olliemaye F. Hamm, 1990.

Hantman, Jeffrey. Statement in "Amherst County Monacan Indians Celebrate History." Lynchburg New and Advance. November 16, 1991.

Harlan, Judith. American Indians Today. New York: Franklin Watts, 1987.

Harris, Ida Johnson. Interview. Madison Heights, Virginia, December 14, 1990.

Harris, Stanley. Interview. Madison Heights, Virginia, January 6, 1991

Haywood, John. "National and Aboriginal History of Tennessee" in Report to
the Bureau of Ethnology, 1823.

Henderson, Eunice Ferguson. Interview. Lynchburg, Virginia, December 24,
1990.

Hening, William Walter. Statutes at Large: A Collection of Laws of Virginia.
Richmond, Virginia: George Cochran, 1823.

Hesson, Edward A. Interview. Stapleton, Virginia, January 16, 1991.

Hibbert, Meg. "Tepees Sprout on Lawn at Amelon Elementary." Amherst New-
Era Progress. November 25,1 993.

Hibbert, Meg. "Tribal Pride." Amherst New Era-Progress. February 13, 1992.

History and Geography Supplement. Bedford, Virginia: Bicentennial
Commission, 1949.

Hopper, Lola Marie. Interview. Stapleton, Virginia, January 18, 1991.

Houck, Peter. Indian Island in Amherst County. Lynchburg, Virginia:
Progress Printing, 1984.

Hudnall, Beulah Morcom. Interview. Stapleton, Virginia, March 16, 1991.

Huffer, Donna. Fare Thee Well, Old Joe Clark--History of the Clark Family of
Rockbridge County. 1985.

Humphreys, A.A. The Battle-Field of Chancellorsville, Virginia. Under the
Authority of the Hon. Secretary of War, 1867.

Indians of Virginia (Cherokee, Meherrin, and Nottoway). Silver Burdett
Company, and Virginia Department of Education, 1983.

Jackson, Mary West. Interview. Madison Heights, Virginia, February 21, 1990.

Jacobson, Daniel. Great Indian Tribes. Hammond Incorporated, 1970.

Jamerson, V., E. Nash, and C. Nash. Appomattox County Marriages, 1854-
1890. Appomattox, Virginia, 1979.

Jefferson, Thomas. "Notes on the State of Virginia." London, England: 1786,
In Lauber, Almon W. Indian Slavery in Colonial Times. Williamstown,

Massachussett, 1970.

Jenkins, Dock. Birth Certificate. October 28, 1912.

Jenkins, Dock. Interview. Amherst, Virginia, April 17, 1991.

Jenkins, Dock. Marriage Certificate. March 8, 1948.

Jewell, George. Marriage Certificate. September 13, 1838.

Johnson, Patricia Givens. The New River Early Settlement. Pulaski, Virginia: Edmonds Printing, Inc., 1983.

Jones, Dorothy V. License for Empire: Colonialism by Treaty in Early America. Chicago: University of Chicago Press.

Jordan, Jerry Wright. Cherokee By Blood. Record of Eastern Cherokee Ancestry in the U.S. Court of Claims, 1906-1910. Bowie, Maryland: Heritage Books, Inc., 1992.

Jordan, Patricia Ferguson. Interview. Madison Heights, Virginia, January 3, 1991.

Jordan, Eleanor West Tinsley. Interview. Madison Heights, Virginia, January 9, 1991.

Jordan, Frances Jenkins Wright. Interview. Amherst, Virginia, November 10, 1990, and March 2, 1991.

Jordan, Robert Quinton. Interview. Madison Heights, Virginia, March 9, 1991

Keel, Bennie C. Cherokee Archaeology. Knoxville, Tennessee: The University of Tennessee Press, 1976.

Kegley, F.B. Kegley's Virginia Frontier--The Beginning of the Southwest. The Roanoke of Colonial Days--1740-1783. Roanoke, Virginia: The Southwest Virginia Historical Society, 1938.

Kennedy, N. Brent. Telephone Interview. March 22, 1994.

Kennedy, N. Brent and Robyn Vaughan Kennedy. The Melungeons: The Resurrection of a Proud People. "An Untold Story of Ethnic Cleansing in America." Macon, Georgia: Mercer University Press, 1994.

Kephart, Calvin. Races of Mankind. Philosophical Library, Inc., 1960.

Lauber, Almon Wheeler. _Indian Slavery in Colonial Times within the Present Limits of the United States._ Corner House Publishers, 1970.

Laubin, Gladys and Reginald Laubin. _Indian Dances of North America._ Norman, Oklahoma: University of Oklahoma, 1976.

Laubin, Reginald and Gladys Laubin. American Indian Archery. Norman, Oklahoma: University of Oklahoma, 1980.

Lawrence, W.D. "The Fergusons--Five Brothers of the Lynchburg Plant." In The Iron Worker. October, 1934.

Laws of Virginia. Chapter LXXVIII, January 1, 1787.

Leavitt, Jerome E. America and Its Indians. Chicago, Illinois: Children's Press, 1962.

Lee, Charlie Rupert. Interview. Galts Mill, Virginia, March 19, 1991.

Matthews, C.M. English Surnames. New York: Charles Scribner's Sons, 1967.

Maxwell, Nan Brown. "Redcross Roots Begin with an Indian." Yorktown Crier. Wednesday, August 8, 1990, p. 3.

McCary, Ben C. Indians in Seventeenth Century Virginia. Charlottesville, Virginia: The University of Virginia Press, 1980.

McCoy, Missie. Interview. Clifton Forge, Virginia, January 19, 1991.

McElwain, Thomas. Our Kind of People. Turin Painoteos, Finland: Swedish Research Council for the Humanities and Social Sciences, 1981.

McGill, John. The Beverley Family of Virginia--Descendants of Major Robert Beverley (1641-1687). Columbia, South Carolina: R. L. Bryan Company, 1956.

McLeRoy, Sherrie and William McLeRoy. Passages--A History of Amherst County. Lynchburg, Virginia: Sherrie S. McLeRoy Printing, 1977.

McLeRoy, William and Sherry. Strangers in their Midst. Bowie, Maryland: Heritage Books, Inc., 1993.

McLoughlin, William. Champions of the Cherokee. Princeton, New Jersey: Princeton University Press, 1990.

Malone, Henry T. Cherokee of the Old South. Athens, Georgia: The University of Georgia Press, 1956.

236

Meade, Bishop W. "Old Churches, Ministers, and Families of Virginia." 2
Vols., Philadelphia: 1878, in Almon Wheeler Lauber, Indian Slavery
in Colonial Times within the Present Limits of the United States.
Williamstown, Massachusetts: Corner House Publishers, 1970.

Miller, Guion. The Miller Report. U.S. Court of Claims, 1906-1910. National
Archives Microfilm (12 rolls, # M685).

Minutes of the Provincial Council of Pennsylvania. Vol. VI, Harrisburg,
Pennsylvania: Printed by Theo. Fenn & Company, 1851.

Minutes of the Unity Council (39 Cherokee Tribes). In Jasper, Tennessee,
October 8-10, 1993, William C. Smith Red Bear, Secretary.

Montell, Lynwood. "The Coe Ridge Colony--A Racial Island Disappears."
In American Anthropologist. 74 (3): 710-719.

Montell, Lynwood. The Saga of Coe Ridge: A Study of Oral History.
Knoxville: University of Tennessee Press, 1970.

Mooney, James. Myths of the Cherokee and Sacred Formulas of the Cherokee.
Nashville, Tennessee: Charles and Randy Elder--Booksellers,
Publishers, 1982.

Mooney, James. "Myths of the Cherokee. Bureau of American Ethnology,
Nineteenth Annual Report. Pt. I, 14.

Moore, I.S. Memoirs. Jones Memorial Library, Lynchburg, Virginia, July
18, 1923.

Morcom, Wood, jr. Interview. Stapleton, Virginia, March 16, 1991.

Morse, Reverend Henry Clay. Interview. Lovingston, Virginia. April 24, 1991.

Moulton, Gary E. John Ross--Cherokee Chief. Athens, Georgia:
The University of Georgia Press, 1978.

Murphy, Joleen (Genealogy Researcher). "The (K)Nuckles Family."
Amherst County Historical Museum, Amherst, Virginia.

Museum of the Cherokee Indian. Journal of Cherokee Studies. Vol. 1, No. 2,
Fall, 1976.

Nabokov, Peter. Native American Testimony. New York: Thomas Y. Crowell,
1978.

Names (Some of theNames) on the Final Rolls of Cherokee. Compiled by

Horace Rice, 1993.

National Archives of the United States, 1934. _1835 Census Roll of the Cherokee of Indians East of the Mississippi_, w/index. T-496.

National Geographic Society. _The World of the American Indians._ Washington, D.C.: 1974.

National Park Service. _Appomattox Court House._ Washington: Nartional Park Service Publication, 1980.

"Native American Center Opening." _The Dominion Post._ Morgantown, West Virginia, June 23, 1989.

Neblett, E., L. Hume, and R. McIvor. _The History of Monroe, Virginia:_ Home Demonstration Club, 196

O'Brien, Robert and Harold H. Martin. _The Encyclopedia of the South._ New York: Facts on File Publications, 1932.

O'Neill, William J. "The Amherst Cherokee--Virginia's Lost Tribe." _The Washington Post--Potomac._ June 15, 1969.

Order Book. Prince Edward County, 1829 (22-57).

Osborne, J.A. _Williamsburg In Colonial Times._ Richmond, Virginia: The Dietz Press, Publishers, 1936.

Owen, Narcissa. _Memoirs of Narcissa Owens--1831-1907._ 1907.

Parker, Thomas Valentine. _The Cherokee Indians._ New York: Grafton Press, 1907.

Page, Barbara. Interview. Piney River, Virginia. April 24, 1991.

Parris, John. _The Cherokee Story._ Asheville, North Carolina: The Stephens Press, 1950.

Pendleton, William C. _History of Tazewell County and Southwest Virginia, 1748-1920._ Johnson City, Tennessee: The Overmountain Press, 1920.

Penn, Bernard Humbles. Interview. Lynchburg, Virginia, November 26, 1990.

Penn, Bernard Humbles. Interview. Lynchburg, Virginia, November 20, 1992.

Penn, Bernard Humbles. Interview. Sewickley, Pennsylvania, July 25, 1994.

Penn, Canolia Johnson. Interview. Madison Heights, Virginia, December 14,

1990.

Penn, Dennis. Interview. Madison Heights, Virginia, December 10, 1992.

Penn, Lawrence. Interview. Covington, Virginia, March 27, 1991.

Penn, Samuel H. Interview. Madison Heights, Virginia, February 24, 1991.

Penn, Samuel H. Written Statement. Madison Heights, Virginia, September 5, 1994.

Percy, Alfred. Exploring the Present and Past--Central Virginia Blue Ridge. Madison Heights, Virginia, Percy Press, 1952.

Percy, Alfred. Old Place Names. Madison Heights, Virginia: Alfred Percy Press, 1950.

Percy, Alfred. Piedmont Apocalypse. Madison Heights, Virginia: Peg and Alfred Percy, Publishing, 1949.

Percy, Alfred. The Amherst County Story. Madison Heights, Virginia: Percy Press, 1961.

Perdue, Theda. The Cherokee. New York: Chelsea House Publishers, 1989.

Pinn, Rolla. Marriage Certificate. June 18, 1827.

Plecker, W.A. "Dr. Plecker Writes on the History of the Irish Creek Indians." County News. 1924, in Withrow's Scrapbook. Washington and Lee University Library.

Plecker, William, M.D., State Registrar of Vital Statistics. Letter with attachments (Surnames of "families striving to pass as Indian or white") to Local Registrars, Physicians, Health Officers, Nurses, School Superintendents, and Clerks of the Courts, January, 1943.

Plecker, William. Letter to Local Registrars, Clerks, Legislators, and others responsible for, and interested in, the prevention of racial intermixture, December, 1943.

Powell, J.W. The First Annual Report of the Bureau of Ethnology to the Secretary of the Smithsonian Institution--1879-80. Washington,

Powell, J.W. Annual Report of 1883-84 to Secretary Spencer Baird, Bureau of Ethnology. Washington, D.C.: Government Printing Office, 1887.

Proclamation by the Governor, State of West Virginia. "Native American Day." June 13, 1989.

Purdue, Theda. The Cherokee. New York: The Chelsea House, Publishers, 1989.

Randolph, Doris Crawford. Interview. Phenix (Charlotte County), Virginia, January 5, 1991.

Read, Donald Wilson and Vivian Wilson Santini. Brief History of and for Northern Tsalagi Tribe of Southwest Virginia. 1989.

Register of St. Peter's Parish. "John, Son of Lucy Redcross." Williamsburg Regional Library, p. 598.

Rice, Horace. Amherst County Marriage Records--Buffalo Ridge Cherokee Ancestors and Relatives. 1993.

Rice, Horace. Appomattox County Marriage Records--Family Members. 1993.

Rice, Horace. Cherokee in Virginia. 1993.

Rice, Horace. Cherokee in West Virginia. 1993.

Rice, Horace. Early Amherst County Marriages--With Cherokee Surnames and Oral Histories. 1993.

Rice, Horace. Some Common Cherokee Surnames in Amherst County and Vicinity (Central Virginia). May 15, 1992.

Rice, Horace. The Buffalo Ridge Cherokee: The Colors and Culture of a Virginian Indian Community. Madison Heights, Virginia: BRC Books.

Rice, Sabra Rogers. Interview. Pacolet, South Carolina, March 10, 1990.

Roanoke Valley Historical Society. Historical Map of Botetourt County, Virginia--1770-1820.

Roanoke Valley Historical Society. Historical Map of Rockbridge County, Virginia, Virginia--1778-1865.

Robertson, Wyndham, and R.A. Brock. Pocahontas. Alias Matoaka, and Her Descendants. Richmond, Virginia,: J.W. Randolph and English, Publishers, 1887.

Robinson, Prentice. A Booklet of Beginning Cherokee Language 1 & 11. Copyright, 1988, Prentice Robinson, 4158 E. 48th Place, Tulsa, Oklahoma 74135.

Rogers, Horace. Interview. Baltimore, Maryland, January 18, 1991.

240

Ross, John. Chief, Keetoowah Band of Cherokee. Letter to the Honorable Governor David Waters, State of Oklahoma, March 10, 1993.

Ross, John, Chief, Keetoowah Band of Cherokee. Letter dated February 14, 1994.

Royce, C.C. Map of the Former Territorial Limits of the Cherokee "Nation of" Indians--Exhibiting the Boundaries of the Warriors Cessions of Land Made by Them to the Colonies and to the United States. Cherokee, North Carolina: The Museum of the Cherokee Indians, 1977.

Royce, C.C.The Cherokee Nation of Indians, in Bureau of Ethnology Fifth Annual Report, 1883-1884. Washington, D.C.: Government Printing Office, 1887.

Saffell, W.T.R. Records of the Revolutionary War. Reprint of 3rd Edition of 1894, with Index to Saffell's List of Virginia Soldiers in the Revolution by J.T. McAllister, 1913. Baltimore, Maryland: Genealogical Publishing Company, 1969.

Salley, Alexander S. Narrative of Early Carolina. New York, 1911.

Salomon, Julian H.B. Indian Crafts and Indian Lore. Harper & Bros., 1928.

Sandidge, William E. Interview. Amherst, Virginia, January 25, 1995.

Santini, Vivian Wilson. Brief History of and for Northern Tsaligi Tribe of Southwest Virginia. 1989.

Santini, Vivian Wilson. Interview. August 23, 1994.

Santini, Vivian Wilson. Documented History of the Wilsons from 1600-- Present. 1989.

Santini, Vivian Wilson. My Own Accounts: Vivian Wilson Santini. February, 1994.

Scott, Jesse. Interview. Concord (Appomattox County), Virginia, August 29, 1994.

Scott, Samuel. Interview. Stapleton, Virginia, November 21, 1990.

Settlers in Amherst County with Cherokee Surnames and Oral Histories, 1739-1834. From Amherst County Marriage Register, compiled by Horace Rice, 1992.

Smith, Conway H. Colonial Days in the Land that Became Pulaski County, Pulaski, Virginia: B.D. Smith & Bros., Publishers, Inc. Pulaski, 1975.

Smith, Elsdon C. The Story of Our Names Detroit, Michigan: Gale Research Company, 1970.

Smith, Lois. Director, Amherst County Historical Museum. Interview. Amherst, Virginia, August 5, 1992.

Smith, William C. "Red Bear." "Cherokee Unity Council Meeting's Minutes." Jasper, Tennessee (Marion County Park), October 8-10, 1993 (with list of 39 Cherokee tribal representatives that were present).

Sparrow, Bartlett. Marriage Certificate. December 26, 1827.

Sparrow, Onie. Interview. Madison Heights, Virginia, December 15, 1990.

Spraggs, Louise Langhorne. Interview. Cumberland, Virginia, May 14, 1991.

Starr, Emmet. Old Cherokee Families--Old Families and Their Genealogy. Norman, Oklahoma, University of Oklahoma Press, 1968.

Stern, Phillip Van Doren. An End to Valor. Boston: Houghton Mifflin Company, 1958.

Stratton, Lizzie. Interview. Madison Heights, Virginia, December 27,1 990.

Summers, Lewis Preston. History of Southwest Virginia, 1746-1786, Washington County, 1777-1870. Baltimore, Maryland: Regional Publishing Company
(Genealogical Publishing Company), 1971.

Swanton, John R. The Indians of the Southeastern United States. Washington, D.C.: Government Printing Office, 1946.

Sweeny, Lenora Higginbotham. Amherst County, Virginia in the Revolution. Lynchburg, Virginia: J.P. Bell Printing.

Taylor, Jonathan. Chief of the Eastern Band of Cherokee Indians, Cherokee, North Carolina, January 18, 1991.

Terrell, John Upton. American Indian Almanac. New York: Thomas Y. Crowell Company, 1971.

The Buffalo Ridge Review. The Buffalo Ridge Cherokee Newsletter, Spring, 1992.

The Commission and Commissioner to the Five Civilized Tribes. The Index and

Final Rolls of Citizens and Freedmen of the Cherokee Tribe in Indian Territory. June 21, 1906.

The Encyclopaedia Americana. Danbury, Connecticut: Grolier Incorporated, 1972.

The Rockfish Baptist Association of Virginia. "Minutes of the One Hundredth Thirteenth Annual Session," June 18-20, 1991

The Southern Bell Telephone Book. June, 1993-94.

The Virginia Gazette. Williamsburg, Virginia, August 3, 1776.

The Virginia Gazette. Williamsburg, Virginia, August 10, 1776.

Thornton, Russell. American Indian Holocaust and Survival--A Population History Since 1492. Norman, Oklahoma: University of Oklahoma Press, 1987.

Tillerson, Thomas M. Interview. Farmville, Virginia, March 24, 1991.

Tippins, Norman. "Archaeologists Excavate Stapleton Indian Mounds" (after 1985 flood). In Amherst New Era-Progress. December 26, 1985.

Tomlin, Jean. Interview. Madison Heights, Virginia. May 30, 1992.

Tompkins, E.P., M.D. "Irish Creek." Rockbridge Historical Society, Washington and Lee University Library.

Tompkins, E.P., M.D. The Natural Bridge and Its Historical Surroundings. Natural Bridge, Virginia: Natural Bridge of Virginia, Incorporated, 1939.

Treaty with the Cherokee, 1866. Preamble, Article 9 (Treaty Document).

Treaty Held with the Catawba and Cherokee Indians, at the Catawba Town and Broad River, February and March , 1756. Williamsburg, Virginia: W. Hunter, Printers, MDCCLVI.

Trigger, Bruce G. Handbook on North American Indians. Washington, D.C.: Smithsonian Institution, 1978.

Tunis, Edwin. Indians Cleveland, Ohio: The World Publishing Company, 1959.

Turner, Dr. Charles. Professor Emeritus, Washington & Lee University, Lexington, Virginia. Letter to Bernard Humbles, dated April 30, 1990.

Tyner, James W. Those Who Cried--The 16,000. Muskogee, Oklahoma: Thomason Printing Company, 1990.

Tyree, Elmore. Interview. Lexington (Whistle Creek area), Virginia, May 21, 1991.

Tyree, Leonard. Interview. Gladstone, Virginia, June 30, 1992.

Tribal Registrations, United Cherokee Indian Tribe of Virginia, Incorporated. Madison Heights, Virginia, June, 1992.

Underwood, Thomas Brian. The Story of the Cherokee People. S.B. Newman Printing Company, 1961.

Uris, Leon, and Dimitrios Harissladis. Exodus Revisited. Garden City, N.Y.: Doubleday & Company, Inc.

U.S. Census, 1790, Virginia.
Amherst County
Buckingham County

U.S. Census, 1810, Virginia. Ronald Vern Jackson and Gary Ronald Teeples, Editors. Bountiful, Utah: Accelerated Indexing Systems.

U.S. Census, 1810
Amherst County
Buckingham County

U.S.Census, 1840.
Amherst County
Buckingham County
Nelson County

U.S. Census, 1850
Amherst County
Alleghany County
Appomattox County
Buckingham County
Nelson County
Rockbridge County

U.S. Census, 1860.
Amherst County
Alleghany County
Appomattox County
Buckingham County
Nelson County

Rockbridge County

U.S. Census, 1870
Amherst County
Appomattox County

U.S. Census, 1880
Amherst County
Appomattox County

U.S. Census, 1900
Amherst County
Appomattox County

Utley, Robert M. and Wilcomb Washburn. History of the Indian Wars. American Heritage Publishing Company, 1977.

Virginia Historical Landmarks Commission Survey. "Stapleton Railroad Station." Form-File No. 05-39, Amherst County.

Vital Statistic Laws of Virginia. Department of Health. Report from the Code of Virginia, 1950 & 1956. Charlottesville, Virginia: The Michie Company, 1956.

Vogel, Virgil J. A Documentary History of the American Indian. New York: Harper & Row, Publishers, 1972.

Waldman, Carl. Encyclopedia of North American Tribes. New York: Facts on File Publications.

Ware, Dr. Larry. Interview. Due West, South Carolina. January 8, 1995.

Weaver, Gallasneed, Chairman. Tribes Recognized by the State of Alabama. Alabama Indian Affairs Commission, Montgomery, Alabama.

Weeks, Jane L. Executive Director, Alabama Indian Affairs Commission. Letter to Wilma Mankiller, Chief, Cherokee Nation, Oklahoma, March 12, 1993.

West, Elizabeth Pettigrew. Interview. Madison Heights, Virginia, February 27, 1991.

West, Oscar. Interview. Madison Heights, Virginia, January 5, 1991.

West, Willis. Marriage Certificate. December 27,1875.

White, Charles. The Hidden and Forgotten. Marceline, Missouri: Walsworth Press, 1985.

White, John Manchip. Everyday Life of the North American Indian. New York: Meier Publishers, Inc., 1979.

White, Vera. Interview. Lynchburg, Virginia, February 25, 1991.

Whitehead, Edgar. "Amherst County Indians: Highly Interesting History of an Old Settlement of Cherokees." The Times-Richmond. Sunday, April 19, 1896.

Wilkinson, Wallace G. Governor of the Commonwealth of Kentucky. Proclamation: The Delilah Whitecloud United Cherokee Indian Tribe of Kentucky, Incorporated. April 12, 1991.

Wilson, Goodridge. Smyth County History and Traditions. Smyth County, Virginia: Centennial Celebration of Smyth County, Virginia, 1932.

Wilson, Martin Walkingbear. Interview. Wytheville, Virginia, July 22, 1994.

Wilson, Martin Walkingbear. The Amonsoquath Tribe of Cherokee. Ozark, Missouri, 1994.

Wilson, Martin Walkingbear. The Amonsoquath Tribe--Heritage of a Proud Race, 1593-1993. 1993.

Wilson, Rachel. Sworn Statement for Pension. 27 March 1833, State of Tennessee, John Ward, Justice of the Peace.

Wise, Jennings Cropper. Col. John Wise of England and Virginia (1617-1675)-- His Ancestors and Descendants. Richmond, Virginia: The Bell Book and Stationery Company, Inc., 1918.

Withrow, Lucy. "Dr. W. Plecker's Letter to Editor, County News" (1924). Withrow Scrapbook. Vol. 3, p. 17, Rockbridge County, Washington and Lee University Library, Lexington, Virginia.

Woodlief, Ann. In River Time. Chapel Hill, North Carolina: Algonquin Books of Chapel Hill, 1985.

Woodson, Robert F. and Isobel B. Woodson. Virginia Tithables, From the Burned Record Counties. Published by Isobel B. Woodson, September, 1970.

Woodward, Grace Steele. The Cherokees. Norman, Oklahoma: University of Oklahoma Press, 1963.

Wright, Evelyn Wright, Chairperson, "Redcross Descendants (Virginia

Peninsular) New Kent and York Counties, 1768-1993." The Redcross Descendants Reunion Planning Committee, 1993.

Wright, Evelyn S. Letter to Redcross Descendants. October 1, 1987.

Wright, Evelyn S. Telephone Interview. Hayes, Virginia, March 10, 1991.

Wright, Evelyn S. The Redcross Report. October 1, 1987.

Wright, Irene Lewis. Interview. Gladstone (Buckingham County), Virginia, February 12, 1991.

Yenne, Bill. The Encyclopedia of North American Indian Tribes. Greenwich, Connecticut: Arch Cape Press, 1986.

254

ABOUT THE AUTHOR

Horace Richard Rice, a native of Pacolet (Spartanburg County), South Carolina, has been working in the field of public education since 1965. His mother, quarter blood Cherokee, was born in Cherokee County, South Carolina, near Pacolet.

He received a B.A. degree from Johnson C. Smith University, Charlotte, North Carolina , in 1965. He was awarded Master of Education (1970) and Doctor of Education (1980) degrees from the University of Virginia, Charlottesville. His areas of specialization were administration and supervision, counseling, and educational research. Dr. Rice, a school division assistant superintendent, has been a social studies teacher, guidance counselor, and elementary, middle and high school principal.

He is an ordained Baptist minister and has been pastoring since 1976.